DREAM THIEF™

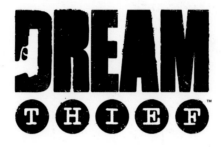

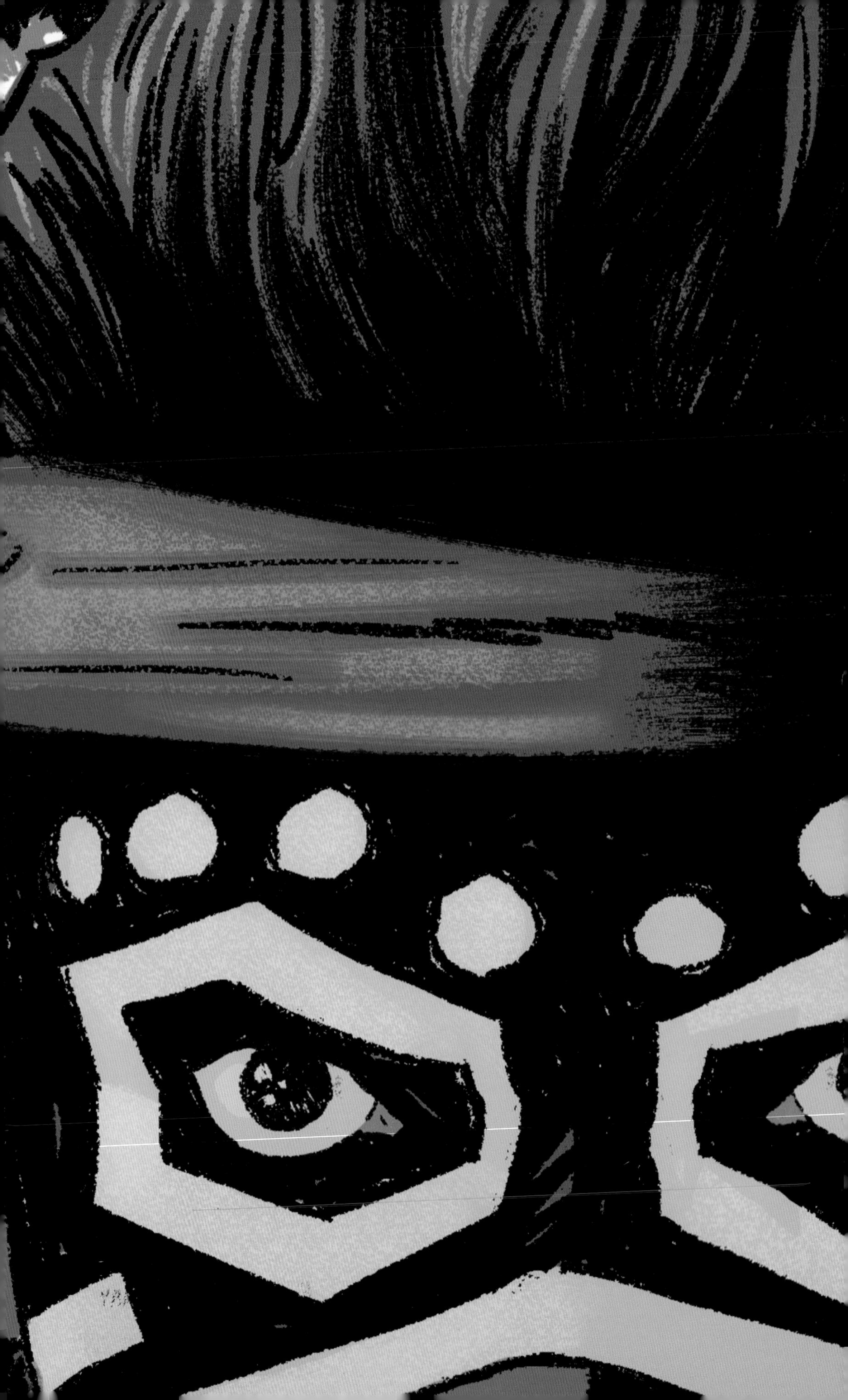

DREAM THIEF

VOLUME 2: ESCAPE

STORY
JAI NITZ

ART & LETTERING (CHAPTERS 1 & 2)
GREG SMALLWOOD

ART (CHAPTERS 3 & 4)
TADD GALUSHA

COLORS (CHAPTERS 3 & 4)
TAMRA BONVILLAIN

LETTERS (CHAPTERS 3 & 4)
RICHARD STARKINGS & COMICRAFT

COVER & CHAPTER BREAKS
GREG SMALLWOOD

DARK HORSE BOOKS

JAI

- For my father, Jerry Nitz.

GREG

- For Jai, my friend and collaborator.
- Special thanks to the Dark Horse crew, Mom, Dad, Megs, Matt, Jacob, and Tiffany.

PUBLISHER Mike Richardson
DESIGNER Rick DeLucco
DIGITAL PRODUCTION Allyson Haller
ASSISTANT EDITOR Everett Patterson
EDITOR Patrick Thorpe

Special thanks to Annie Gullion.

This volume collects issues #1 through #4 of Dark Horse Comics' series *Dream Thief: Escape*.

Published by
Dark Horse Books
A division of Dark Horse Comics, Inc.
10956 SE Main Street
Milwaukie, OR 97222

DarkHorse.com

To find a comics shop in your area, call the Comic Shop Locator Service toll-free at (888) 266-4226.
International Licensing: (503) 905-2377

First edition: January 2015
ISBN 978-1-61655-513-9

Printed in China
10 9 8 7 6 5 4 3 2 1

CHAPTER 1

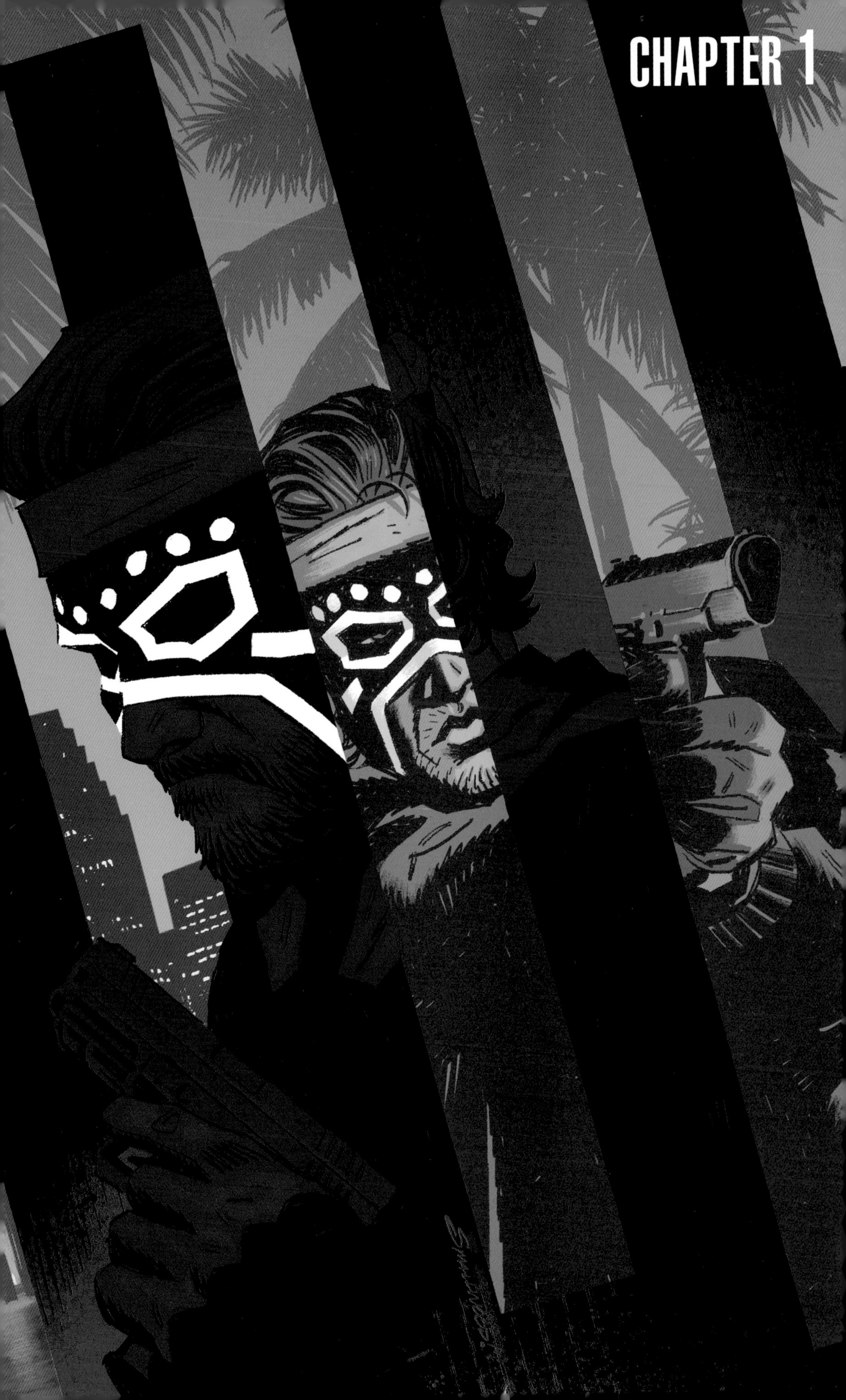

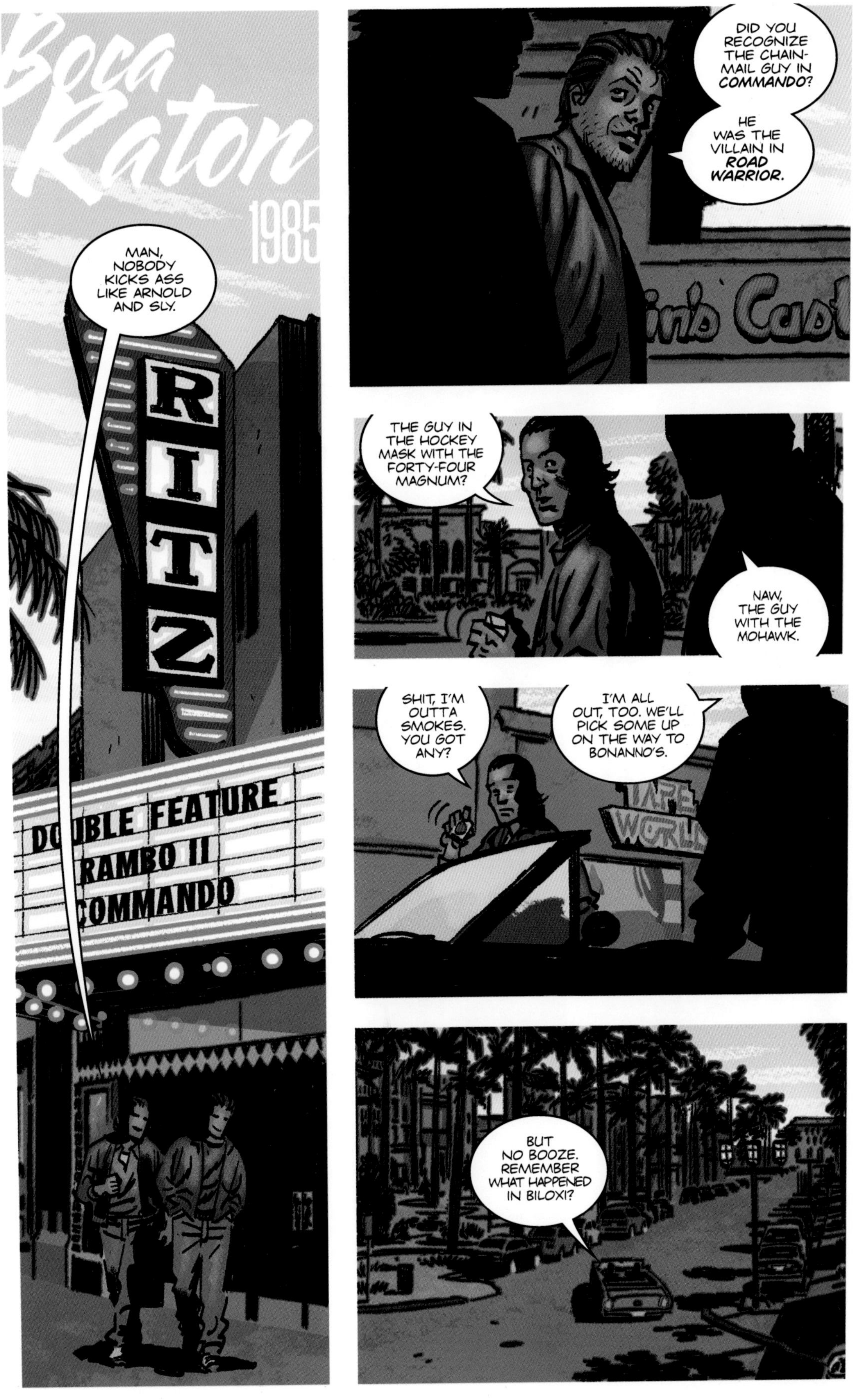
Boca Raton
1985
RITZ
DOUBLE FEATURE
RAMBO II
COMMANDO
MAN, NOBODY KICKS ASS LIKE ARNOLD AND SLY.
DID YOU RECOGNIZE THE CHAIN-MAIL GUY IN ***COMMANDO?***
HE WAS THE VILLAIN IN ***ROAD WARRIOR.***
THE GUY IN THE HOCKEY MASK WITH THE FORTY-FOUR MAGNUM?
NAW, THE GUY WITH THE MOHAWK.
SHIT, I'M OUTTA SMOKES. YOU GOT ANY?
I'M ALL OUT, TOO. WE'LL PICK SOME UP ON THE WAY TO BONANNO'S.
BUT NO BOOZE. REMEMBER WHAT HAPPENED IN BILOXI?

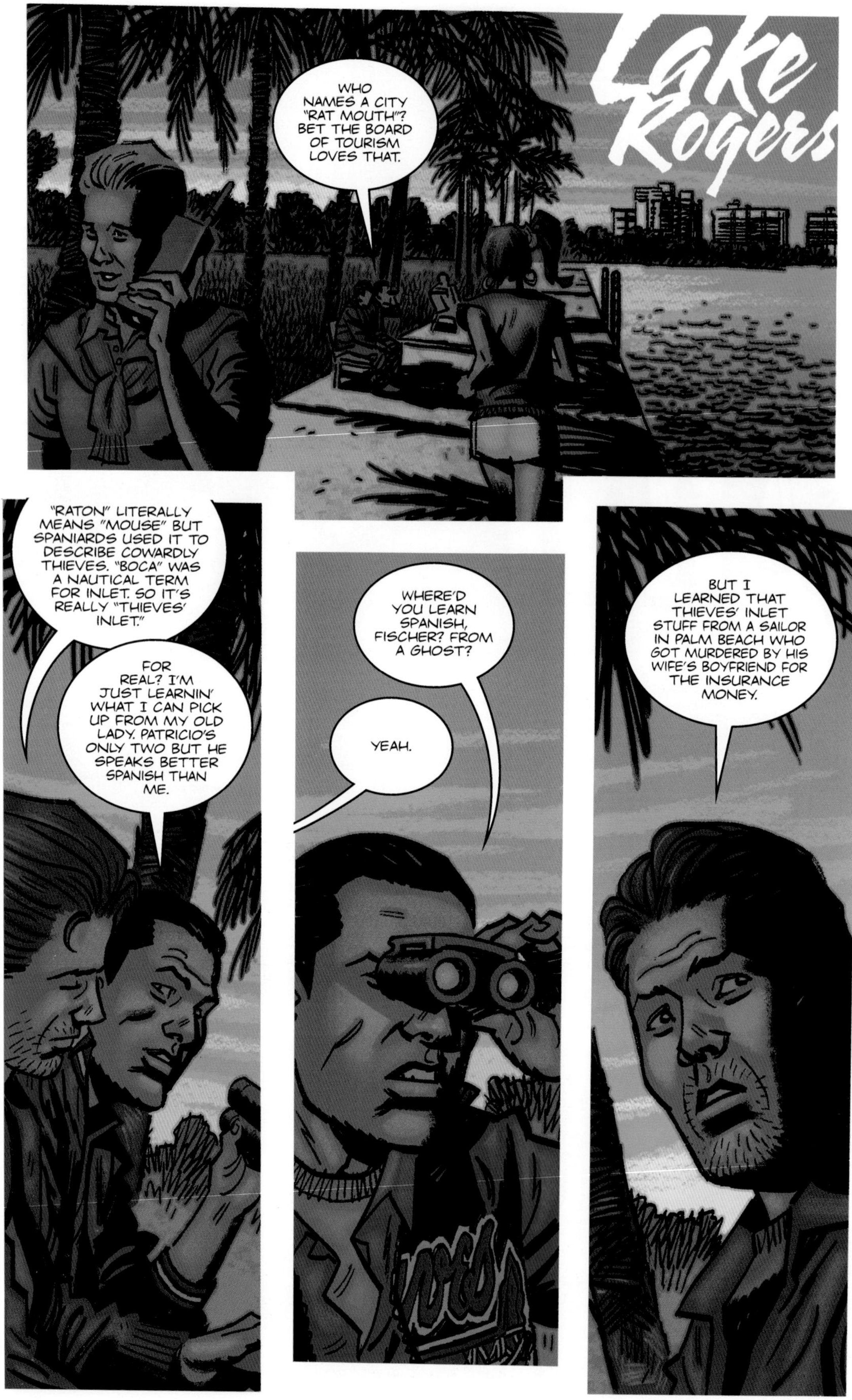
Lake Rogers
WHO NAMES A CITY "RAT MOUTH"? BET THE BOARD OF TOURISM LOVES THAT.
"RATON" LITERALLY MEANS "MOUSE" BUT SPANIARDS USED IT TO DESCRIBE COWARDLY THIEVES. "BOCA" WAS A NAUTICAL TERM FOR INLET. SO IT'S REALLY "THIEVES' INLET."
FOR REAL? I'M JUST LEARNIN' WHAT I CAN PICK UP FROM MY OLD LADY. PATRICIO'S ONLY TWO BUT HE SPEAKS BETTER SPANISH THAN ME.
WHERE'D YOU LEARN SPANISH, FISCHER? FROM A GHOST?
YEAH.
BUT I LEARNED THAT THIEVES' INLET STUFF FROM A SAILOR IN PALM BEACH WHO GOT MURDERED BY HIS WIFE'S BOYFRIEND FOR THE INSURANCE MONEY.

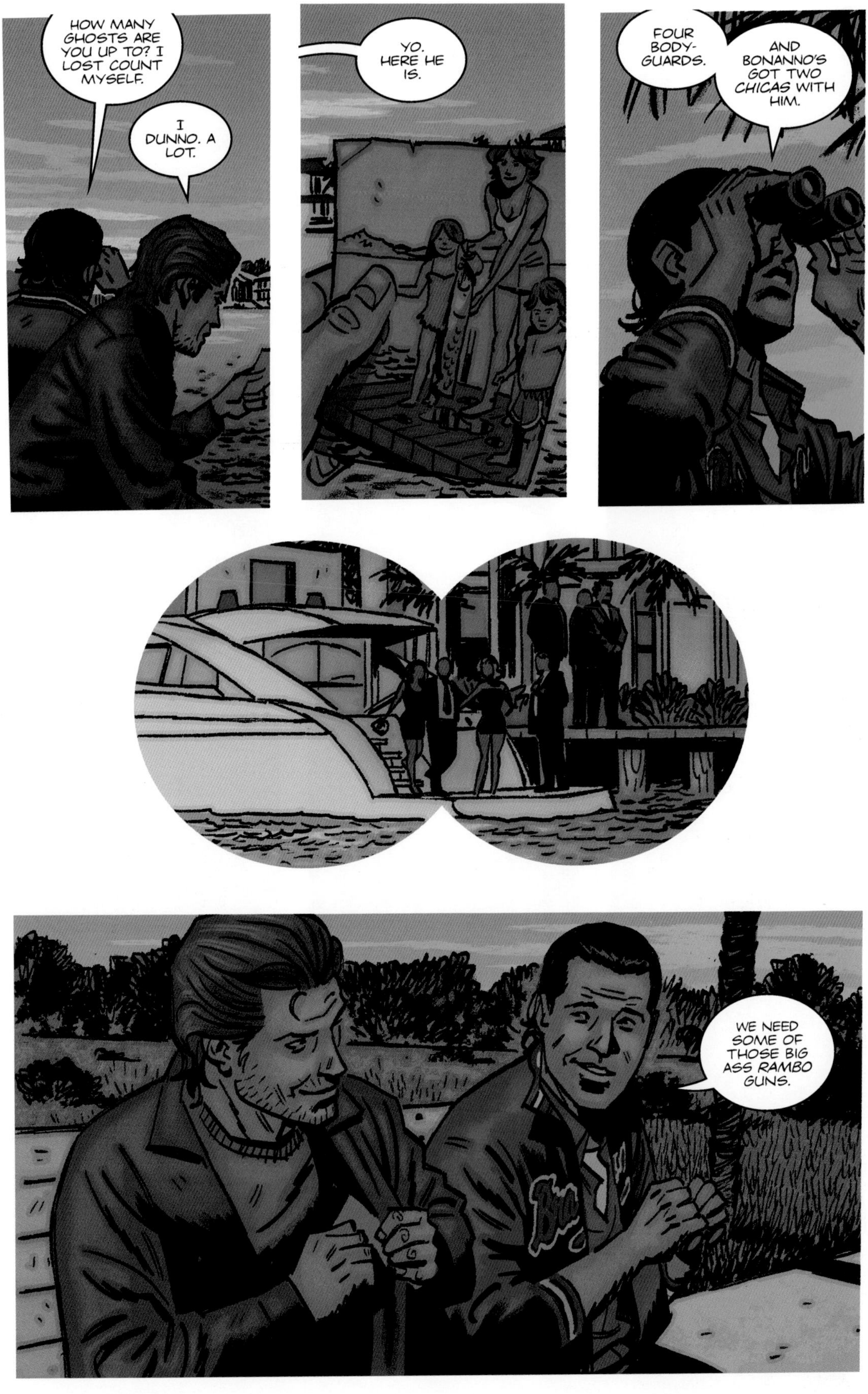
HOW MANY GHOSTS ARE YOU UP TO? I LOST COUNT MYSELF.
I DUNNO. A LOT.
YO. HERE HE IS.
FOUR BODY-GUARDS.
AND BONANNO'S GOT TWO *CHICAS* WITH HIM.
WE NEED SOME OF THOSE BIG ASS *RAMBO* GUNS.

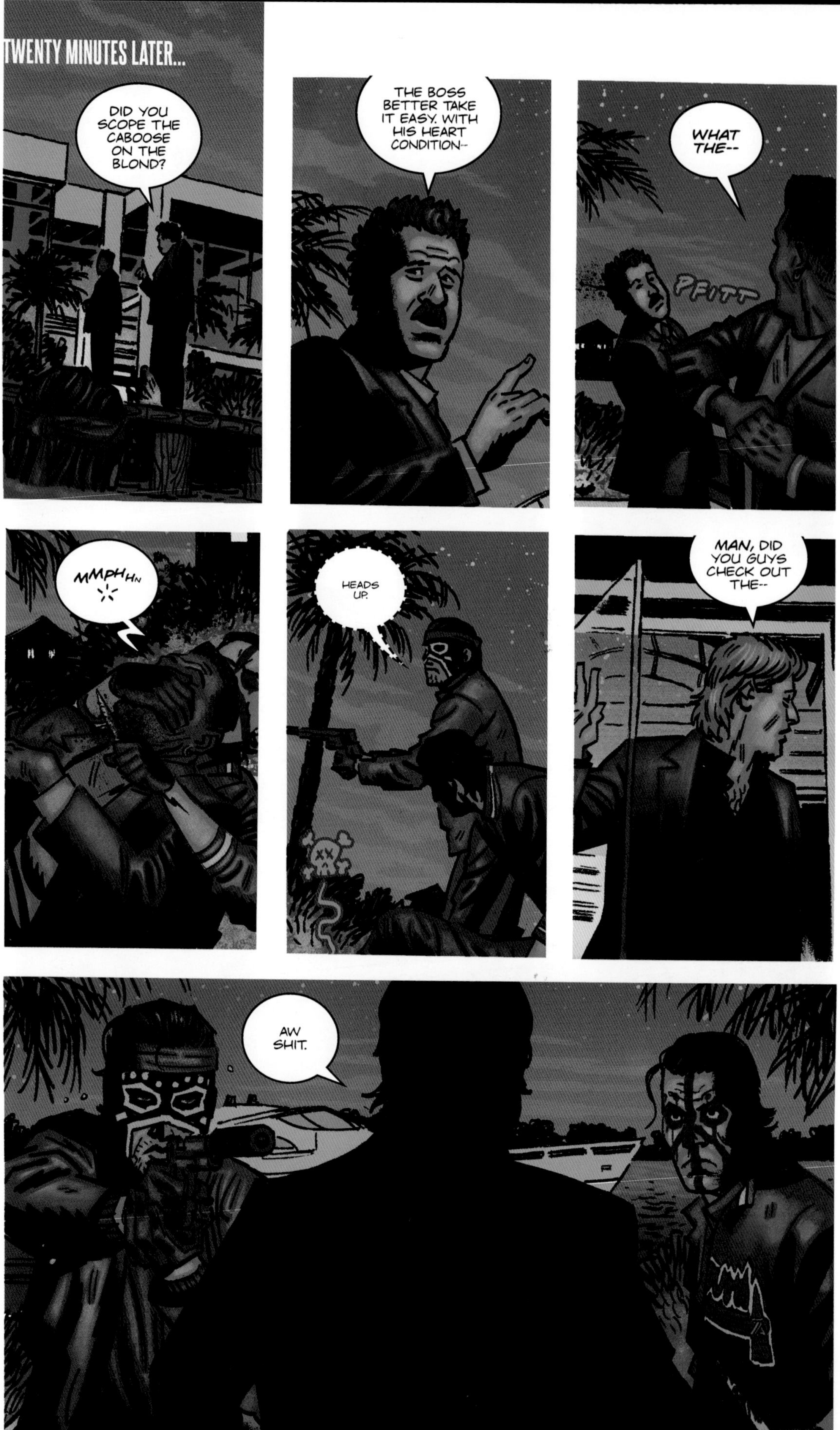
TWENTY MINUTES LATER...
DID YOU SCOPE THE CABOOSE ON THE BLOND?
THE BOSS BETTER TAKE IT EASY. WITH HIS HEART CONDITION--
WHAT THE--
PFITT
MMPHHN
HEADS UP.
MAN, DID YOU GUYS CHECK OUT THE--
AW SHIT.

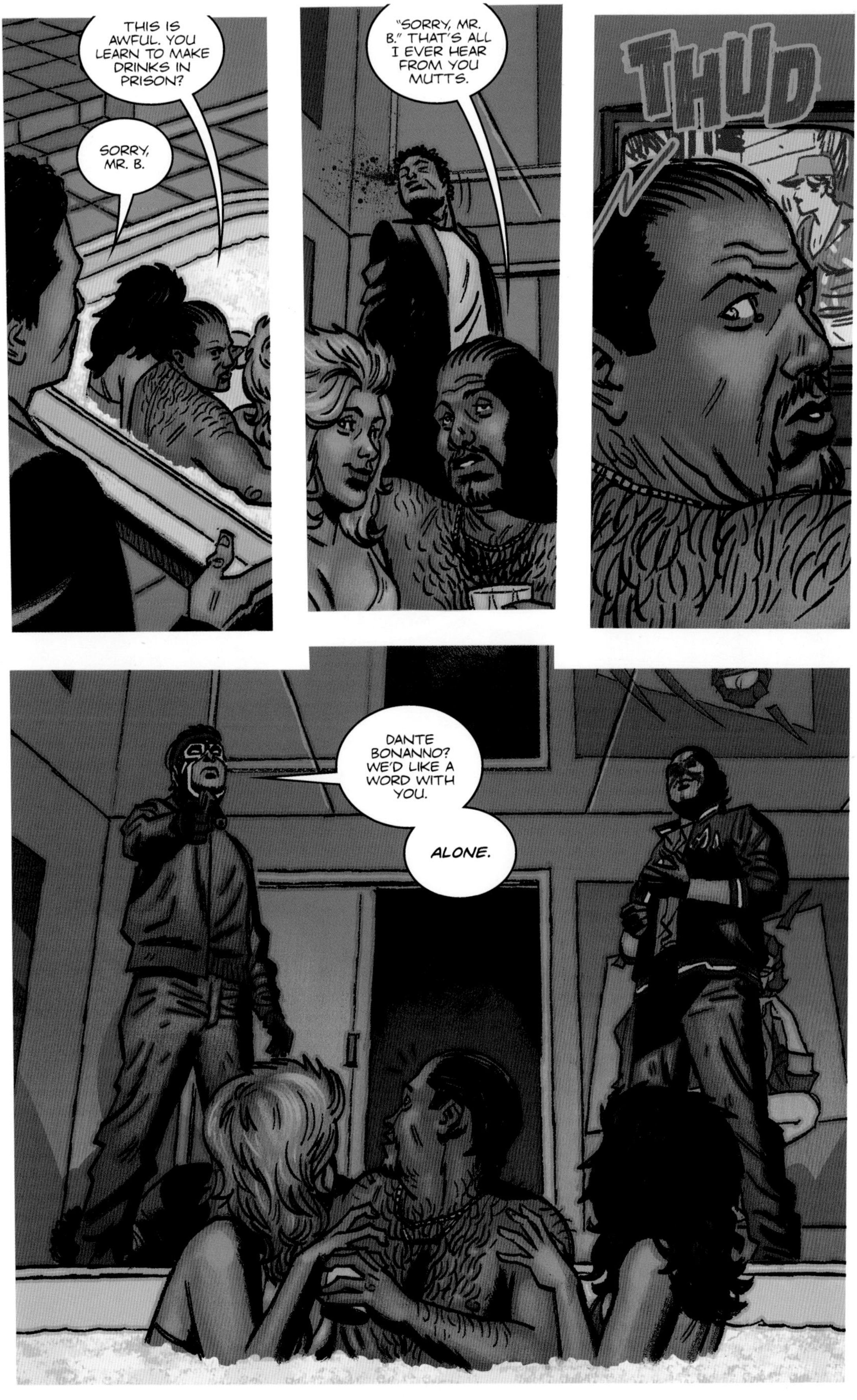

THIS IS AWFUL. YOU LEARN TO MAKE DRINKS IN PRISON?
SORRY, MR. B.
"SORRY, MR. B." THAT'S ALL I EVER HEAR FROM YOU MUTTS.
THUD
DANTE BONANNO? WE'D LIKE A WORD WITH YOU.
ALONE.

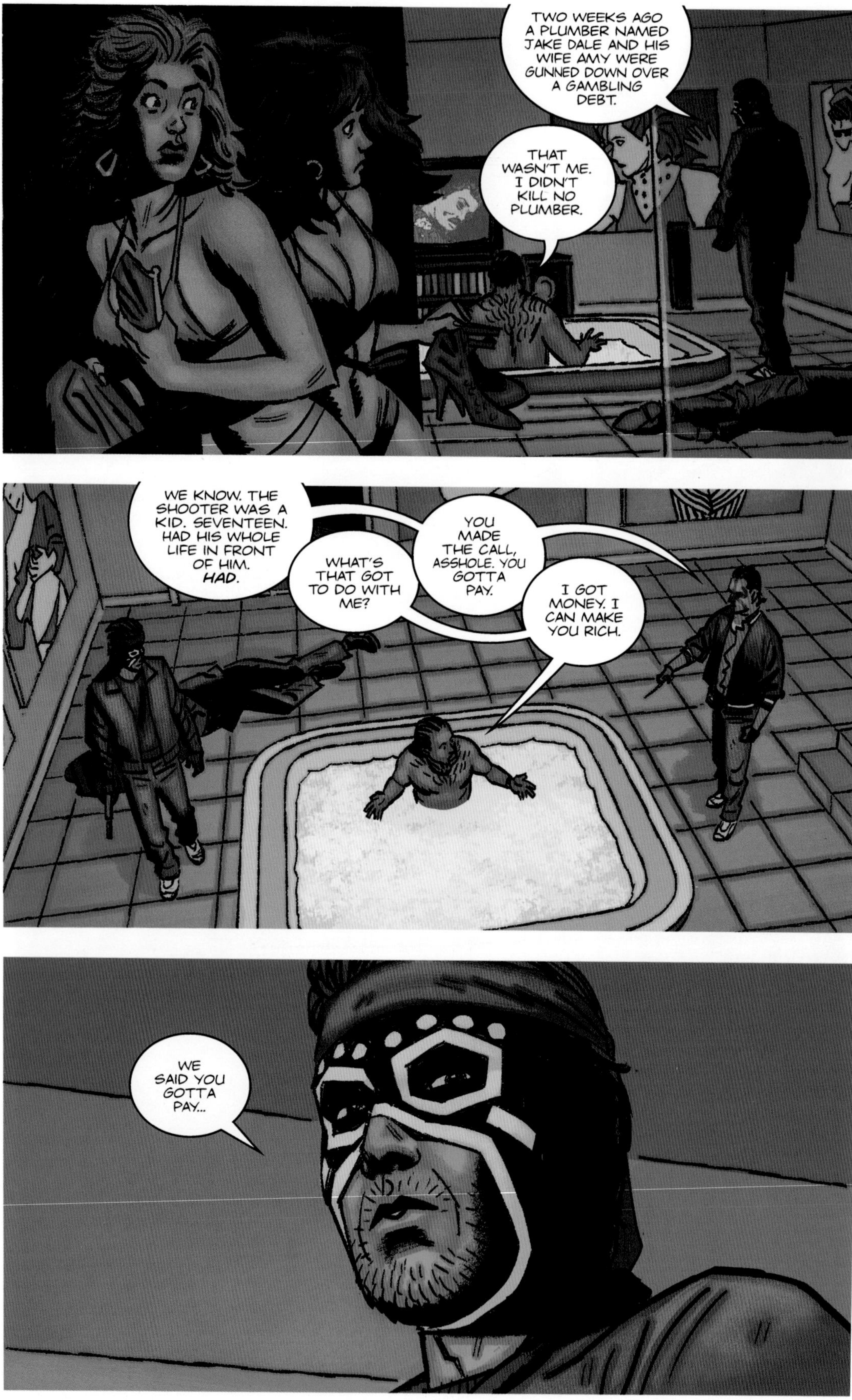
TWO WEEKS AGO A PLUMBER NAMED JAKE DALE AND HIS WIFE AMY WERE GUNNED DOWN OVER A GAMBLING DEBT.
THAT WASN'T ME. I DIDN'T KILL NO PLUMBER.
WE KNOW. THE SHOOTER WAS A KID. SEVENTEEN. HAD HIS WHOLE LIFE IN FRONT OF HIM. **HAD**.
WHAT'S THAT GOT TO DO WITH ME?
YOU MADE THE CALL, ASSHOLE. YOU GOTTA PAY.
I GOT MONEY. I CAN MAKE YOU RICH.
WE SAID YOU GOTTA PAY...

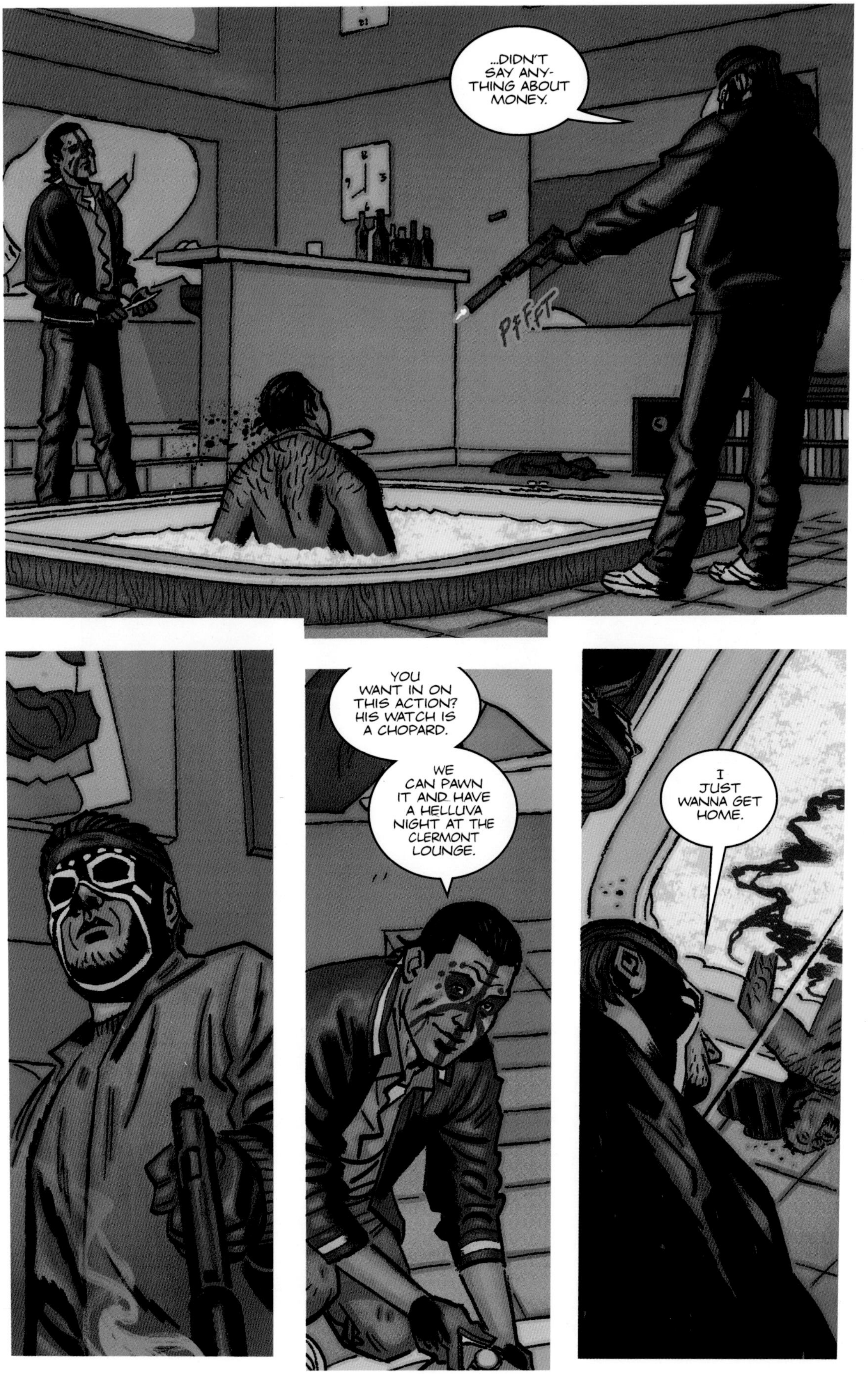
...DIDN'T SAY ANY-THING ABOUT MONEY.
PFFFT
YOU WANT IN ON THIS ACTION? HIS WATCH IS A CHOPARD.
WE CAN PAWN IT AND HAVE A HELLUVA NIGHT AT THE CLERMONT LOUNGE.
I JUST WANNA GET HOME.

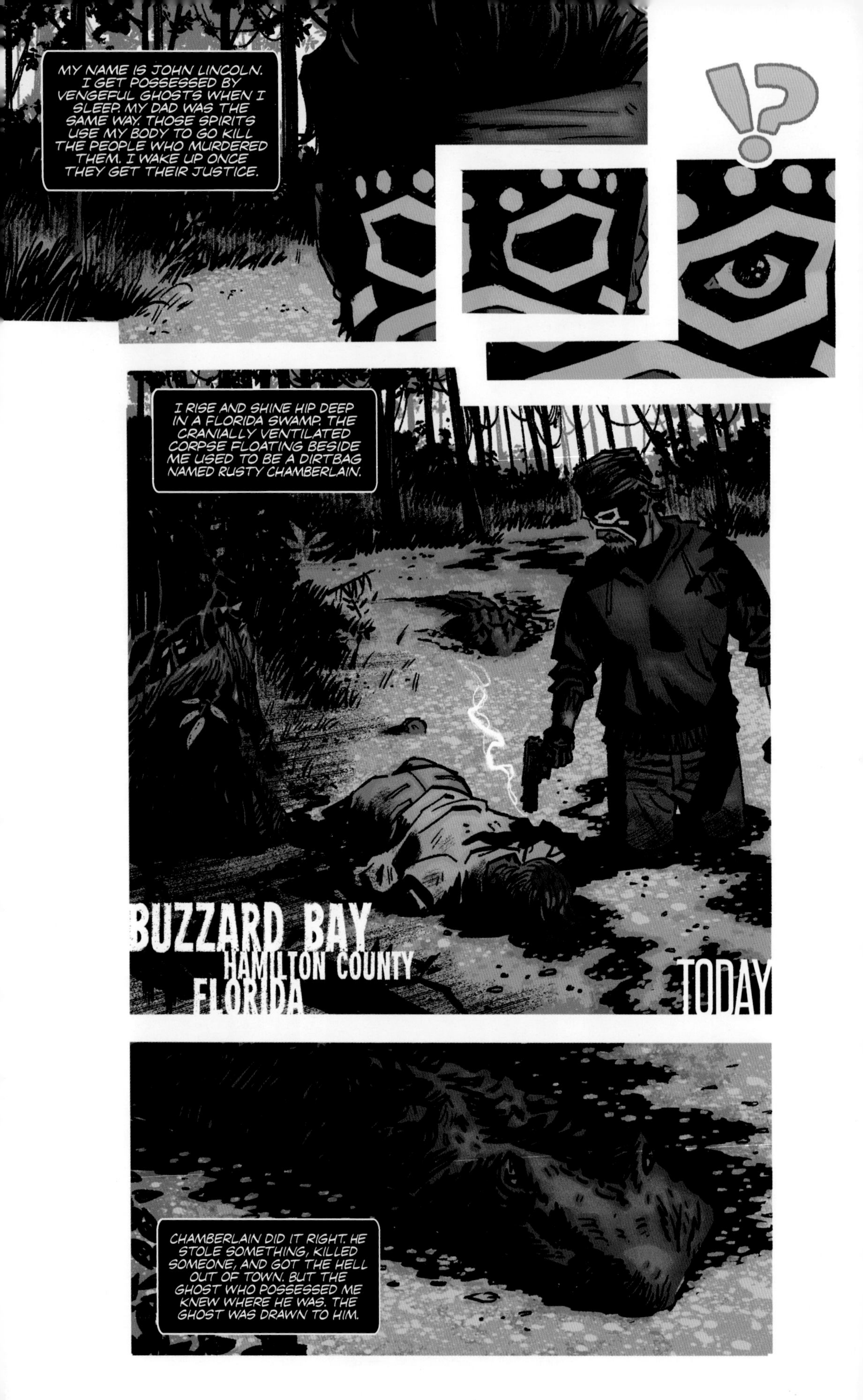
MY NAME IS JOHN LINCOLN. I GET POSSESSED BY VENGEFUL GHOSTS WHEN I SLEEP. MY DAD WAS THE SAME WAY. THOSE SPIRITS USE MY BODY TO GO KILL THE PEOPLE WHO MURDERED THEM. I WAKE UP ONCE THEY GET THEIR JUSTICE.
!?
I RISE AND SHINE HIP DEEP IN A FLORIDA SWAMP. THE CRANIALLY VENTILATED CORPSE FLOATING BESIDE ME USED TO BE A DIRTBAG NAMED RUSTY CHAMBERLAIN.
BUZZARD BAY
HAMILTON COUNTY
FLORIDA
TODAY
CHAMBERLAIN DID IT RIGHT. HE STOLE SOMETHING, KILLED SOMEONE, AND GOT THE HELL OUT OF TOWN. BUT THE GHOST WHO POSSESSED ME KNEW WHERE HE WAS. THE GHOST WAS DRAWN TO HIM.

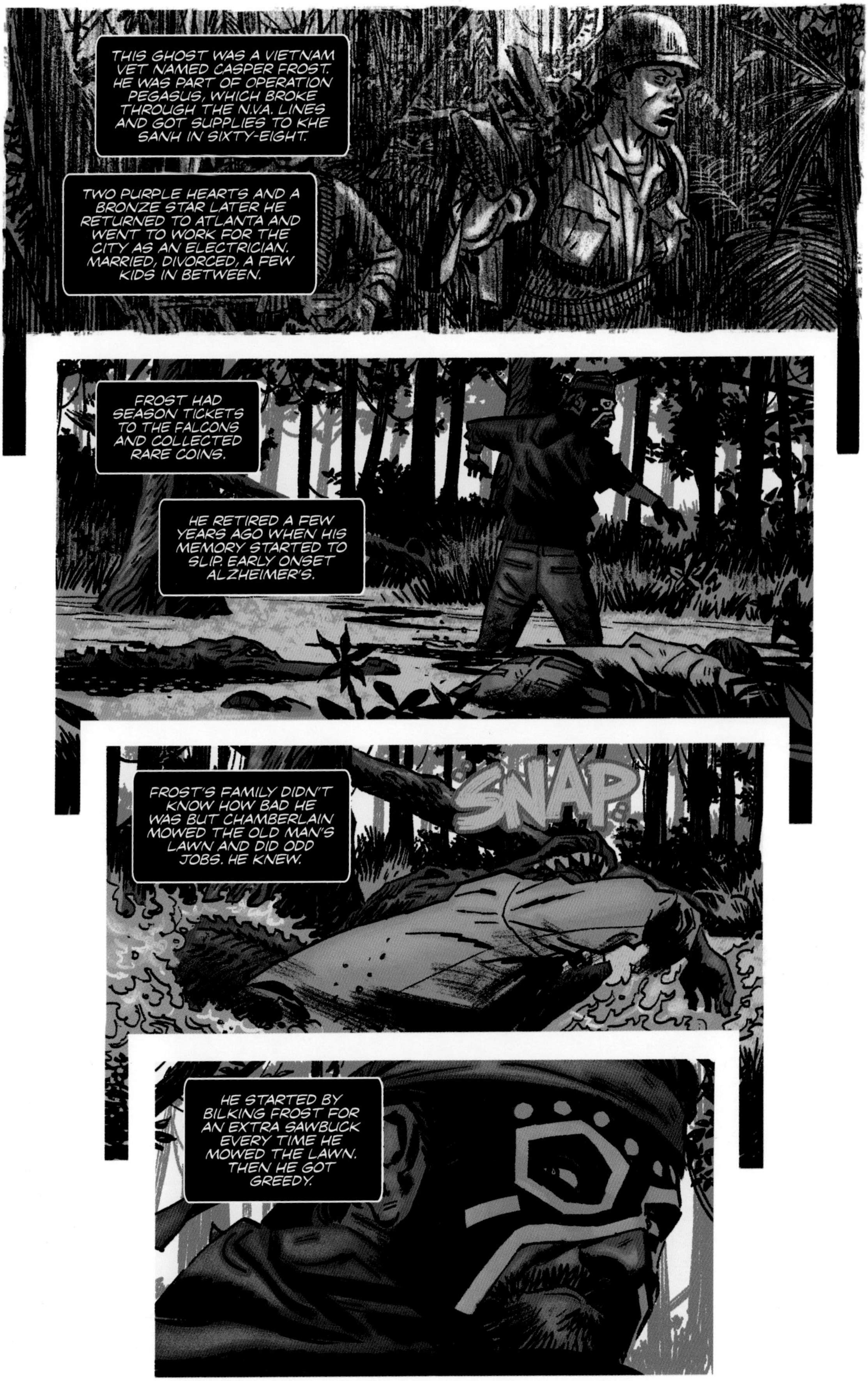
THIS GHOST WAS A VIETNAM VET NAMED CASPER FROST. HE WAS PART OF OPERATION PEGASUS, WHICH BROKE THROUGH THE N.V.A. LINES AND GOT SUPPLIES TO KHE SANH IN SIXTY-EIGHT.
TWO PURPLE HEARTS AND A BRONZE STAR LATER HE RETURNED TO ATLANTA AND WENT TO WORK FOR THE CITY AS AN ELECTRICIAN. MARRIED, DIVORCED, A FEW KIDS IN BETWEEN.
FROST HAD SEASON TICKETS TO THE FALCONS AND COLLECTED RARE COINS.
HE RETIRED A FEW YEARS AGO WHEN HIS MEMORY STARTED TO SLIP. EARLY ONSET ALZHEIMER'S.
FROST'S FAMILY DIDN'T KNOW HOW BAD HE WAS BUT CHAMBERLAIN MOWED THE OLD MAN'S LAWN AND DID ODD JOBS. HE KNEW.
SNAP
HE STARTED BY BILKING FROST FOR AN EXTRA SAWBUCK EVERY TIME HE MOWED THE LAWN. THEN HE GOT GREEDY.

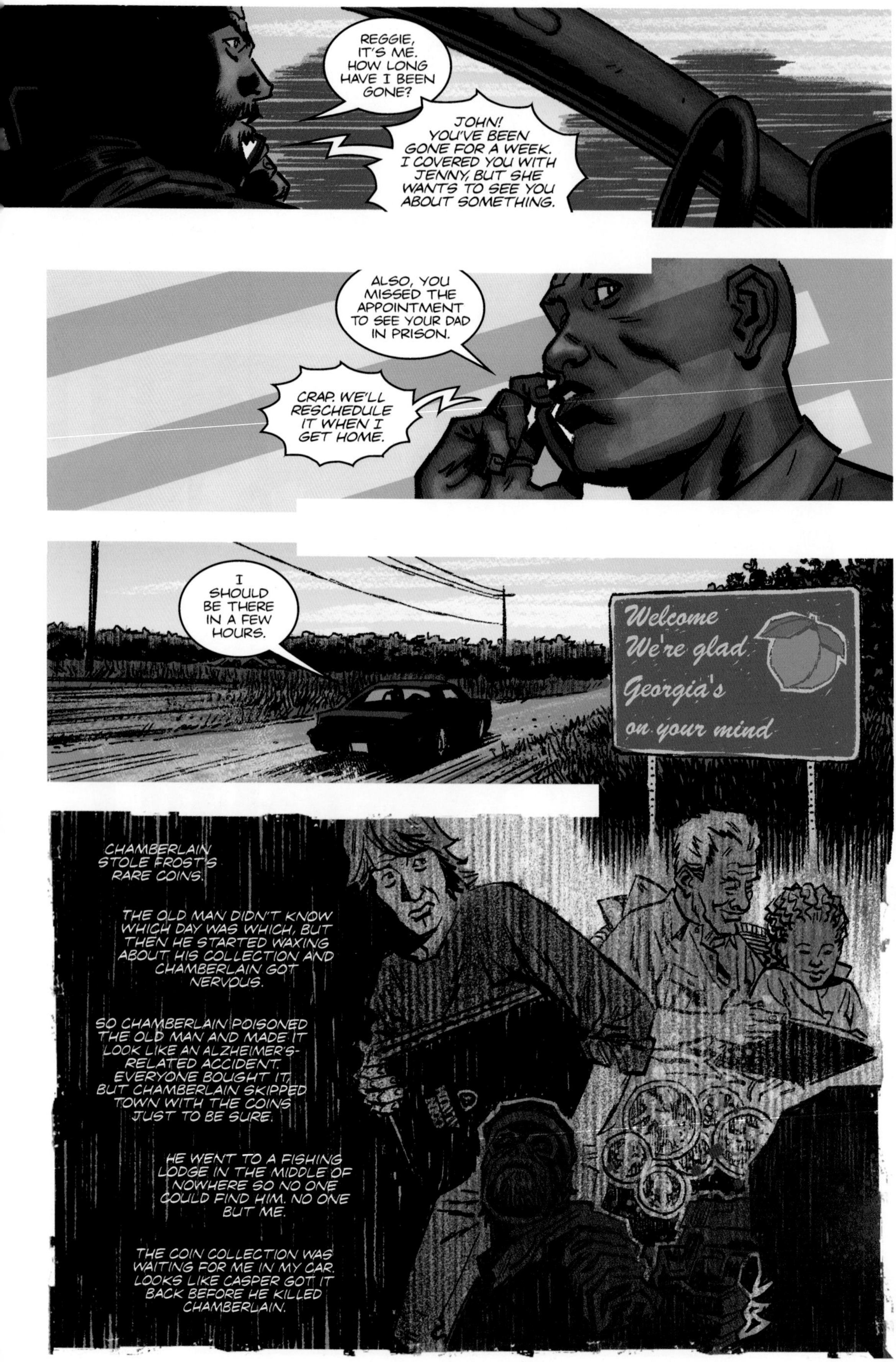
REGGIE, IT'S ME. HOW LONG HAVE I BEEN GONE?
JOHN! YOU'VE BEEN GONE FOR A WEEK. I COVERED YOU WITH JENNY, BUT SHE WANTS TO SEE YOU ABOUT SOMETHING.
ALSO, YOU MISSED THE APPOINTMENT TO SEE YOUR DAD IN PRISON.
CRAP. WE'LL RESCHEDULE IT WHEN I GET HOME.
I SHOULD BE THERE IN A FEW HOURS.
Welcome We're glad Georgia's on your mind
CHAMBERLAIN STOLE FROST'S RARE COINS.
THE OLD MAN DIDN'T KNOW WHICH DAY WAS WHICH, BUT THEN HE STARTED WAXING ABOUT HIS COLLECTION AND CHAMBERLAIN GOT NERVOUS.
SO CHAMBERLAIN POISONED THE OLD MAN AND MADE IT LOOK LIKE AN ALZHEIMER'S-RELATED ACCIDENT. EVERYONE BOUGHT IT, BUT CHAMBERLAIN SKIPPED TOWN WITH THE COINS JUST TO BE SURE.
HE WENT TO A FISHING LODGE IN THE MIDDLE OF NOWHERE SO NO ONE COULD FIND HIM. NO ONE BUT ME.
THE COIN COLLECTION WAS WAITING FOR ME IN MY CAR. LOOKS LIKE CASPER GOT IT BACK BEFORE HE KILLED CHAMBERLAIN.

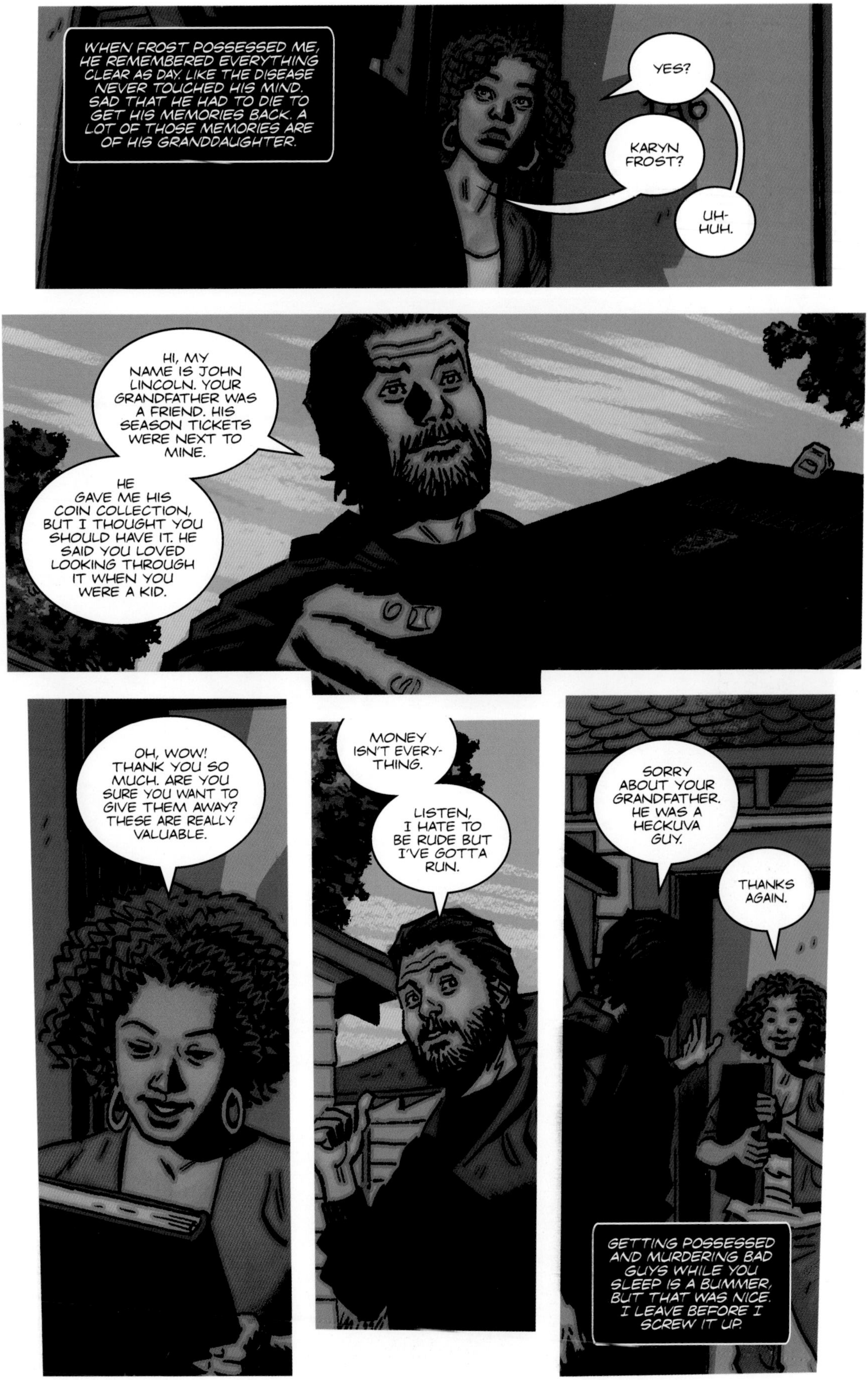
WHEN FROST POSSESSED ME, HE REMEMBERED EVERYTHING CLEAR AS DAY. LIKE THE DISEASE NEVER TOUCHED HIS MIND. SAD THAT HE HAD TO DIE TO GET HIS MEMORIES BACK. A LOT OF THOSE MEMORIES ARE OF HIS GRANDDAUGHTER.
YES?
KARYN FROST?
UH-HUH.
HI, MY NAME IS JOHN LINCOLN. YOUR GRANDFATHER WAS A FRIEND. HIS SEASON TICKETS WERE NEXT TO MINE.
HE GAVE ME HIS COIN COLLECTION, BUT I THOUGHT YOU SHOULD HAVE IT. HE SAID YOU LOVED LOOKING THROUGH IT WHEN YOU WERE A KID.
OH, WOW! THANK YOU SO MUCH. ARE YOU SURE YOU WANT TO GIVE THEM AWAY? THESE ARE REALLY VALUABLE.
MONEY ISN'T EVERY-THING.
LISTEN, I HATE TO BE RUDE BUT I'VE GOTTA RUN.
SORRY ABOUT YOUR GRANDFATHER. HE WAS A HECKUVA GUY.
THANKS AGAIN.
GETTING POSSESSED AND MURDERING BAD GUYS WHILE YOU SLEEP IS A BUMMER, BUT THAT WAS NICE. I LEAVE BEFORE I SCREW IT UP.

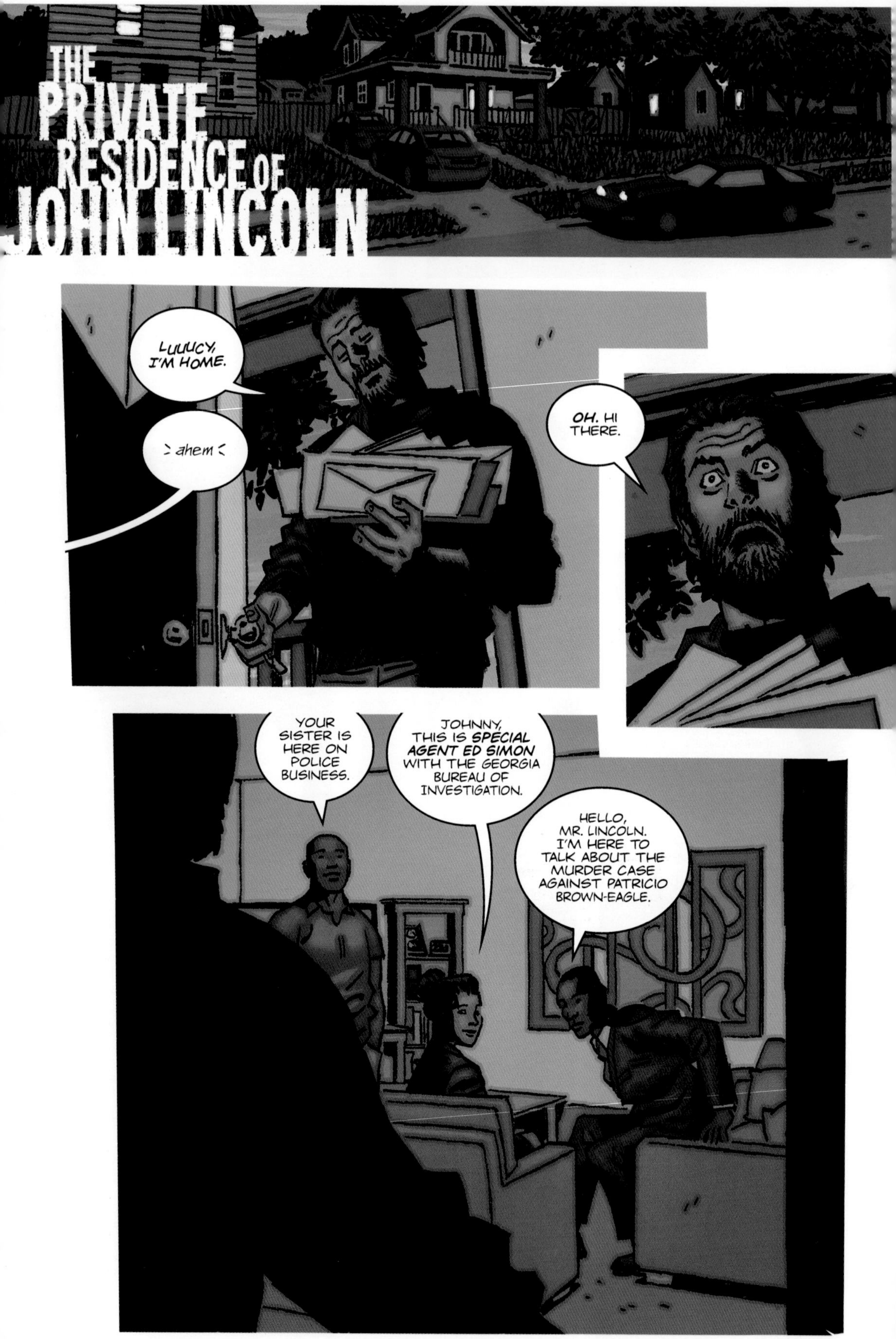
THE PRIVATE RESIDENCE OF JOHN LINCOLN
LUUUCY, I'M HOME.
> ahem <
OH. HI THERE.
YOUR SISTER IS HERE ON POLICE BUSINESS.
JOHNNY, THIS IS SPECIAL AGENT ED SIMON WITH THE GEORGIA BUREAU OF INVESTIGATION.
HELLO, MR. LINCOLN. I'M HERE TO TALK ABOUT THE MURDER CASE AGAINST PATRICIO BROWN-EAGLE.

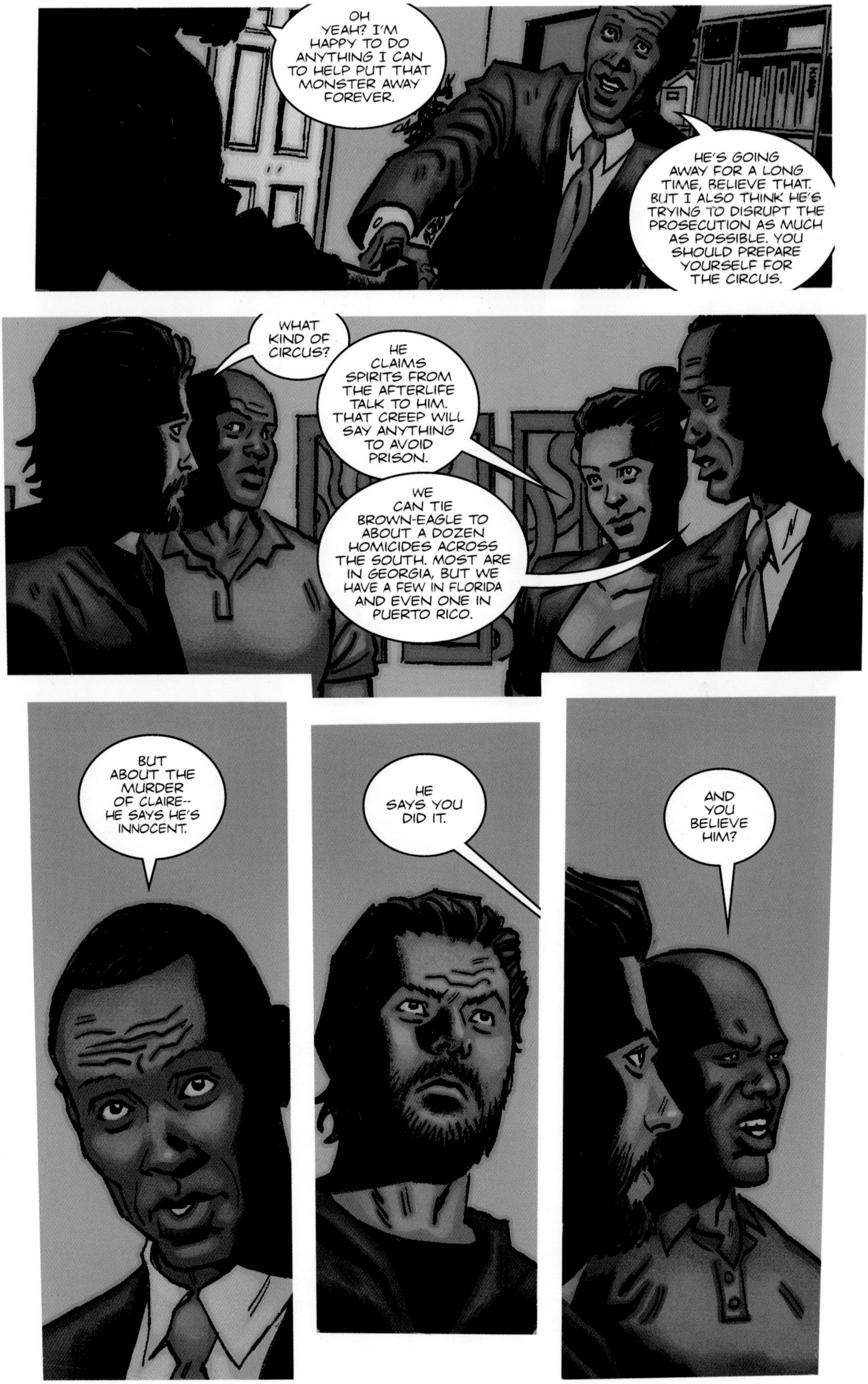
OH YEAH? I'M HAPPY TO DO ANYTHING I CAN TO HELP PUT THAT MONSTER AWAY FOREVER.
HE'S GOING AWAY FOR A LONG TIME, BELIEVE THAT. BUT I ALSO THINK HE'S TRYING TO DISRUPT THE PROSECUTION AS MUCH AS POSSIBLE. YOU SHOULD PREPARE YOURSELF FOR THE CIRCUS.
WHAT KIND OF CIRCUS?
HE CLAIMS SPIRITS FROM THE AFTERLIFE TALK TO HIM. THAT CREEP WILL SAY ANYTHING TO AVOID PRISON.
WE CAN TIE BROWN-EAGLE TO ABOUT A DOZEN HOMICIDES ACROSS THE SOUTH. MOST ARE IN GEORGIA, BUT WE HAVE A FEW IN FLORIDA AND EVEN ONE IN PUERTO RICO.
BUT ABOUT THE MURDER OF CLAIRE-- HE SAYS HE'S INNOCENT.
HE SAYS YOU DID IT.
AND YOU BELIEVE HIM?

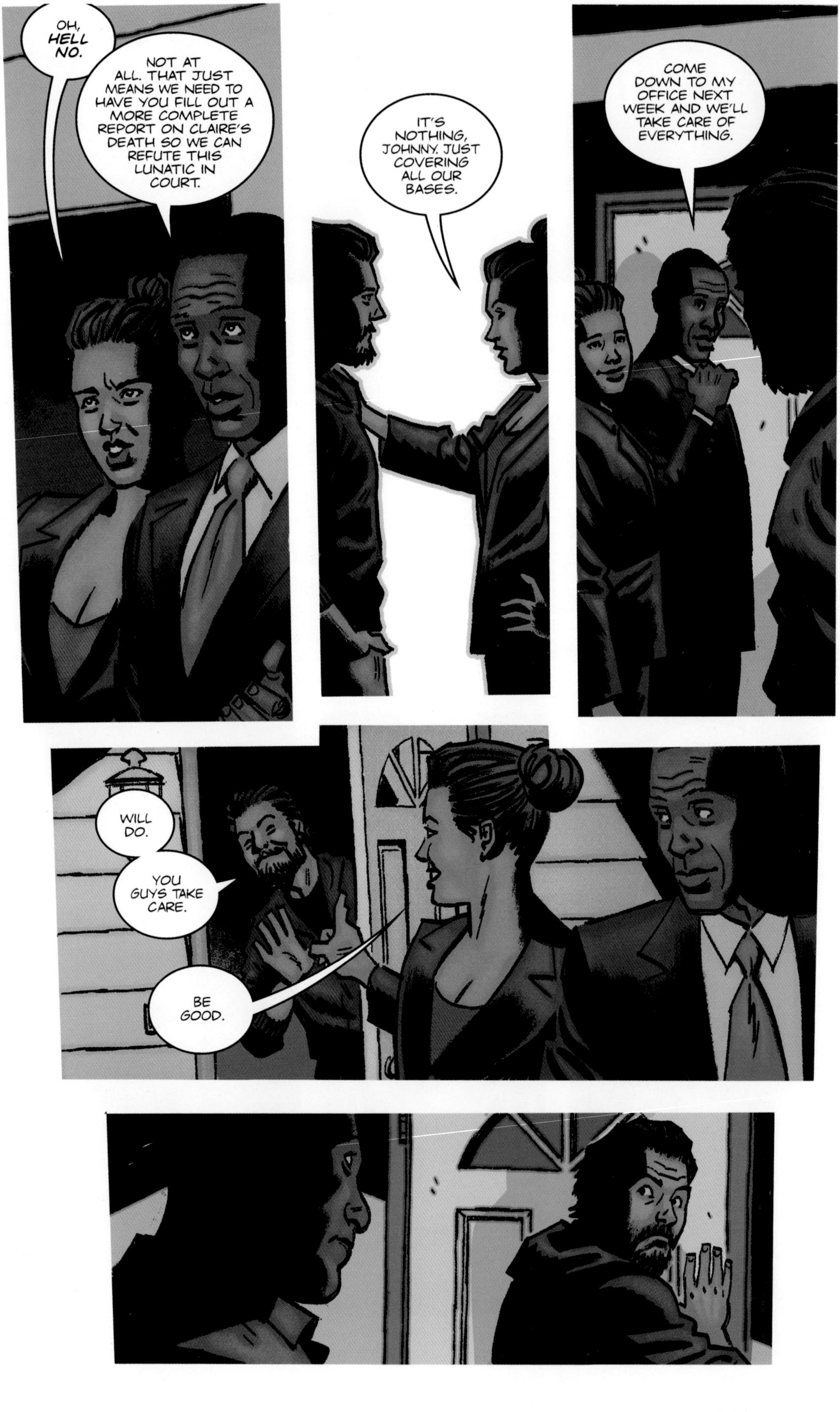
OH, HELL NO.
NOT AT ALL. THAT JUST MEANS WE NEED TO HAVE YOU FILL OUT A MORE COMPLETE REPORT ON CLAIRE'S DEATH SO WE CAN REFUTE THIS LUNATIC IN COURT.
IT'S NOTHING, JOHNNY. JUST COVERING ALL OUR BASES.
COME DOWN TO MY OFFICE NEXT WEEK AND WE'LL TAKE CARE OF EVERYTHING.
WILL DO.
YOU GUYS TAKE CARE.
BE GOOD.

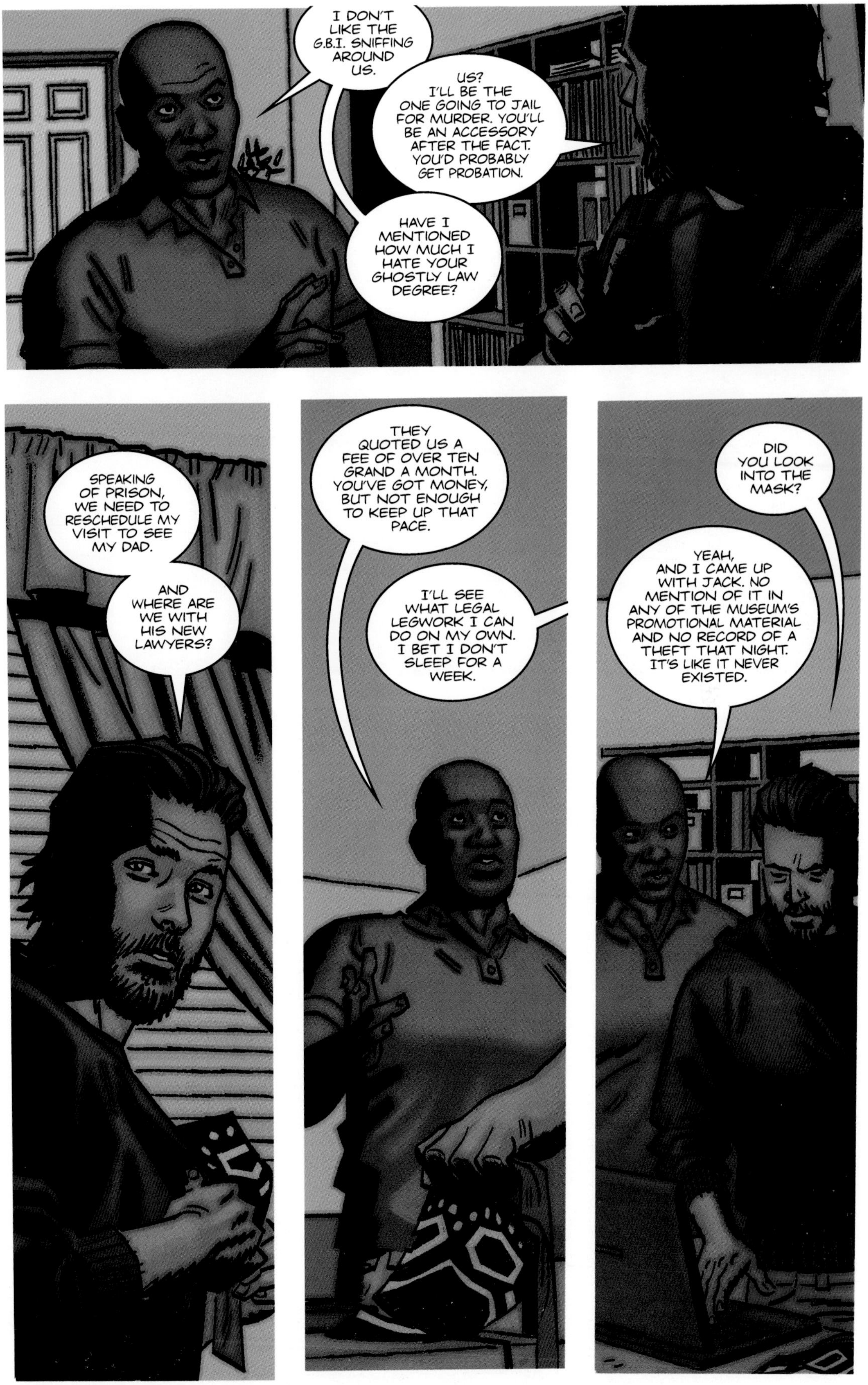
I DON'T LIKE THE G.B.I. SNIFFING AROUND US.
US? I'LL BE THE ONE GOING TO JAIL FOR MURDER. YOU'LL BE AN ACCESSORY AFTER THE FACT. YOU'D PROBABLY GET PROBATION.
HAVE I MENTIONED HOW MUCH I HATE YOUR GHOSTLY LAW DEGREE?
SPEAKING OF PRISON, WE NEED TO RESCHEDULE MY VISIT TO SEE MY DAD.
AND WHERE ARE WE WITH HIS NEW LAWYERS?
THEY QUOTED US A FEE OF OVER TEN GRAND A MONTH. YOU'VE GOT MONEY, BUT NOT ENOUGH TO KEEP UP THAT PACE.
I'LL SEE WHAT LEGAL LEGWORK I CAN DO ON MY OWN. I BET I DON'T SLEEP FOR A WEEK.
DID YOU LOOK INTO THE MASK?
YEAH, AND I CAME UP WITH JACK. NO MENTION OF IT IN ANY OF THE MUSEUM'S PROMOTIONAL MATERIAL AND NO RECORD OF A THEFT THAT NIGHT. IT'S LIKE IT NEVER EXISTED.

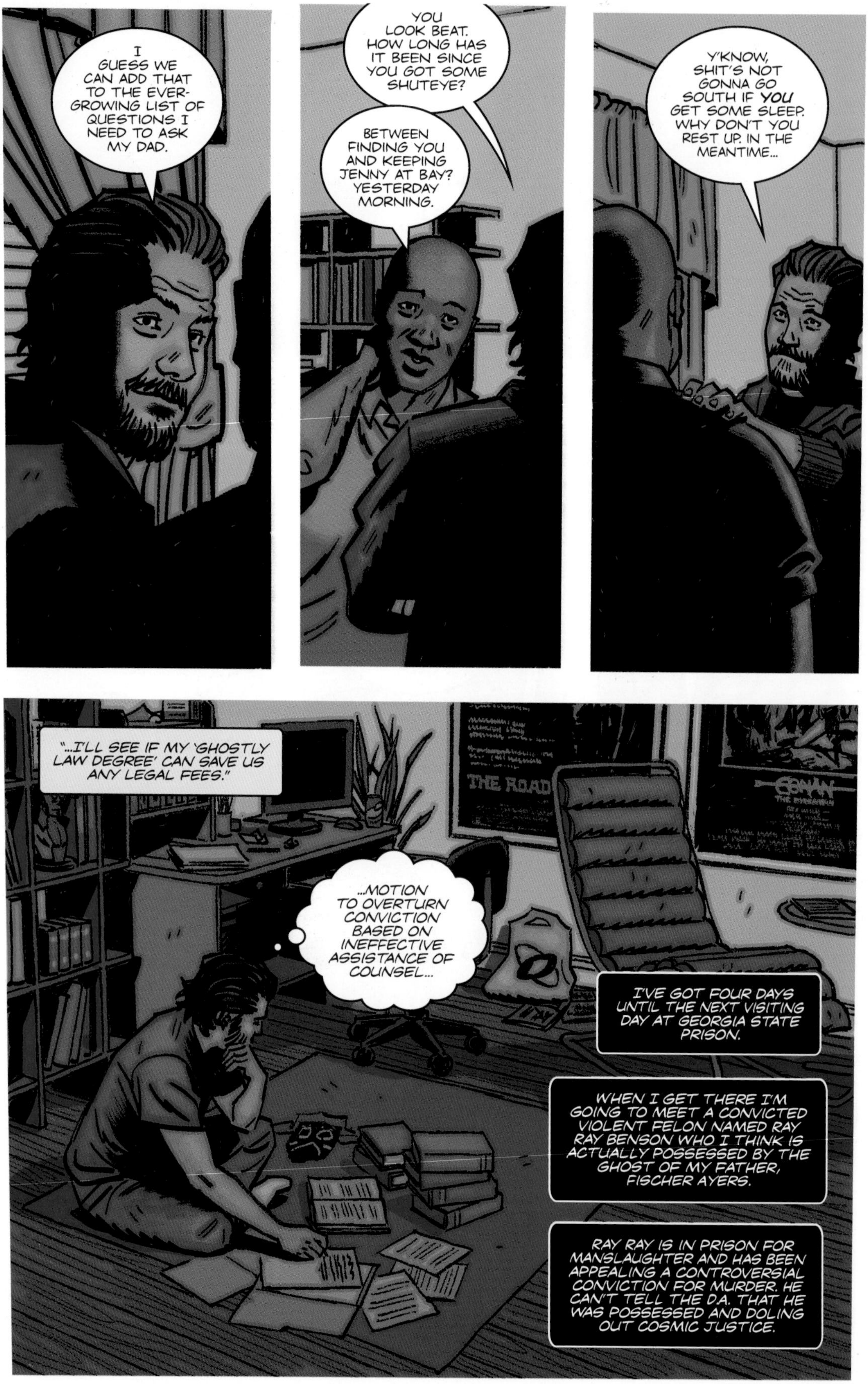
I GUESS WE CAN ADD THAT TO THE EVER-GROWING LIST OF QUESTIONS I NEED TO ASK MY DAD.
YOU LOOK BEAT. HOW LONG HAS IT BEEN SINCE YOU GOT SOME SHUTEYE?
BETWEEN FINDING YOU AND KEEPING JENNY AT BAY? YESTERDAY MORNING.
Y'KNOW, SHIT'S NOT GONNA GO SOUTH IF YOU GET SOME SLEEP. WHY DON'T YOU REST UP. IN THE MEANTIME...
"...I'LL SEE IF MY 'GHOSTLY LAW DEGREE' CAN SAVE US ANY LEGAL FEES."
...MOTION TO OVERTURN CONVICTION BASED ON INEFFECTIVE ASSISTANCE OF COUNSEL...
I'VE GOT FOUR DAYS UNTIL THE NEXT VISITING DAY AT GEORGIA STATE PRISON.
WHEN I GET THERE I'M GOING TO MEET A CONVICTED VIOLENT FELON NAMED RAY RAY BENSON WHO I THINK IS ACTUALLY POSSESSED BY THE GHOST OF MY FATHER, FISCHER AYERS.
RAY RAY IS IN PRISON FOR MANSLAUGHTER AND HAS BEEN APPEALING A CONTROVERSIAL CONVICTION FOR MURDER. HE CAN'T TELL THE DA. THAT HE WAS POSSESSED AND DOLING OUT COSMIC JUSTICE.

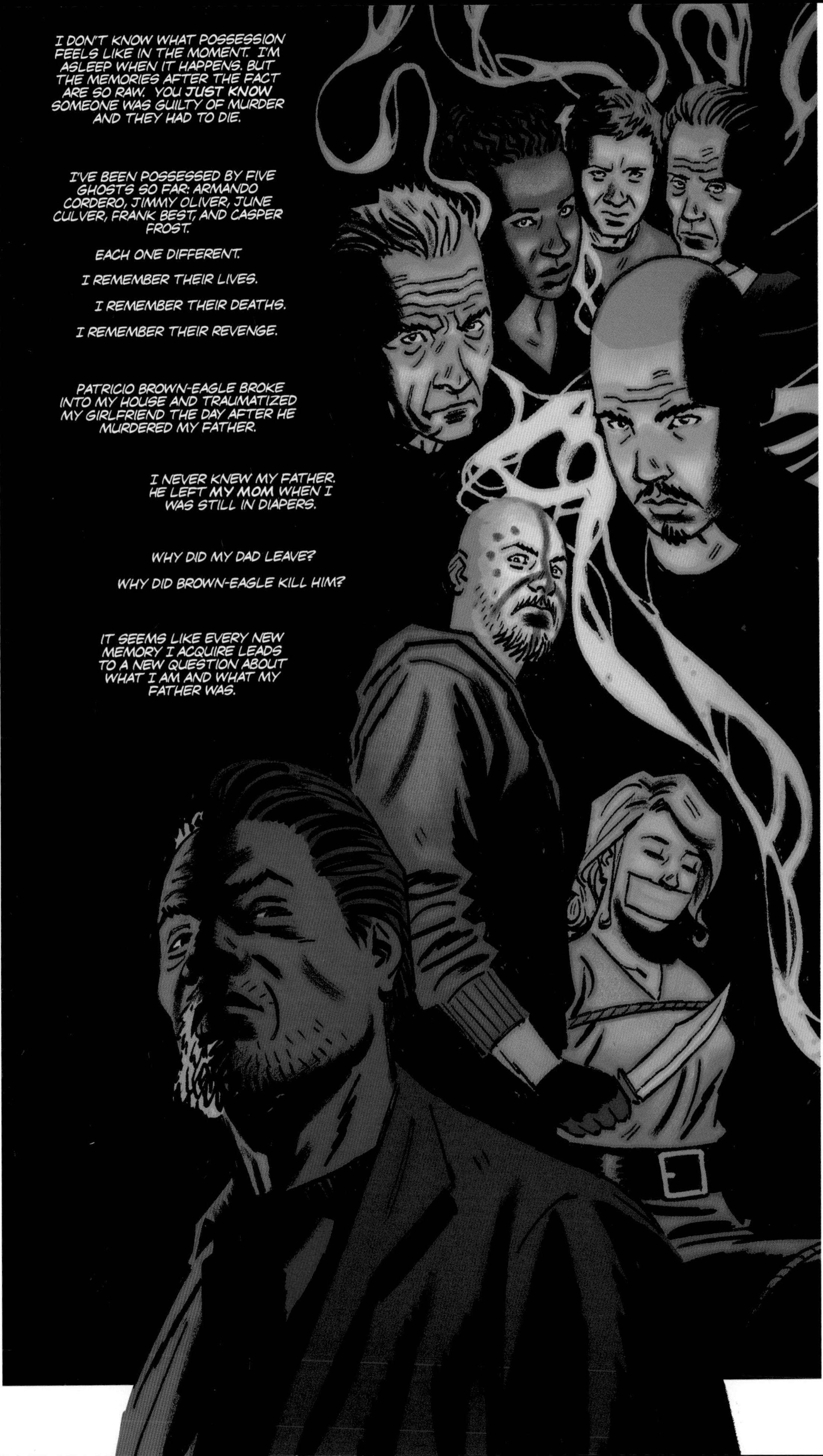
I DON'T KNOW WHAT POSSESSION FEELS LIKE IN THE MOMENT. I'M ASLEEP WHEN IT HAPPENS. BUT THE MEMORIES AFTER THE FACT ARE SO RAW. YOU JUST KNOW SOMEONE WAS GUILTY OF MURDER AND THEY HAD TO DIE.
I'VE BEEN POSSESSED BY FIVE GHOSTS SO FAR: ARMANDO CORDERO, JIMMY OLIVER, JUNE CULVER, FRANK BEST, AND CASPER FROST.
EACH ONE DIFFERENT.
I REMEMBER THEIR LIVES.
I REMEMBER THEIR DEATHS.
I REMEMBER THEIR REVENGE.
PATRICIO BROWN-EAGLE BROKE INTO MY HOUSE AND TRAUMATIZED MY GIRLFRIEND THE DAY AFTER HE MURDERED MY FATHER.
I NEVER KNEW MY FATHER. HE LEFT MY MOM WHEN I WAS STILL IN DIAPERS.
WHY DID MY DAD LEAVE?
WHY DID BROWN-EAGLE KILL HIM?
IT SEEMS LIKE EVERY NEW MEMORY I ACQUIRE LEADS TO A NEW QUESTION ABOUT WHAT I AM AND WHAT MY FATHER WAS.

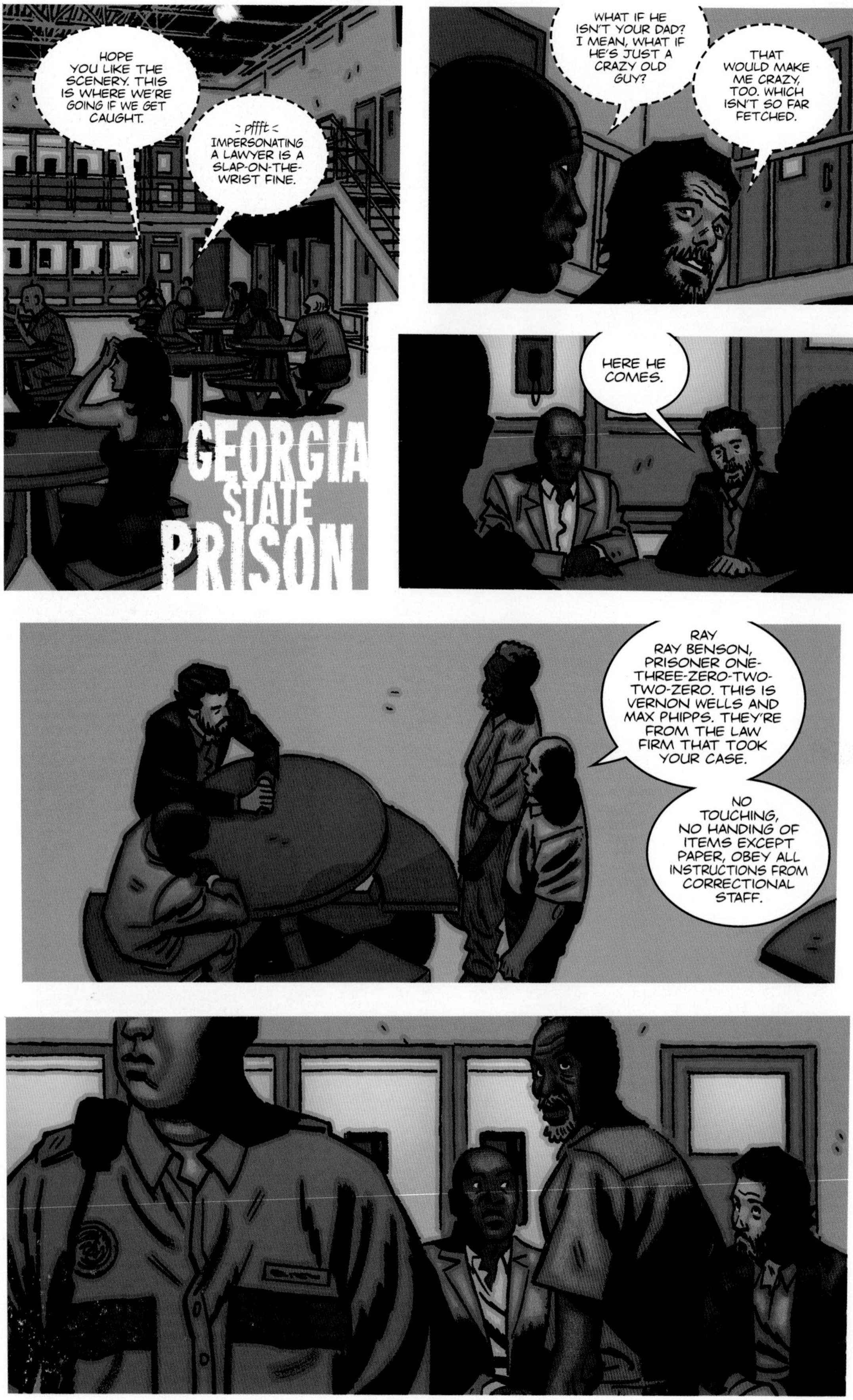
HOPE YOU LIKE THE SCENERY. THIS IS WHERE WE'RE GOING IF WE GET CAUGHT.
> pffft <
IMPERSONATING A LAWYER IS A SLAP-ON-THE-WRIST FINE.
GEORGIA STATE PRISON
WHAT IF HE ISN'T YOUR DAD? I MEAN, WHAT IF HE'S JUST A CRAZY OLD GUY?
THAT WOULD MAKE ME CRAZY, TOO. WHICH ISN'T SO FAR FETCHED.
HERE HE COMES.
RAY RAY BENSON, PRISONER ONE-THREE-ZERO-TWO-TWO-ZERO. THIS IS VERNON WELLS AND MAX PHIPPS. THEY'RE FROM THE LAW FIRM THAT TOOK YOUR CASE.
NO TOUCHING, NO HANDING OF ITEMS EXCEPT PAPER, OBEY ALL INSTRUCTIONS FROM CORRECTIONAL STAFF.

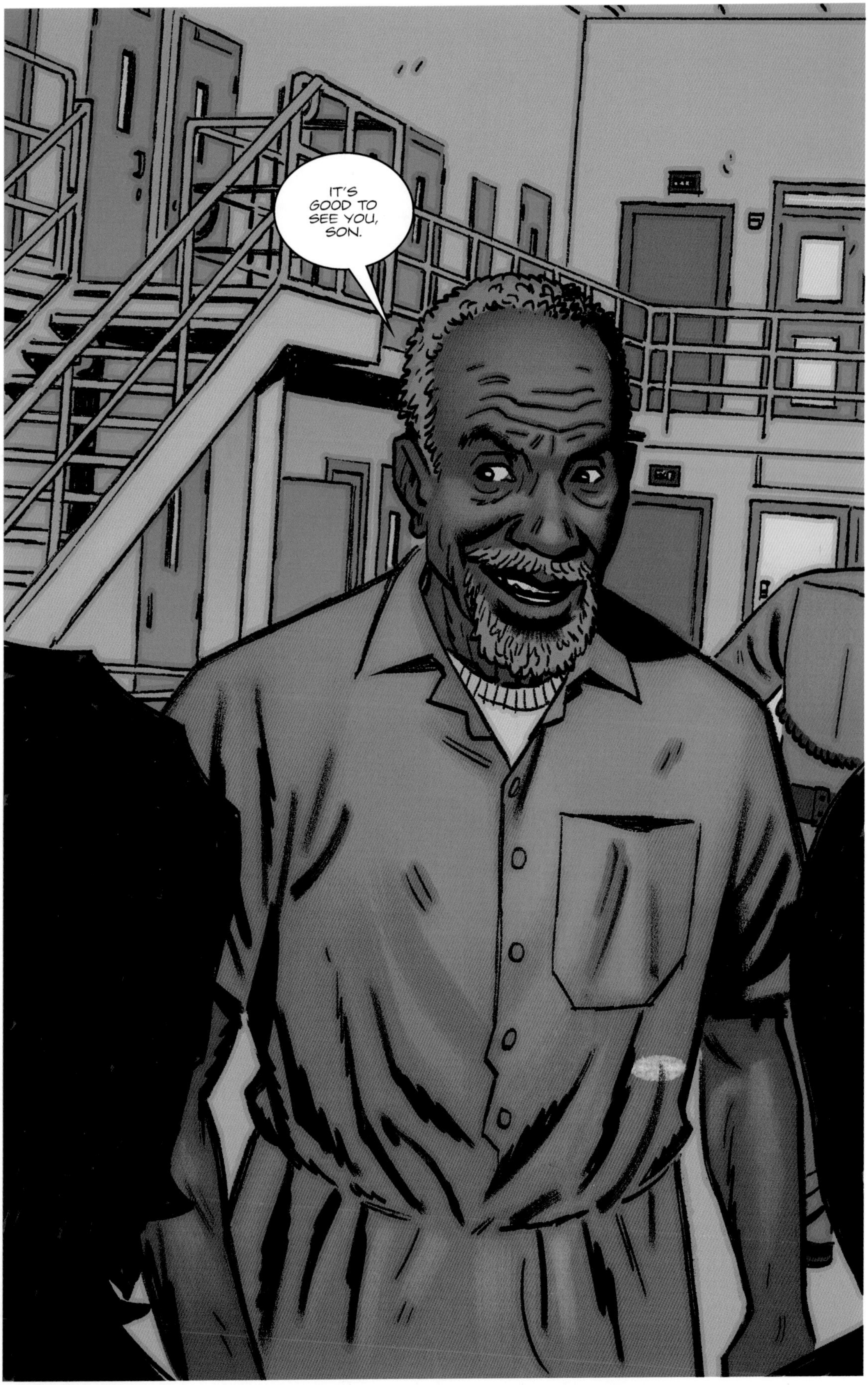
IT'S GOOD TO SEE YOU, SON.

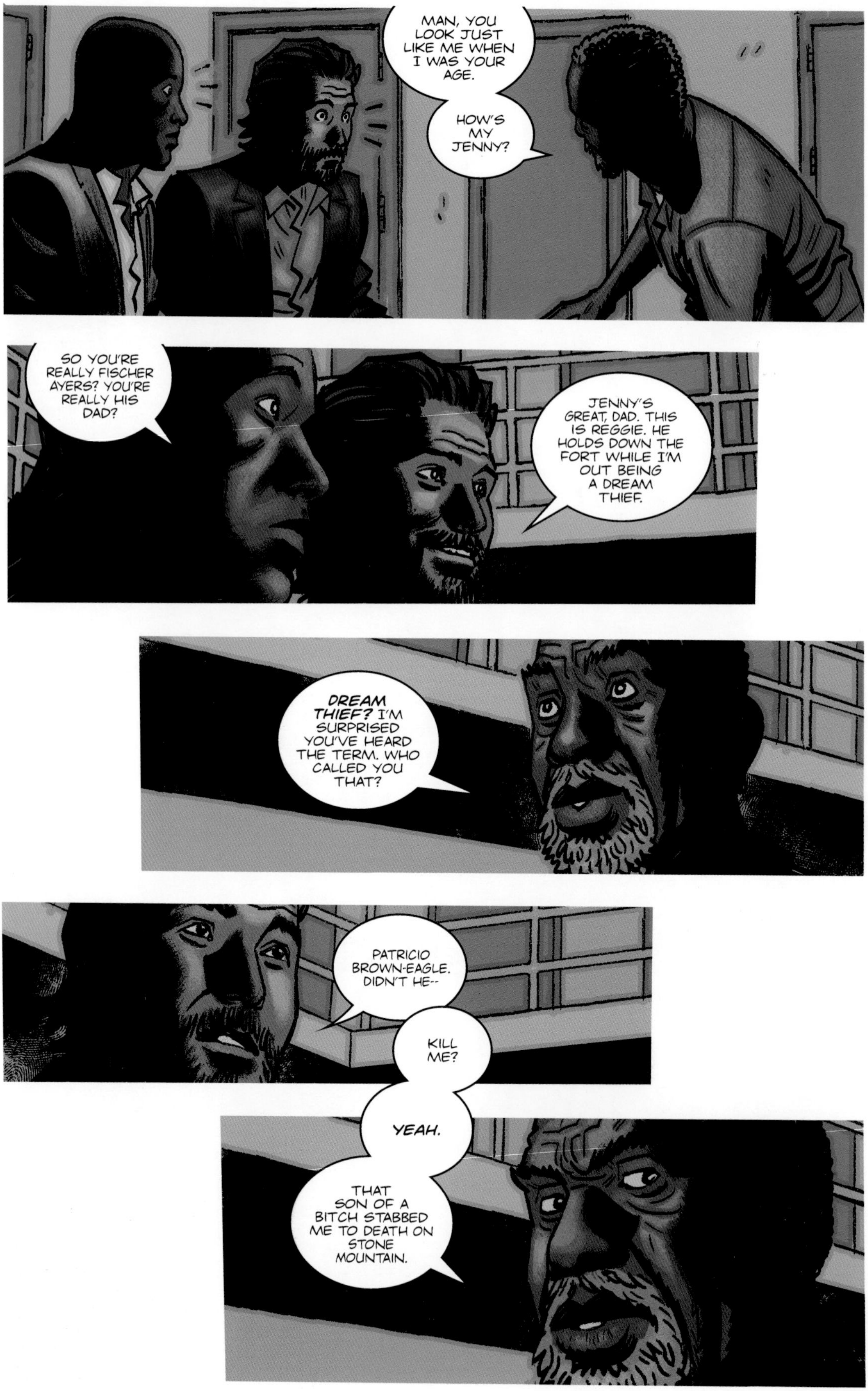
MAN, YOU LOOK JUST LIKE ME WHEN I WAS YOUR AGE.
HOW'S MY JENNY?
SO YOU'RE REALLY FISCHER AYERS? YOU'RE REALLY HIS DAD?
JENNY'S GREAT, DAD. THIS IS REGGIE. HE HOLDS DOWN THE FORT WHILE I'M OUT BEING A DREAM THIEF.
DREAM THIEF? I'M SURPRISED YOU'VE HEARD THE TERM. WHO CALLED YOU THAT?
PATRICIO BROWN-EAGLE. DIDN'T HE--
KILL ME?
YEAH.
THAT SON OF A BITCH STABBED ME TO DEATH ON STONE MOUNTAIN.

HE TRIED TO KILL ME, TOO. THREATENED JENNY AND CLAIRE. HE SAID IT'S ABOUT THE MASK.

I GOT WASTED ONE NIGHT AND STOLE AN ABORIGINAL MASK FROM THE FERNBANK.

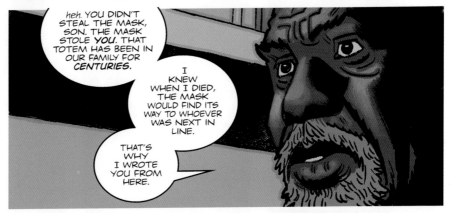

heh. YOU DIDN'T STEAL THE MASK, SON. THE MASK STOLE *YOU*. THAT TOTEM HAS BEEN IN OUR FAMILY FOR *CENTURIES*.

I KNEW WHEN I DIED, THE MASK WOULD FIND ITS WAY TO WHOEVER WAS NEXT IN LINE.

THAT'S WHY I WROTE YOU FROM HERE.

WHY NOT JENNY? SHE'S OLDER.

FEMALE DREAM THIEVES ARE RARE. I HAD AN OLDER SISTER AND IT SKIPPED HER. SAME THING WITH NATHAN BROWN-EAGLE.

PATRICIO'S DAD?

IT'S A LONG STORY.

LISTEN, I KNOW YOU HAVE A LOT OF QUESTIONS BUT I REALLY NEED YOU TO FOCUS ON GETTING ME OUT OF HERE FIRST.

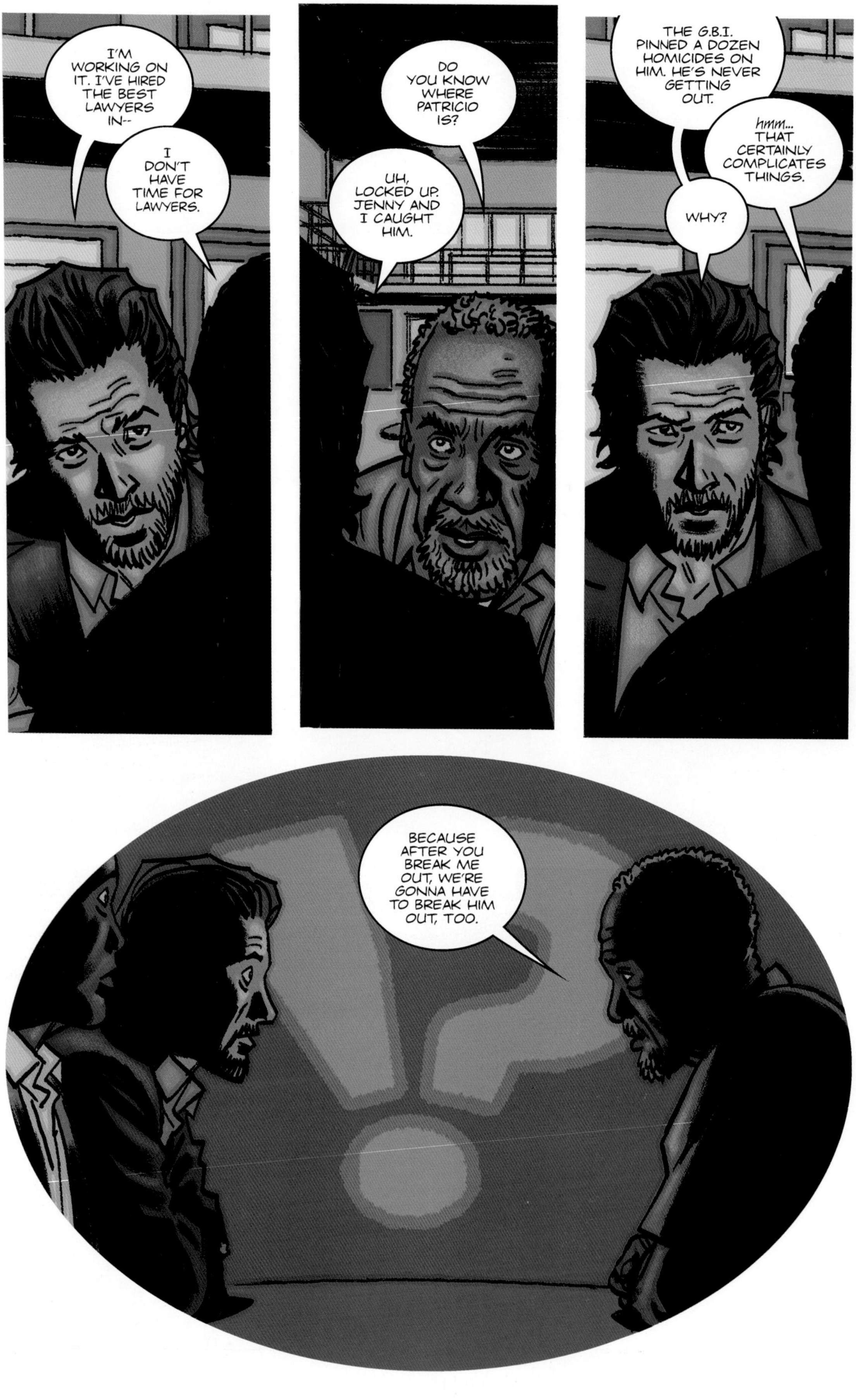
I'M WORKING ON IT. I'VE HIRED THE BEST LAWYERS IN--
I DON'T HAVE TIME FOR LAWYERS.
DO YOU KNOW WHERE PATRICIO IS?
UH, LOCKED UP. JENNY AND I CAUGHT HIM.
THE G.B.I. PINNED A DOZEN HOMICIDES ON HIM. HE'S NEVER GETTING OUT.
hmm... THAT CERTAINLY COMPLICATES THINGS.
WHY?
BECAUSE AFTER YOU BREAK ME OUT, WE'RE GONNA HAVE TO BREAK HIM OUT, TOO.

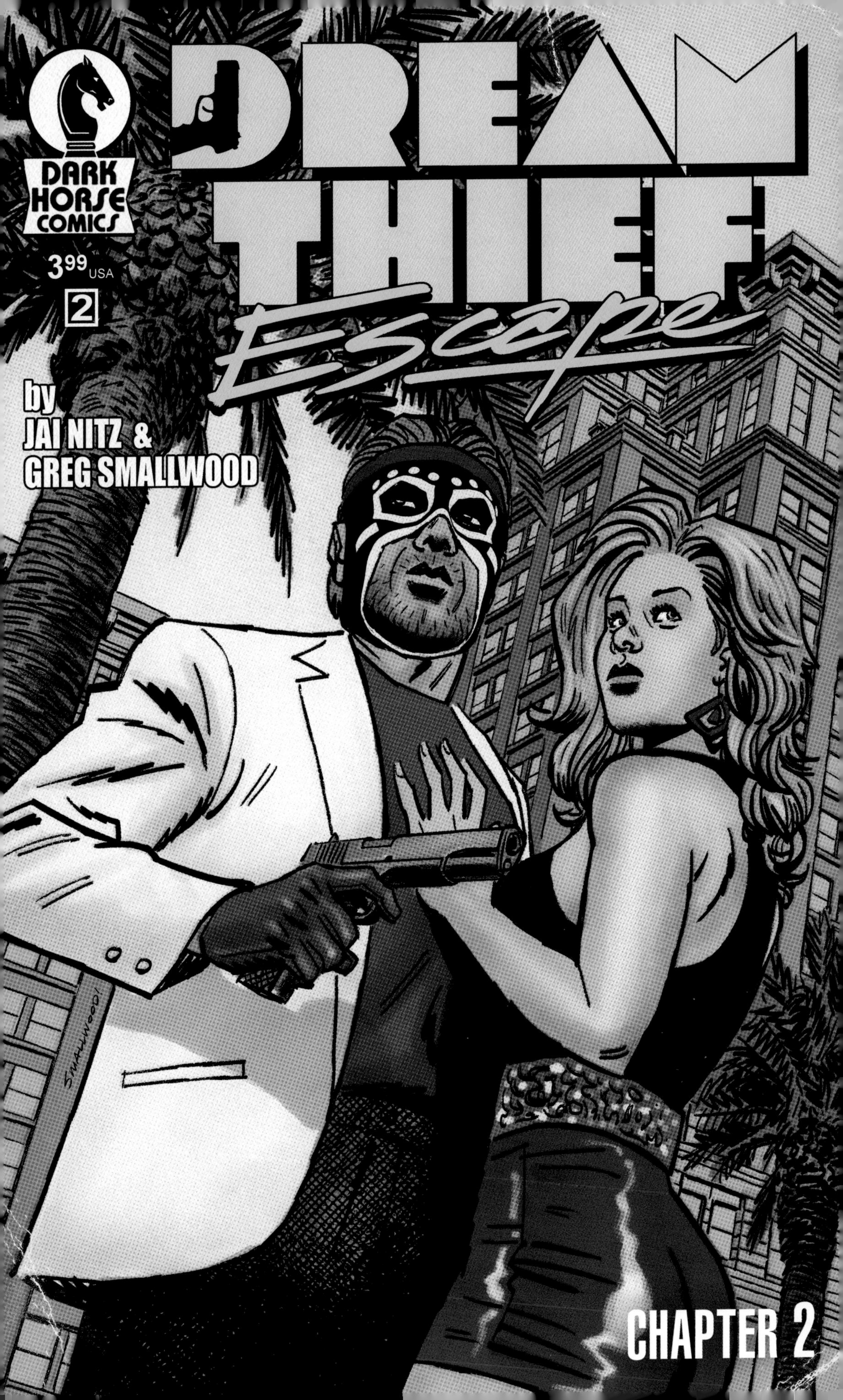
DARK HORSE COMICS
DREAM THIEF
Escape
3.99 USA
2
by
JAI NITZ &
GREG SMALLWOOD
SMALLWOOD!
CHAPTER 2

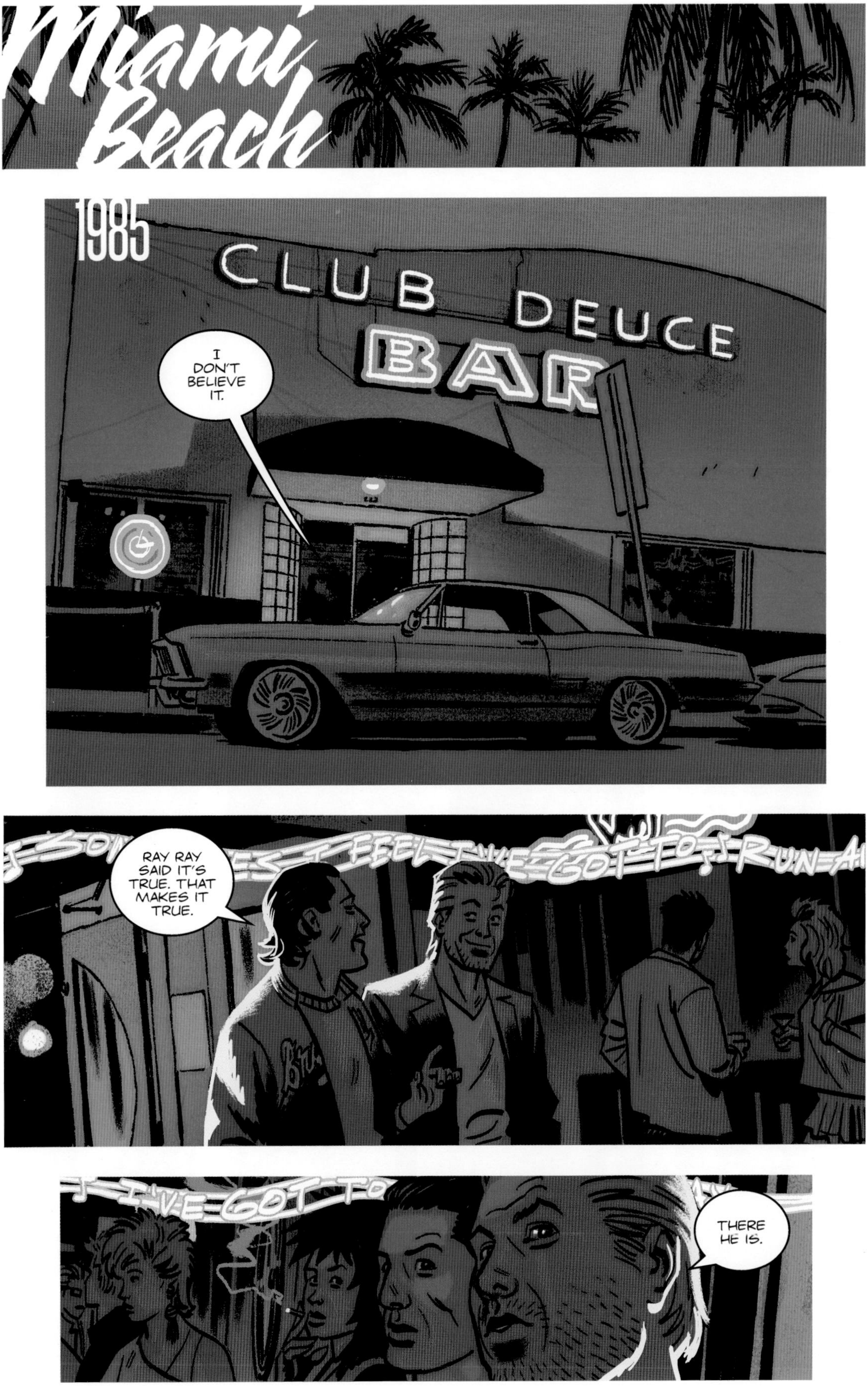
Miami Beach
1985
CLUB DEUCE
BAR
I DON'T BELIEVE IT.
RAY RAY SAID IT'S TRUE. THAT MAKES IT TRUE.
THERE HE IS.

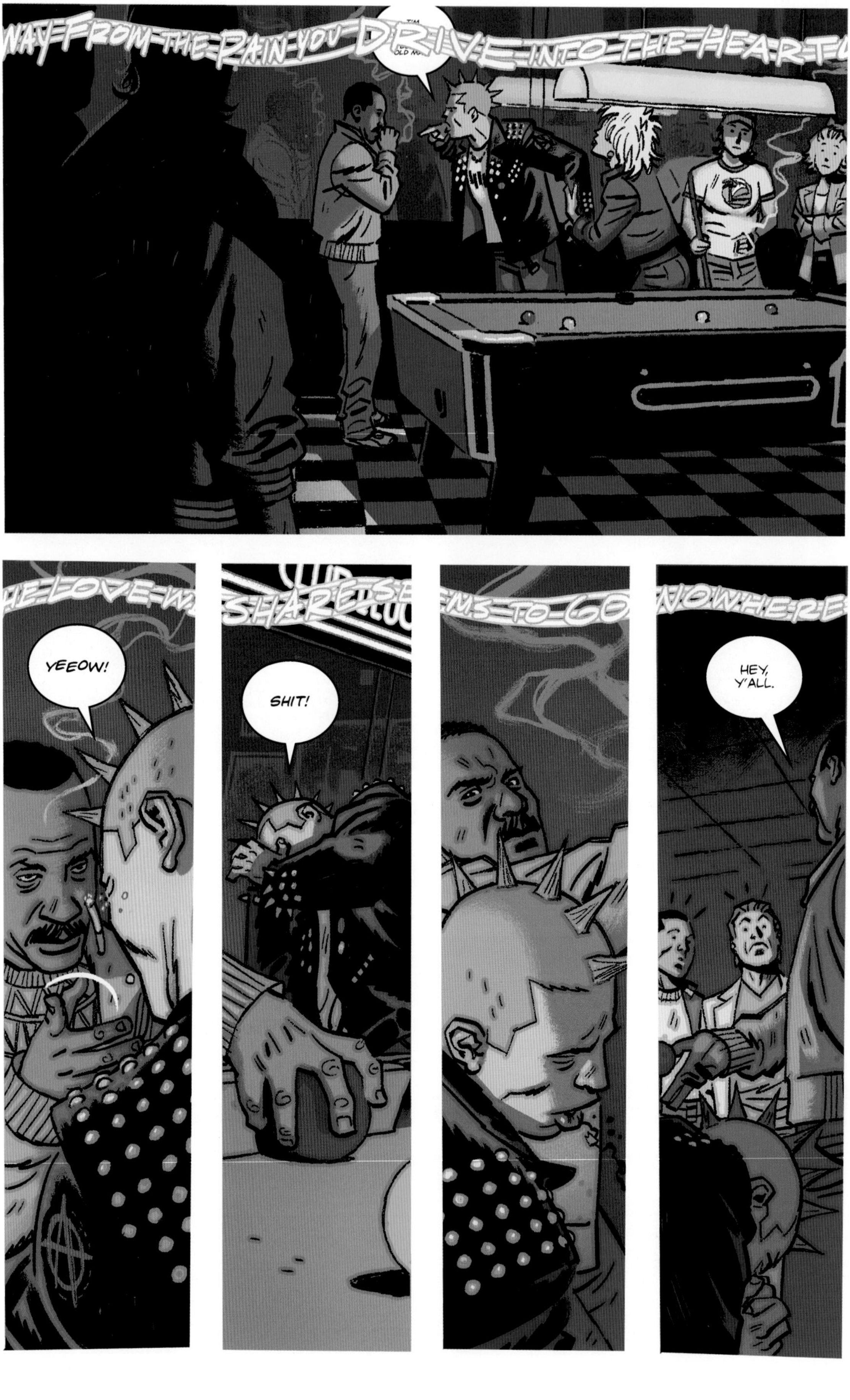
WAY FROM THE RAIN YOU DRIVE INTO THE HEART
HE LOVE W SHARE SE MS TO GO NOWHERE
YEEOW!
SHIT!
HEY, Y'ALL.

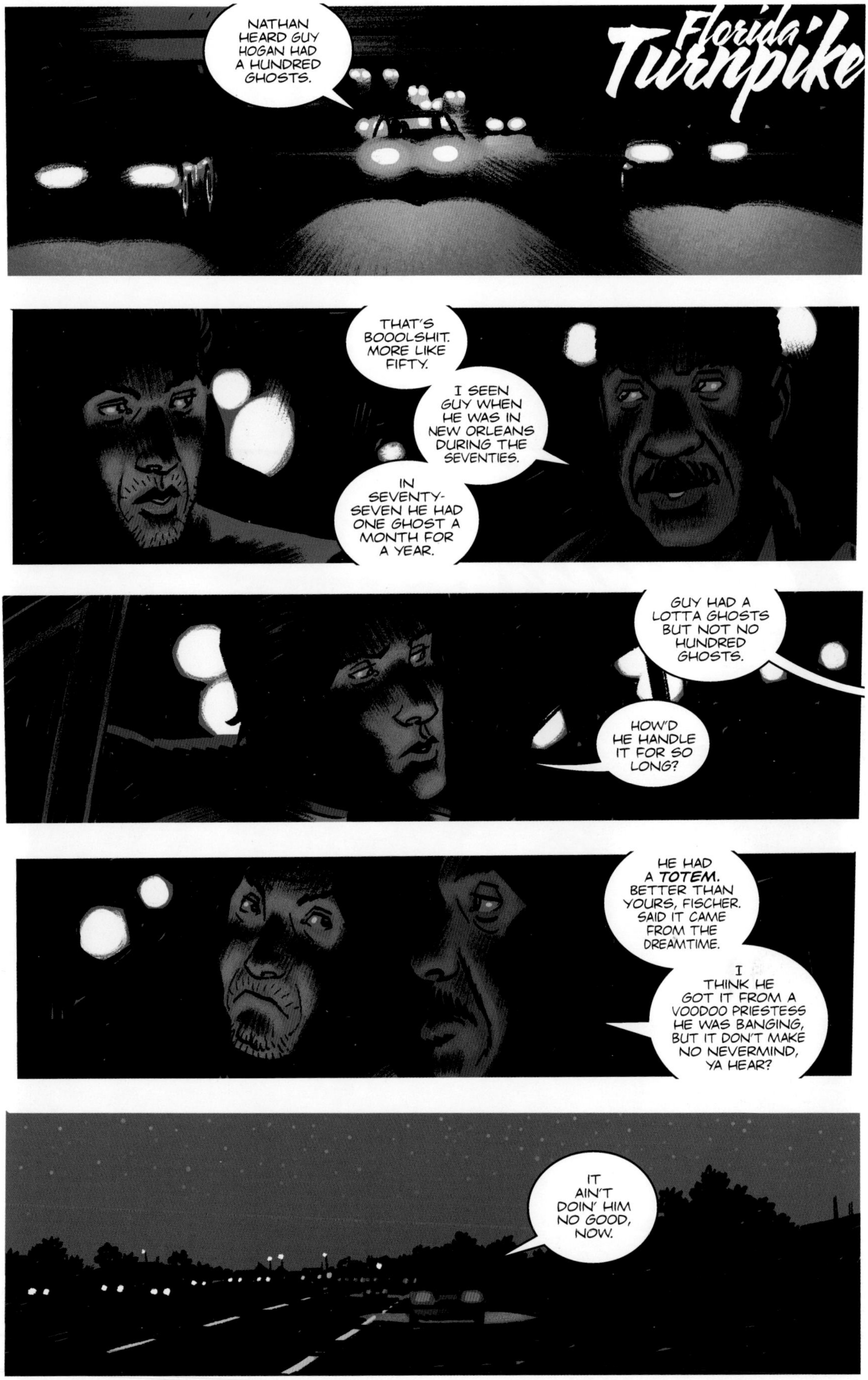
Florida Turnpike
NATHAN HEARD GUY HOGAN HAD A HUNDRED GHOSTS.
THAT'S BOOOLSHIT. MORE LIKE FIFTY.
I SEEN GUY WHEN HE WAS IN NEW ORLEANS DURING THE SEVENTIES.
IN SEVENTY-SEVEN HE HAD ONE GHOST A MONTH FOR A YEAR.
GUY HAD A LOTTA GHOSTS BUT NOT NO HUNDRED GHOSTS.
HOW'D HE HANDLE IT FOR SO LONG?
HE HAD A **TOTEM.** BETTER THAN YOURS, FISCHER. SAID IT CAME FROM THE DREAMTIME.
I THINK HE GOT IT FROM A VOODOO PRIESTESS HE WAS BANGING, BUT IT DON'T MAKE NO NEVERMIND, YA HEAR?
IT AIN'T DOIN' HIM NO GOOD, NOW.

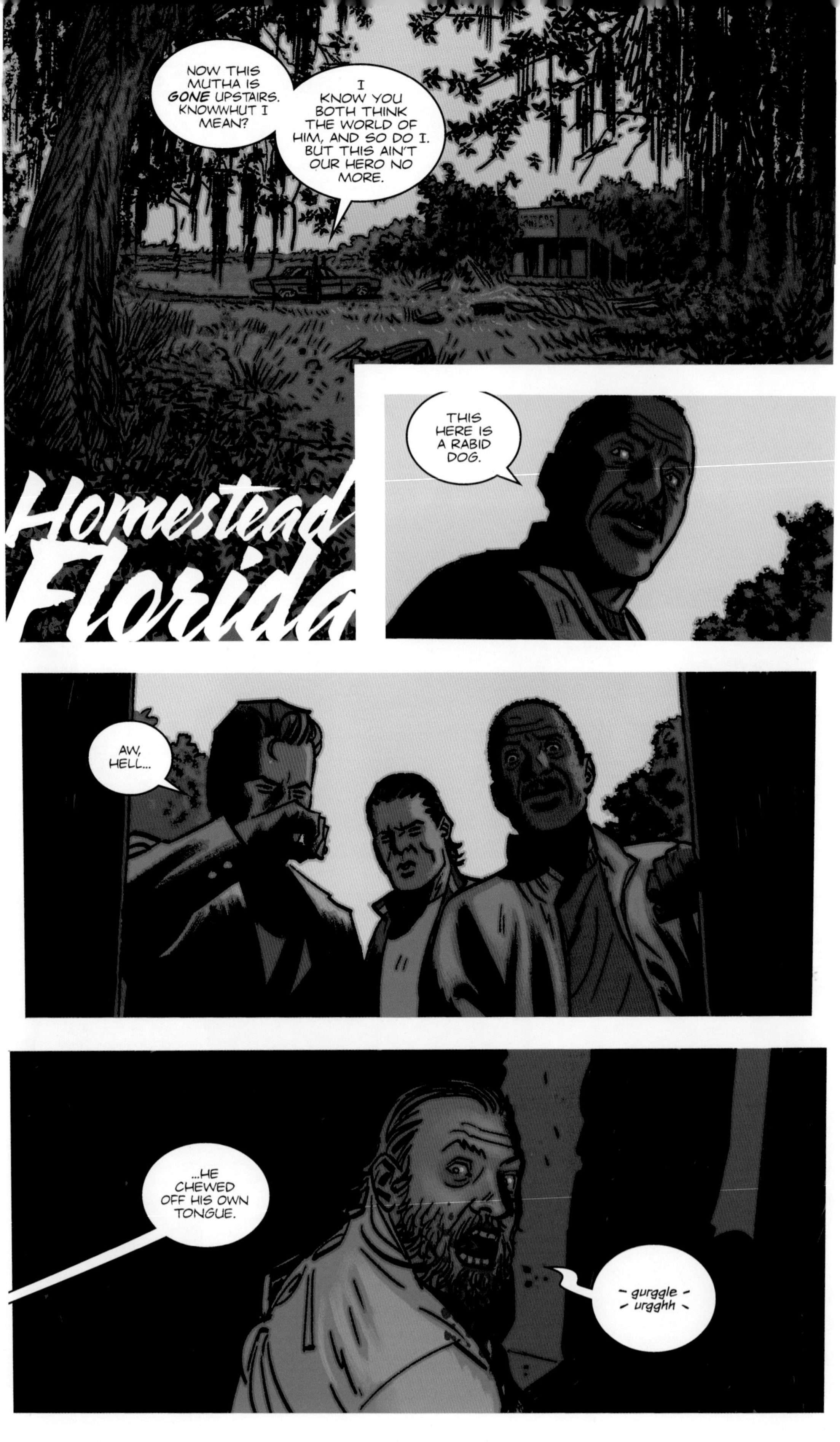
NOW THIS MUTHA IS GONE UPSTAIRS. KNOWWHUT I MEAN?
I KNOW YOU BOTH THINK THE WORLD OF HIM, AND SO DO I. BUT THIS AIN'T OUR HERO NO MORE.
Homestead Florida
THIS HERE IS A RABID DOG.
AW, HELL...
...HE CHEWED OFF HIS OWN TONGUE.
~ gurggle ~ ~ urgghh ~

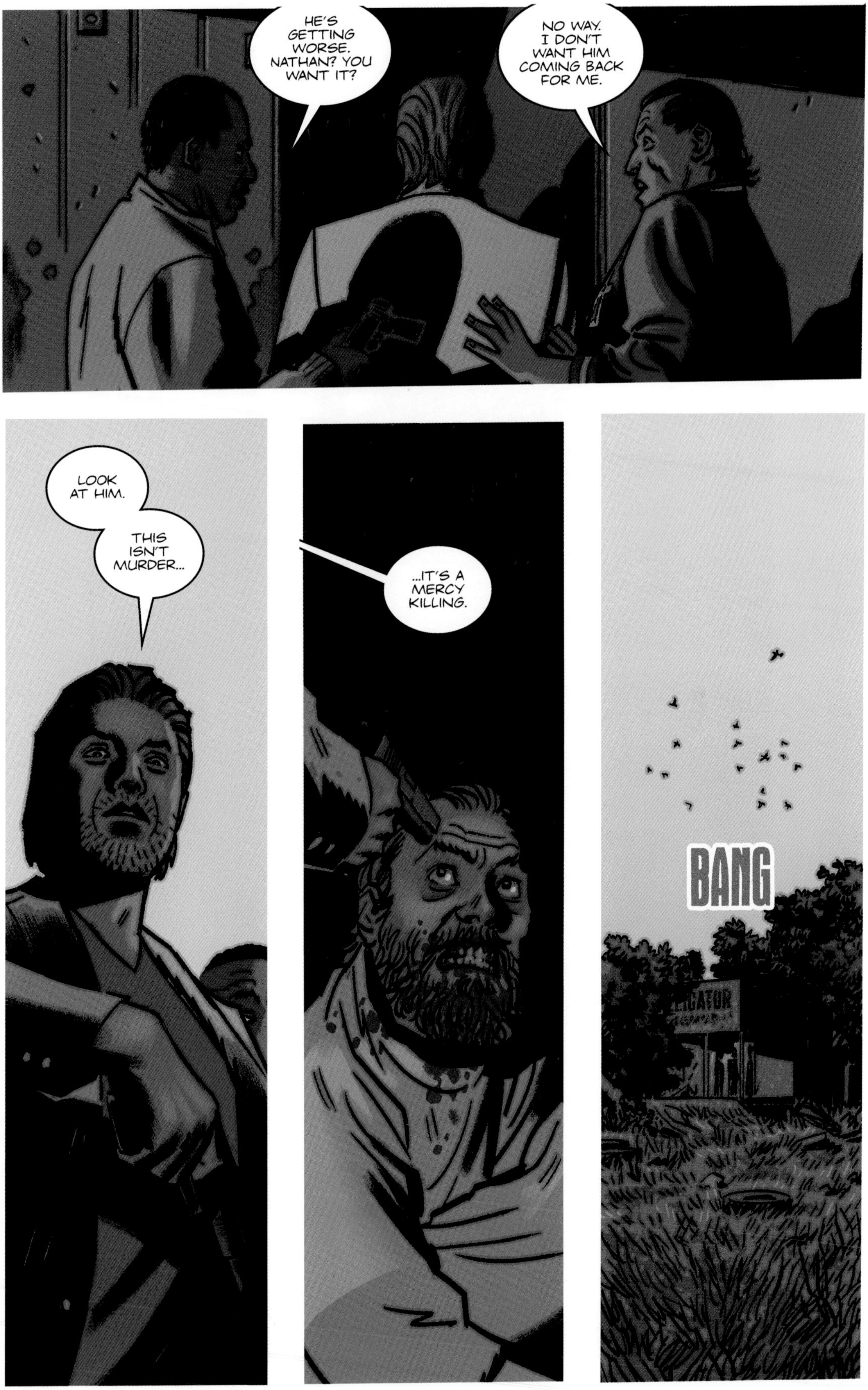
HE'S GETTING WORSE. NATHAN? YOU WANT IT?
NO WAY. I DON'T WANT HIM COMING BACK FOR ME.
LOOK AT HIM.
THIS ISN'T MURDER...
...IT'S A MERCY KILLING.
BANG

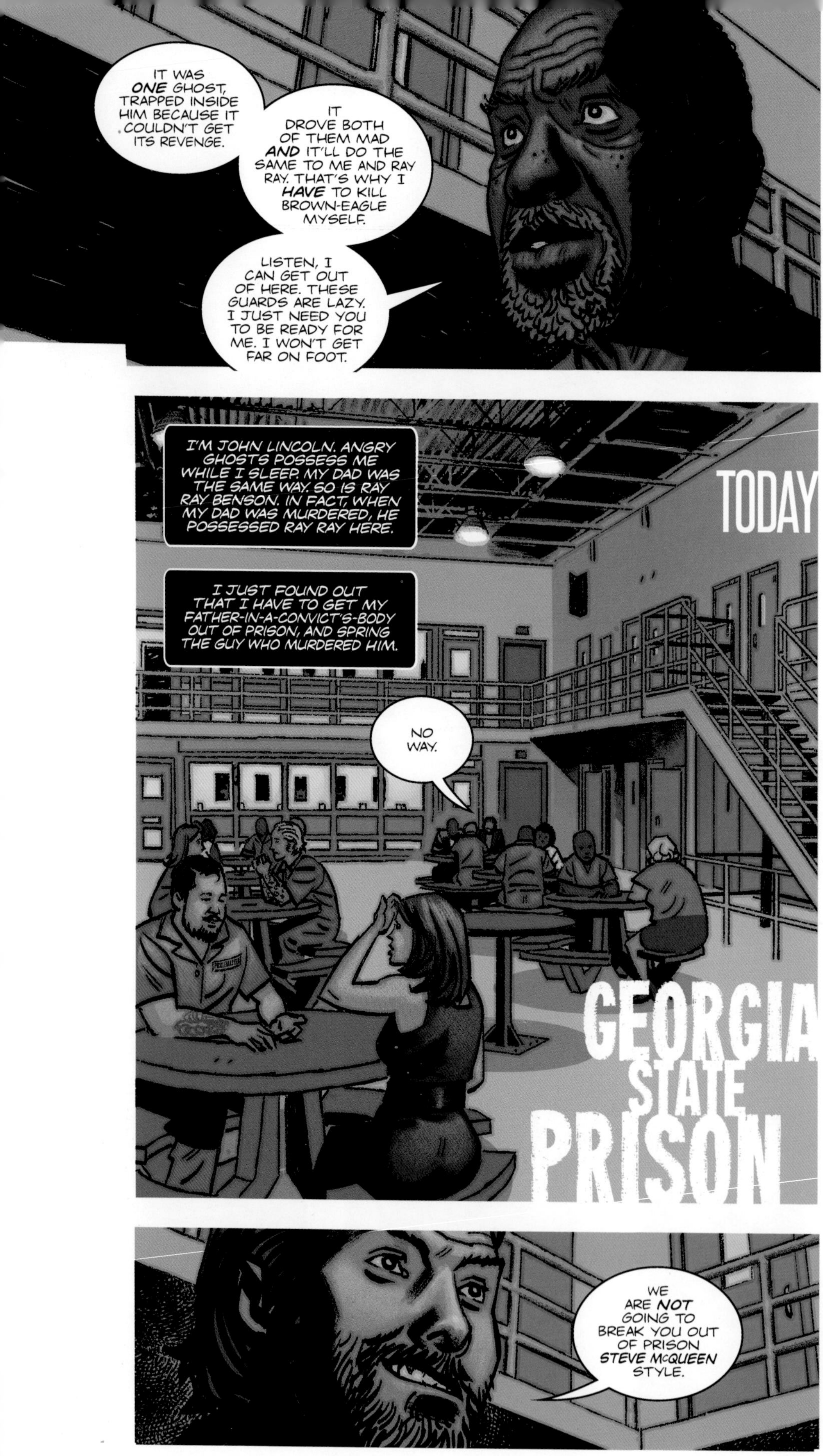
IT WAS ONE GHOST, TRAPPED INSIDE HIM BECAUSE IT COULDN'T GET ITS REVENGE.
IT DROVE BOTH OF THEM MAD AND IT'LL DO THE SAME TO ME AND RAY RAY. THAT'S WHY I HAVE TO KILL BROWN-EAGLE MYSELF.
LISTEN, I CAN GET OUT OF HERE. THESE GUARDS ARE LAZY. I JUST NEED YOU TO BE READY FOR ME. I WON'T GET FAR ON FOOT.
I'M JOHN LINCOLN. ANGRY GHOSTS POSSESS ME WHILE I SLEEP. MY DAD WAS THE SAME WAY. SO IS RAY RAY BENSON. IN FACT, WHEN MY DAD WAS MURDERED, HE POSSESSED RAY RAY HERE.
TODAY
I JUST FOUND OUT THAT I HAVE TO GET MY FATHER-IN-A-CONVICT'S-BODY OUT OF PRISON, AND SPRING THE GUY WHO MURDERED HIM.
NO WAY.
GEORGIA STATE PRISON
WE ARE NOT GOING TO BREAK YOU OUT OF PRISON STEVE McQUEEN STYLE.

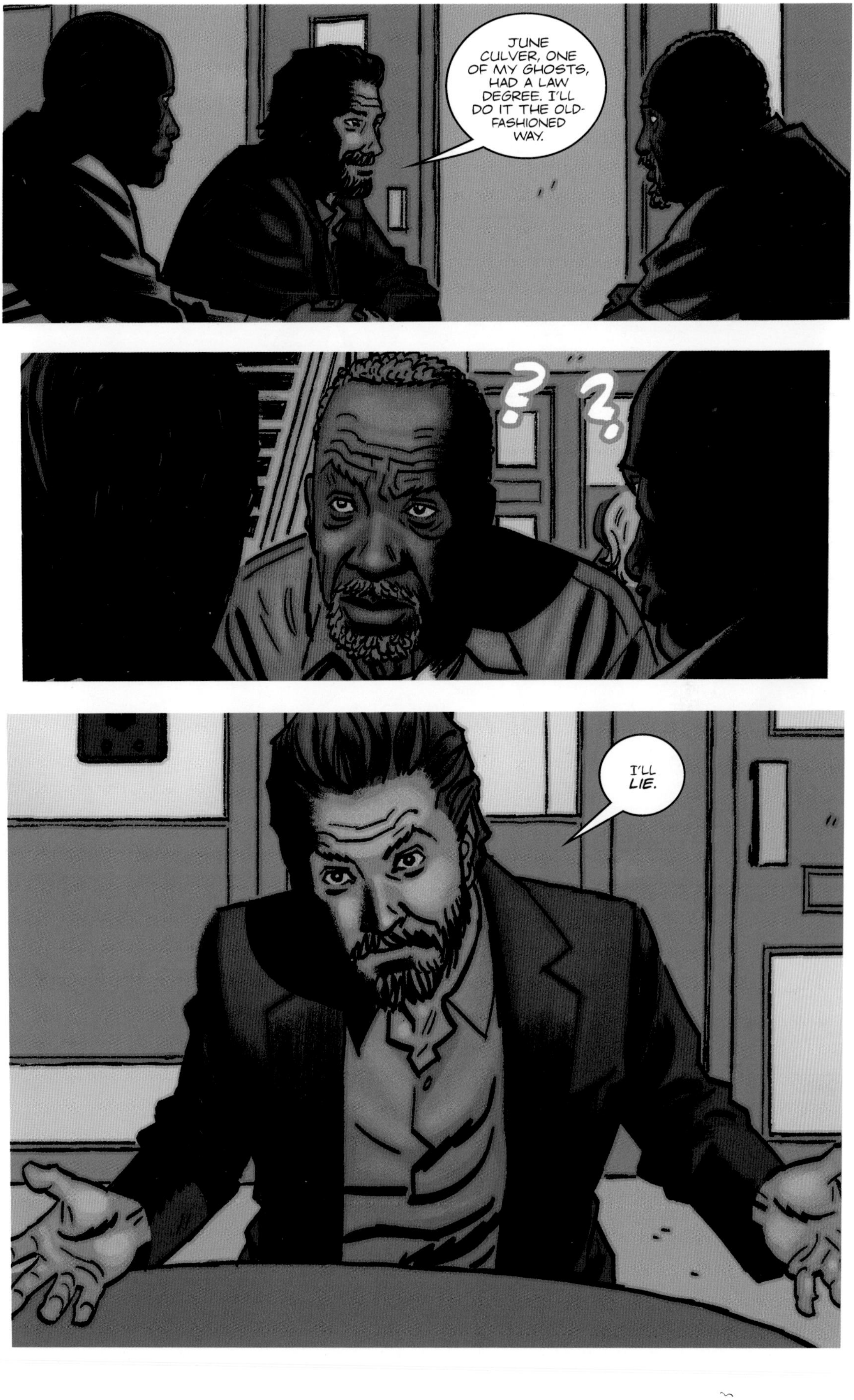
JUNE CULVER, ONE OF MY GHOSTS, HAD A LAW DEGREE. I'LL DO IT THE OLD-FASHIONED WAY.
??
I'LL LIE.

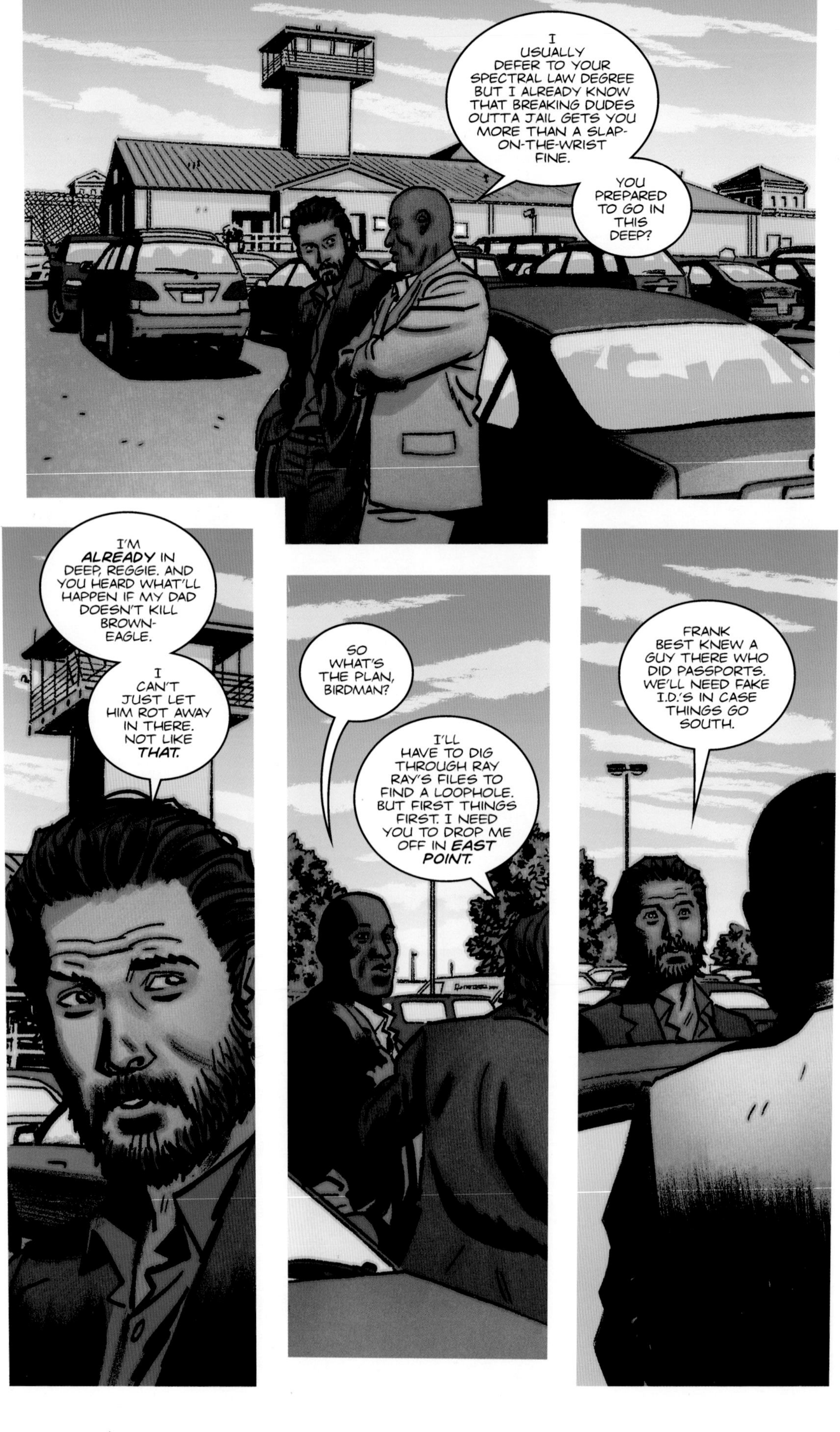
I USUALLY DEFER TO YOUR SPECTRAL LAW DEGREE BUT I ALREADY KNOW THAT BREAKING DUDES OUTTA JAIL GETS YOU MORE THAN A SLAP-ON-THE-WRIST FINE.
YOU PREPARED TO GO IN THIS DEEP?
I'M *ALREADY* IN DEEP, REGGIE. AND YOU HEARD WHAT'LL HAPPEN IF MY DAD DOESN'T KILL BROWN-EAGLE.
I CAN'T JUST LET HIM ROT AWAY IN THERE. NOT LIKE *THAT.*
SO WHAT'S THE PLAN, BIRDMAN?
I'LL HAVE TO DIG THROUGH RAY RAY'S FILES TO FIND A LOOPHOLE. BUT FIRST THINGS FIRST. I NEED YOU TO DROP ME OFF IN *EAST POINT.*
FRANK BEST KNEW A GUY THERE WHO DID PASSPORTS. WE'LL NEED FAKE I.D.'S IN CASE THINGS GO SOUTH.

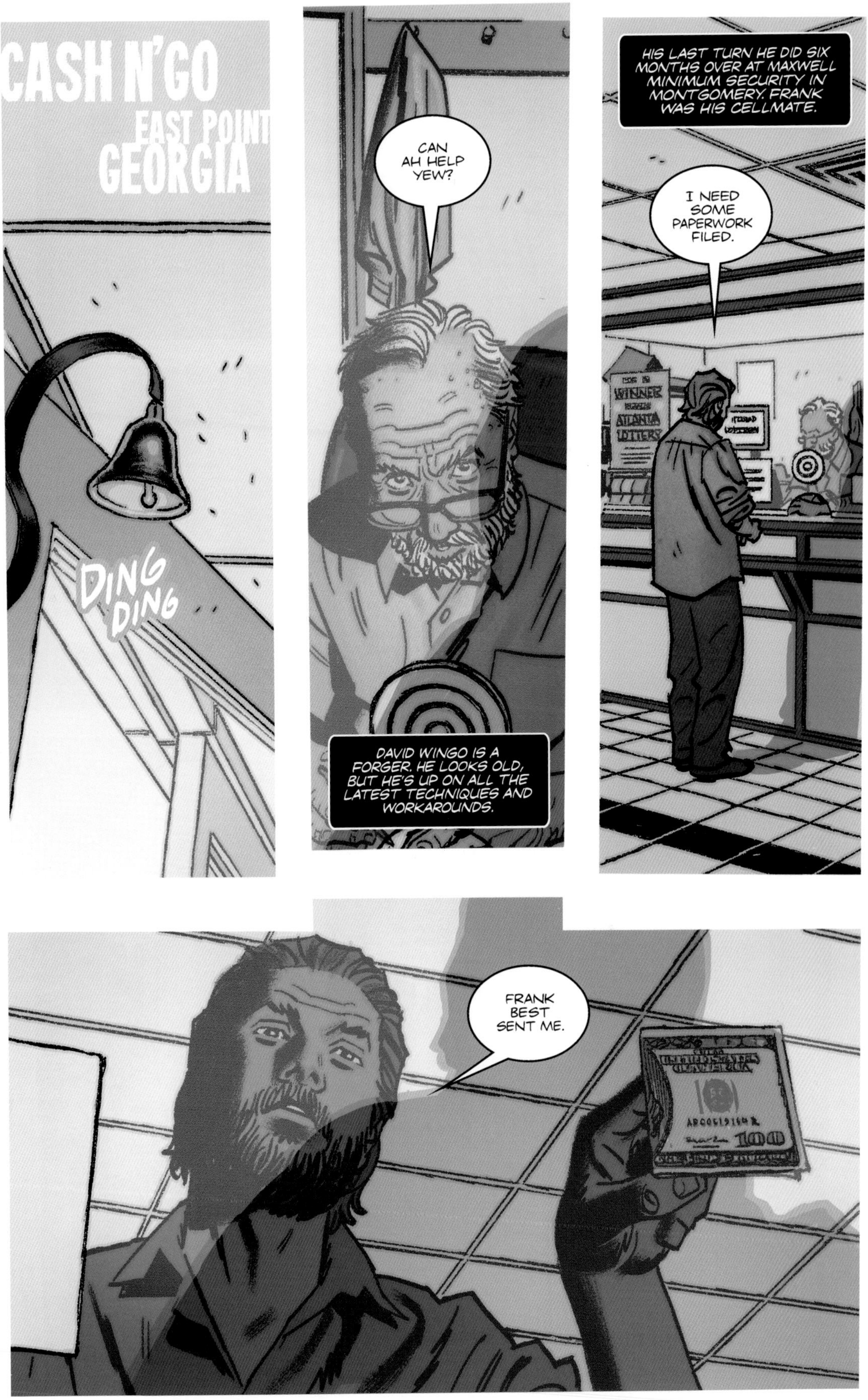
CASH N'GO
EAST POINT
GEORGIA
DING DING
CAN AH HELP YEW?
DAVID WINGO IS A FORGER. HE LOOKS OLD, BUT HE'S UP ON ALL THE LATEST TECHNIQUES AND WORKAROUNDS.
HIS LAST TURN HE DID SIX MONTHS OVER AT MAXWELL MINIMUM SECURITY IN MONTGOMERY. FRANK WAS HIS CELLMATE.
I NEED SOME PAPERWORK FILED.
WINNER
ATLANTA LOTTERY
FRANK BEST SENT ME.

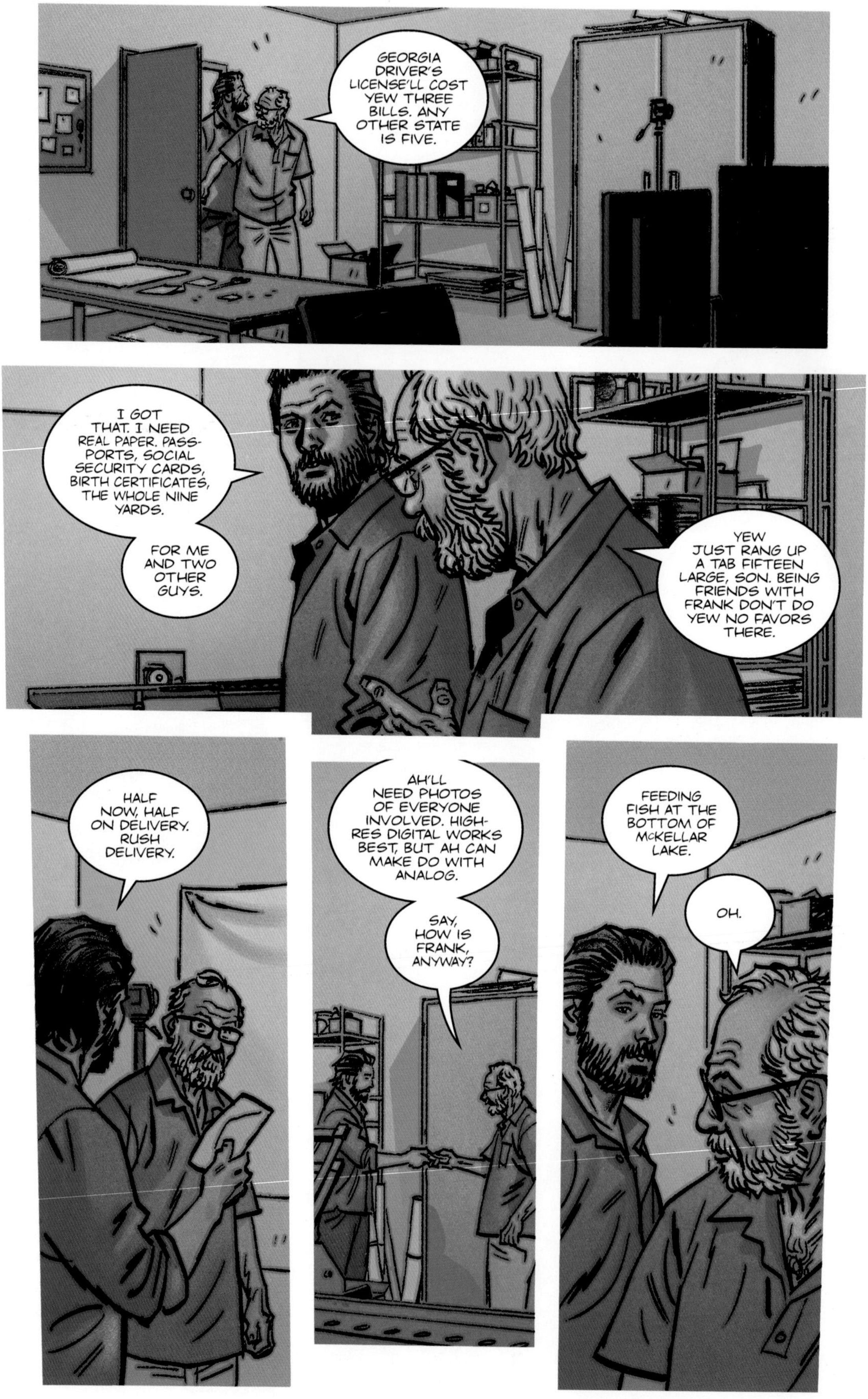
GEORGIA DRIVER'S LICENSE'LL COST YEW THREE BILLS. ANY OTHER STATE IS FIVE.
I GOT THAT. I NEED REAL PAPER. PASS-PORTS, SOCIAL SECURITY CARDS, BIRTH CERTIFICATES, THE WHOLE NINE YARDS.
FOR ME AND TWO OTHER GUYS.
YEW JUST RANG UP A TAB FIFTEEN LARGE, SON. BEING FRIENDS WITH FRANK DON'T DO YEW NO FAVORS THERE.
HALF NOW, HALF ON DELIVERY. RUSH DELIVERY.
AH'LL NEED PHOTOS OF EVERYONE INVOLVED. HIGH-RES DIGITAL WORKS BEST, BUT AH CAN MAKE DO WITH ANALOG.
SAY, HOW IS FRANK, ANYWAY?
FEEDING FISH AT THE BOTTOM OF McKELLAR LAKE.
OH.

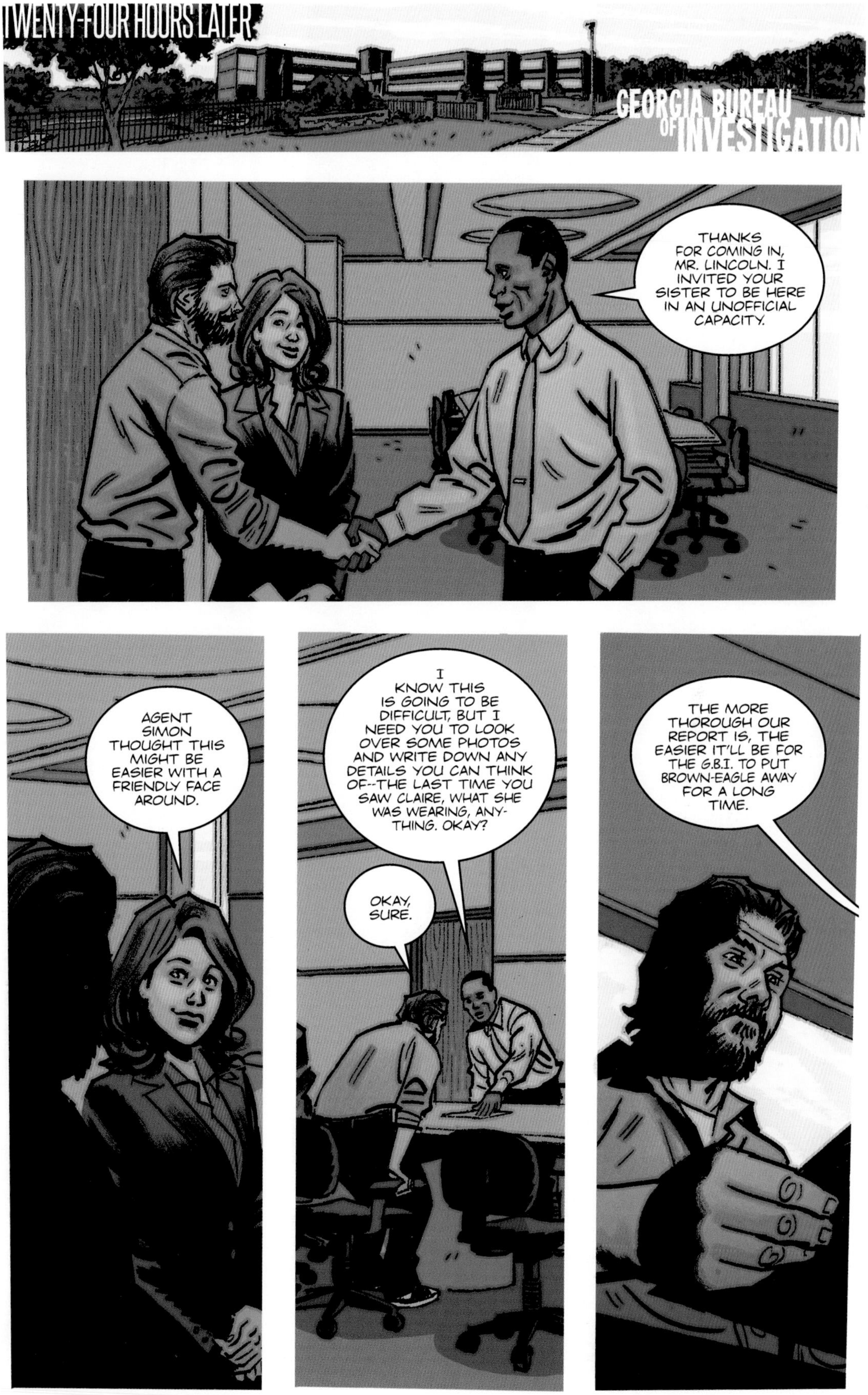
TWENTY-FOUR HOURS LATER
GEORGIA BUREAU OF INVESTIGATION
THANKS FOR COMING IN, MR. LINCOLN. I INVITED YOUR SISTER TO BE HERE IN AN UNOFFICIAL CAPACITY.
AGENT SIMON THOUGHT THIS MIGHT BE EASIER WITH A FRIENDLY FACE AROUND.
I KNOW THIS IS GOING TO BE DIFFICULT, BUT I NEED YOU TO LOOK OVER SOME PHOTOS AND WRITE DOWN ANY DETAILS YOU CAN THINK OF--THE LAST TIME YOU SAW CLAIRE, WHAT SHE WAS WEARING, ANYTHING. OKAY?
OKAY, SURE.
THE MORE THOROUGH OUR REPORT IS, THE EASIER IT'LL BE FOR THE G.B.I. TO PUT BROWN-EAGLE AWAY FOR A LONG TIME.

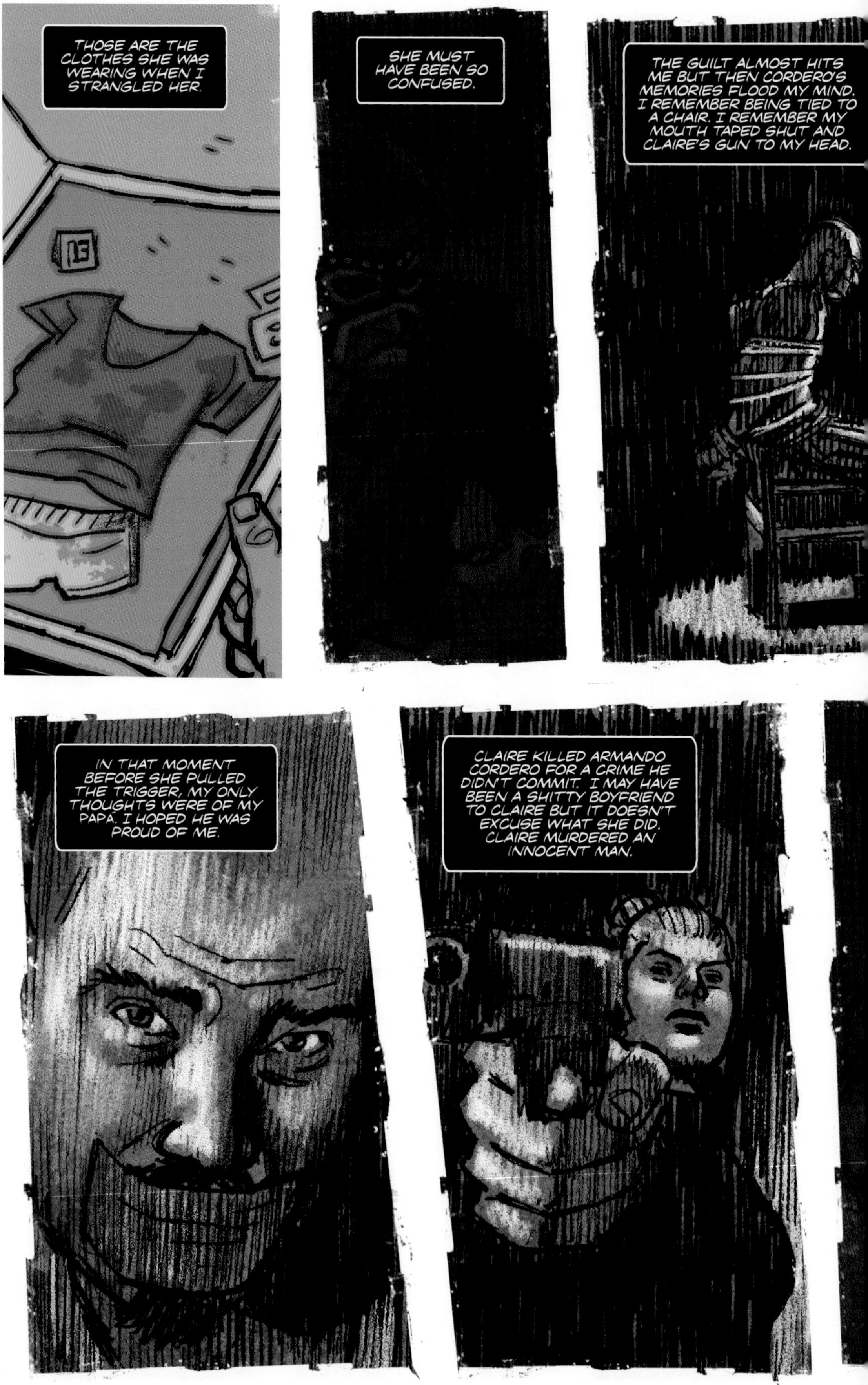
THOSE ARE THE CLOTHES SHE WAS WEARING WHEN I STRANGLED HER.
13
SHE MUST HAVE BEEN SO CONFUSED.
THE GUILT ALMOST HITS ME BUT THEN CORDERO'S MEMORIES FLOOD MY MIND. I REMEMBER BEING TIED TO A CHAIR. I REMEMBER MY MOUTH TAPED SHUT AND CLAIRE'S GUN TO MY HEAD.
IN THAT MOMENT BEFORE SHE PULLED THE TRIGGER, MY ONLY THOUGHTS WERE OF MY PAPA. I HOPED HE WAS PROUD OF ME.
CLAIRE KILLED ARMANDO CORDERO FOR A CRIME HE DIDN'T COMMIT. I MAY HAVE BEEN A SHITTY BOYFRIEND TO CLAIRE BUT IT DOESN'T EXCUSE WHAT SHE DID. CLAIRE MURDERED AN INNOCENT MAN.

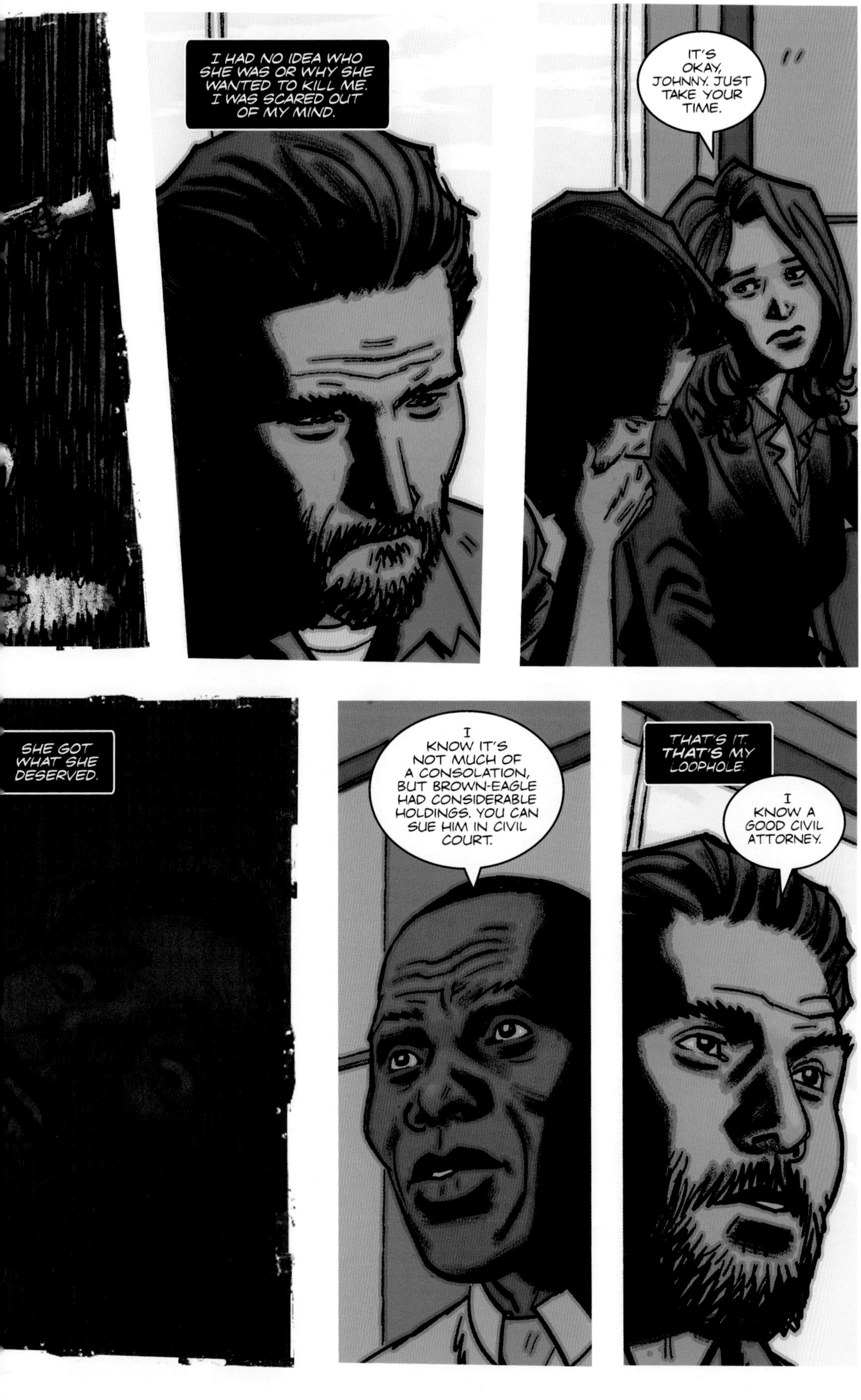
I HAD NO IDEA WHO SHE WAS OR WHY SHE WANTED TO KILL ME. I WAS SCARED OUT OF MY MIND.
IT'S OKAY, JOHNNY. JUST TAKE YOUR TIME.
SHE GOT WHAT SHE DESERVED.
I KNOW IT'S NOT MUCH OF A CONSOLATION, BUT BROWN-EAGLE HAD CONSIDERABLE HOLDINGS. YOU CAN SUE HIM IN CIVIL COURT.
THAT'S IT. THAT'S MY LOOPHOLE.
I KNOW A GOOD CIVIL ATTORNEY.

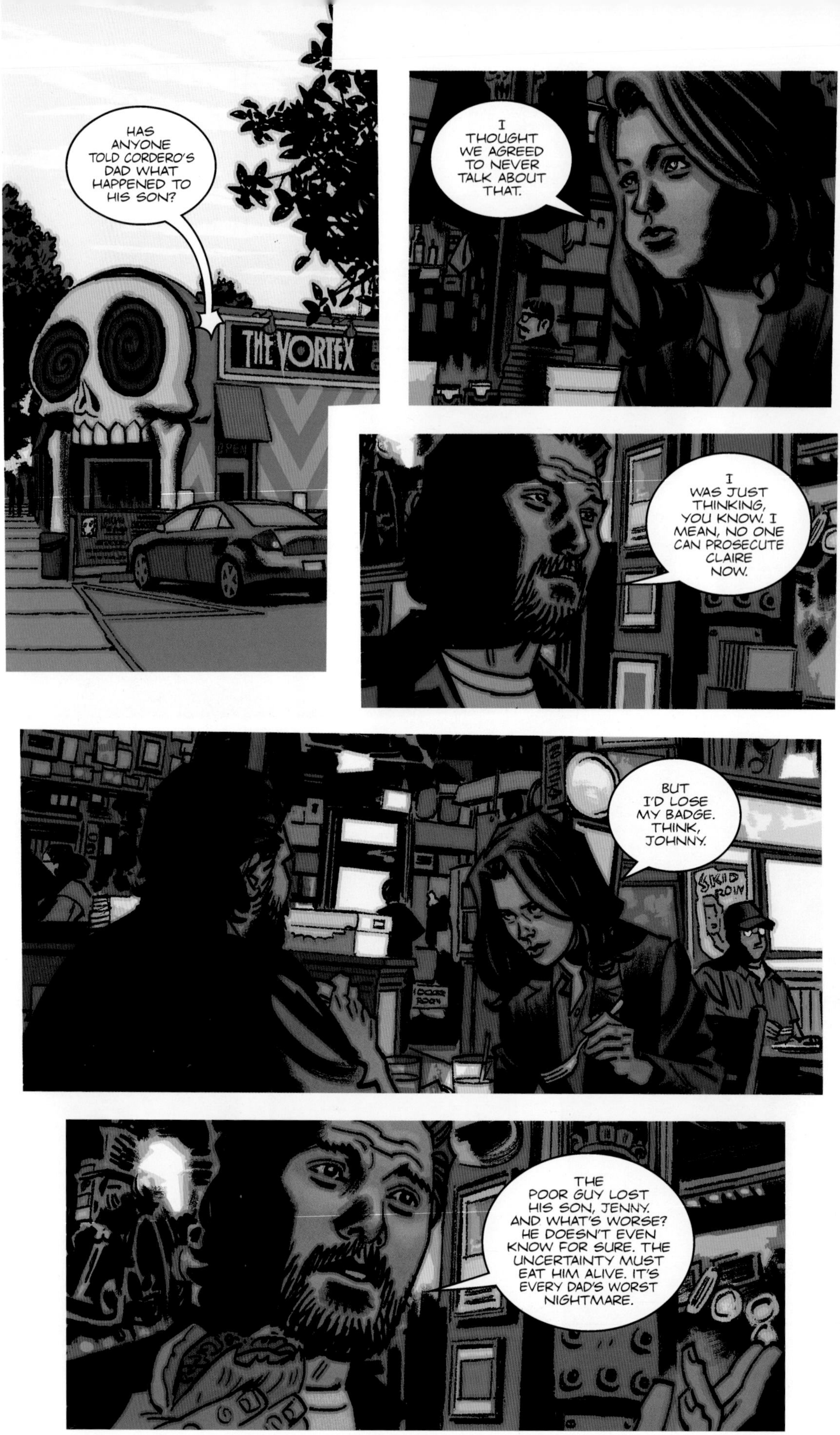
HAS ANYONE TOLD CORDERO'S DAD WHAT HAPPENED TO HIS SON?
THE VORTEX
OPEN
I THOUGHT WE AGREED TO NEVER TALK ABOUT THAT.
I WAS JUST THINKING, YOU KNOW. I MEAN, NO ONE CAN PROSECUTE CLAIRE NOW.
BUT I'D LOSE MY BADGE. THINK, JOHNNY.
SKID ROW
THE POOR GUY LOST HIS SON, JENNY. AND WHAT'S WORSE? HE DOESN'T EVEN KNOW FOR SURE. THE UNCERTAINTY MUST EAT HIM ALIVE. IT'S EVERY DAD'S WORST NIGHTMARE.

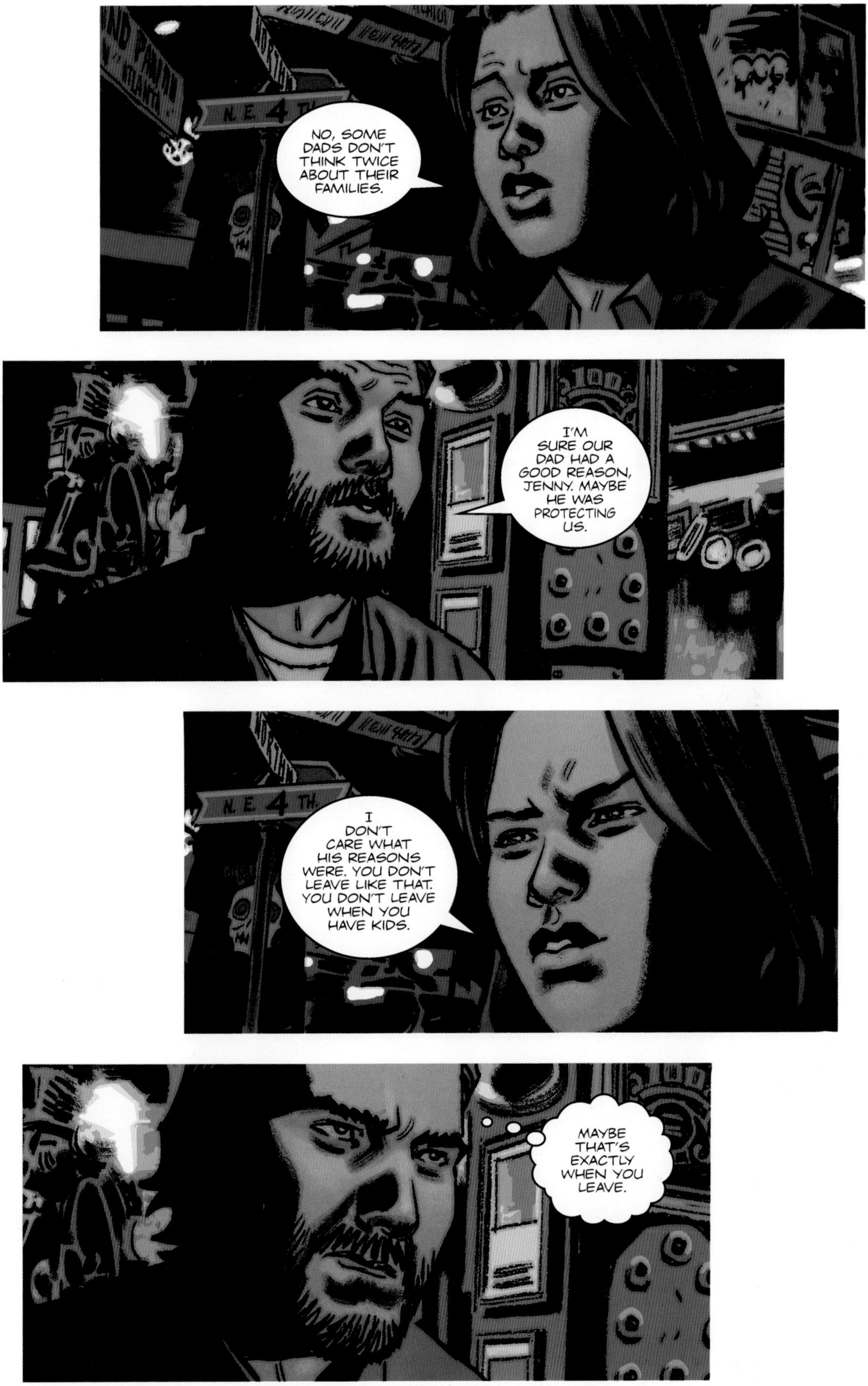
N. E. 4 TH.
NO, SOME DADS DON'T THINK TWICE ABOUT THEIR FAMILIES.
I'M SURE OUR DAD HAD A GOOD REASON, JENNY. MAYBE HE WAS PROTECTING US.
N. E. 4 TH.
I DON'T CARE WHAT HIS REASONS WERE. YOU DON'T LEAVE LIKE THAT. YOU DON'T LEAVE WHEN YOU HAVE KIDS.
MAYBE THAT'S EXACTLY WHEN YOU LEAVE.

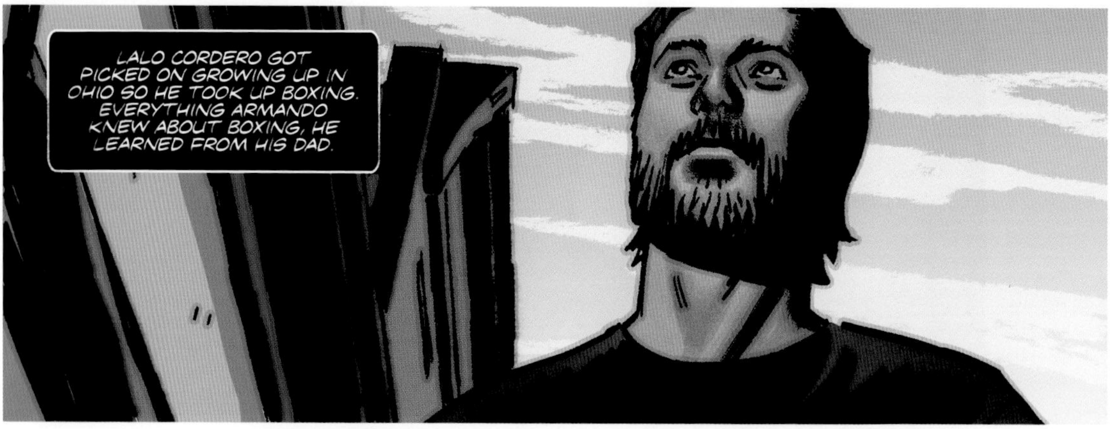
LALO CORDERO GOT PICKED ON GROWING UP IN OHIO SO HE TOOK UP BOXING. EVERYTHING ARMANDO KNEW ABOUT BOXING, HE LEARNED FROM HIS DAD.

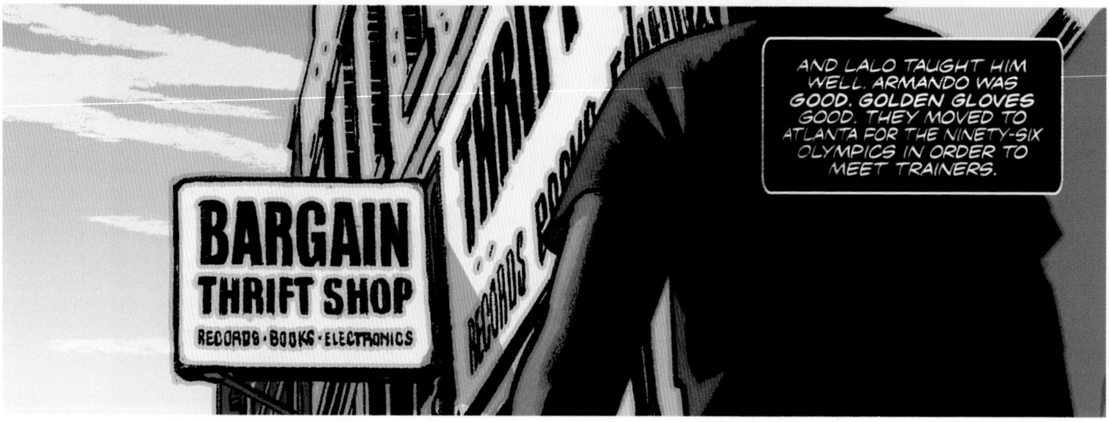
BARGAIN THRIFT SHOP
RECORDS · BOOKS · ELECTRONICS
AND LALO TAUGHT HIM WELL. ARMANDO WAS GOOD. **GOLDEN GLOVES** GOOD. THEY MOVED TO ATLANTA FOR THE NINETY-SIX OLYMPICS IN ORDER TO MEET TRAINERS.

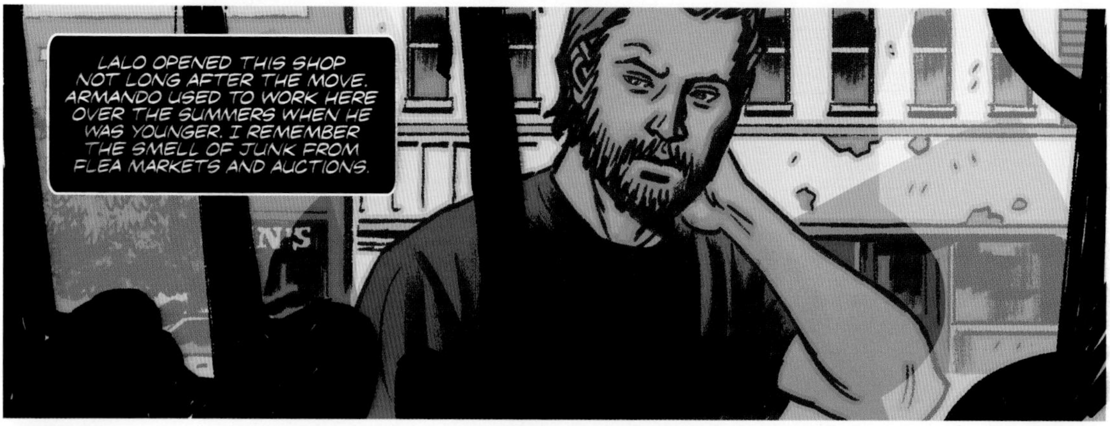
LALO OPENED THIS SHOP NOT LONG AFTER THE MOVE. ARMANDO USED TO WORK HERE OVER THE SUMMERS WHEN HE WAS YOUNGER. I REMEMBER THE SMELL OF JUNK FROM FLEA MARKETS AND AUCTIONS.

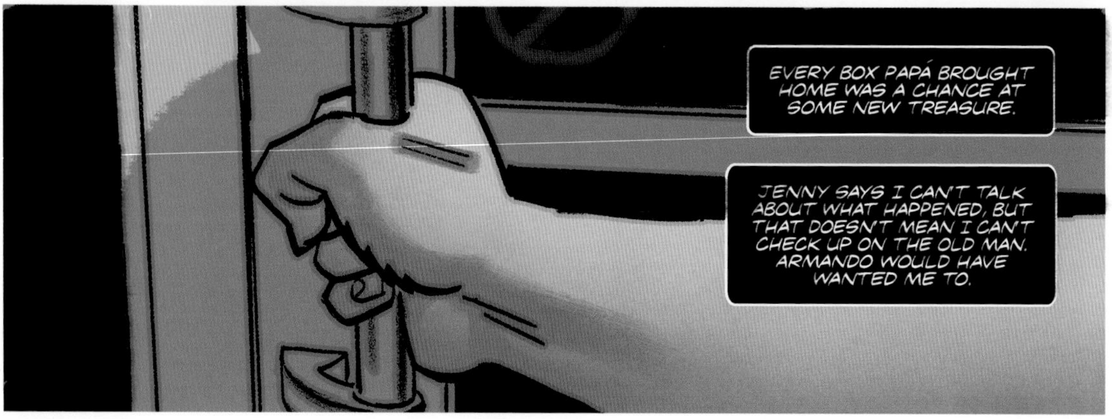
EVERY BOX PAPÁ BROUGHT HOME WAS A CHANCE AT SOME NEW TREASURE.
JENNY SAYS I CAN'T TALK ABOUT WHAT HAPPENED, BUT THAT DOESN'T MEAN I CAN'T CHECK UP ON THE OLD MAN. ARMANDO WOULD HAVE WANTED ME TO.

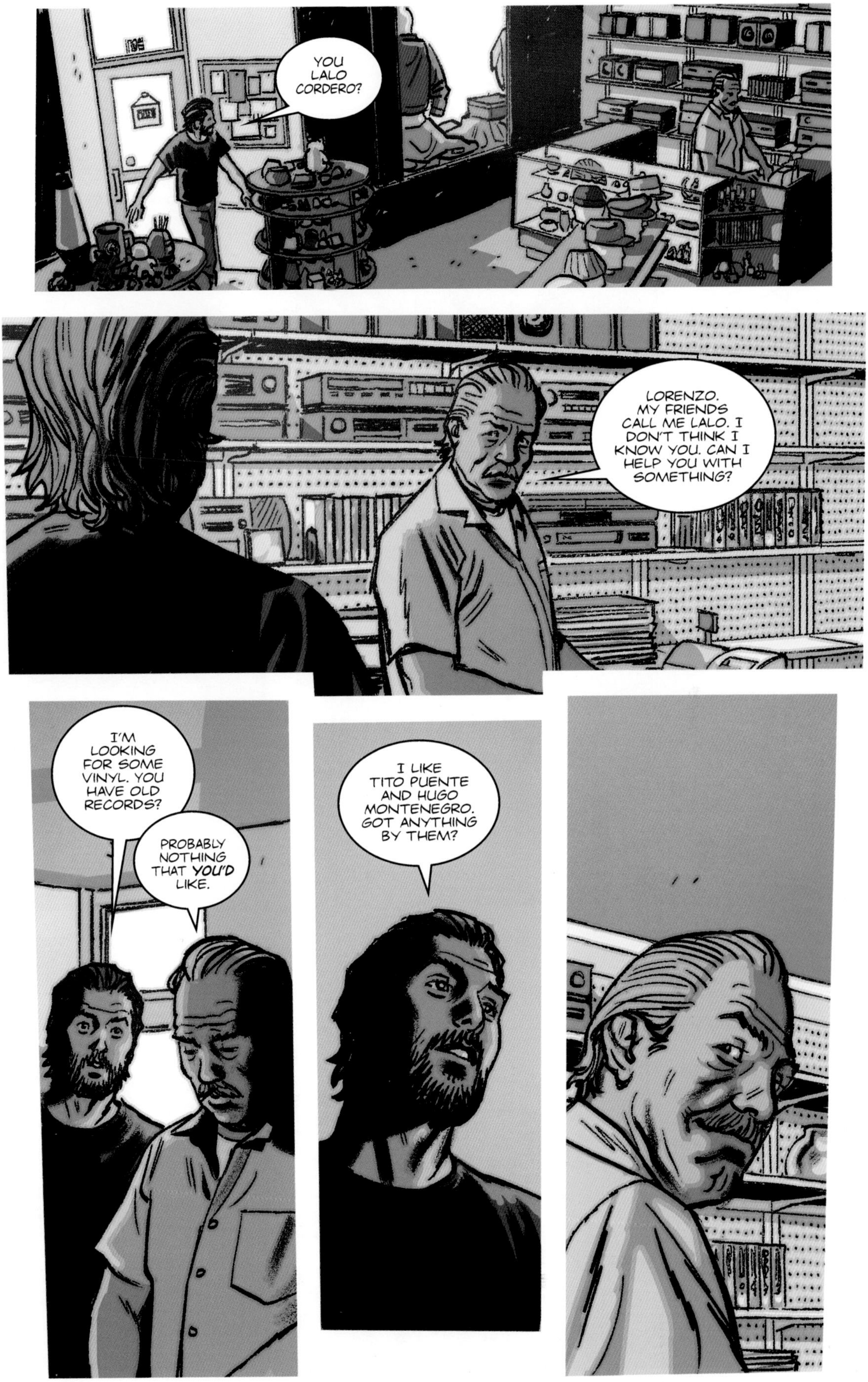
YOU LALO CORDERO?
LORENZO. MY FRIENDS CALL ME LALO. I DON'T THINK I KNOW YOU. CAN I HELP YOU WITH SOMETHING?
I'M LOOKING FOR SOME VINYL. YOU HAVE OLD RECORDS?
PROBABLY NOTHING THAT *YOU'D* LIKE.
I LIKE TITO PUENTE AND HUGO MONTENEGRO. GOT ANYTHING BY THEM?

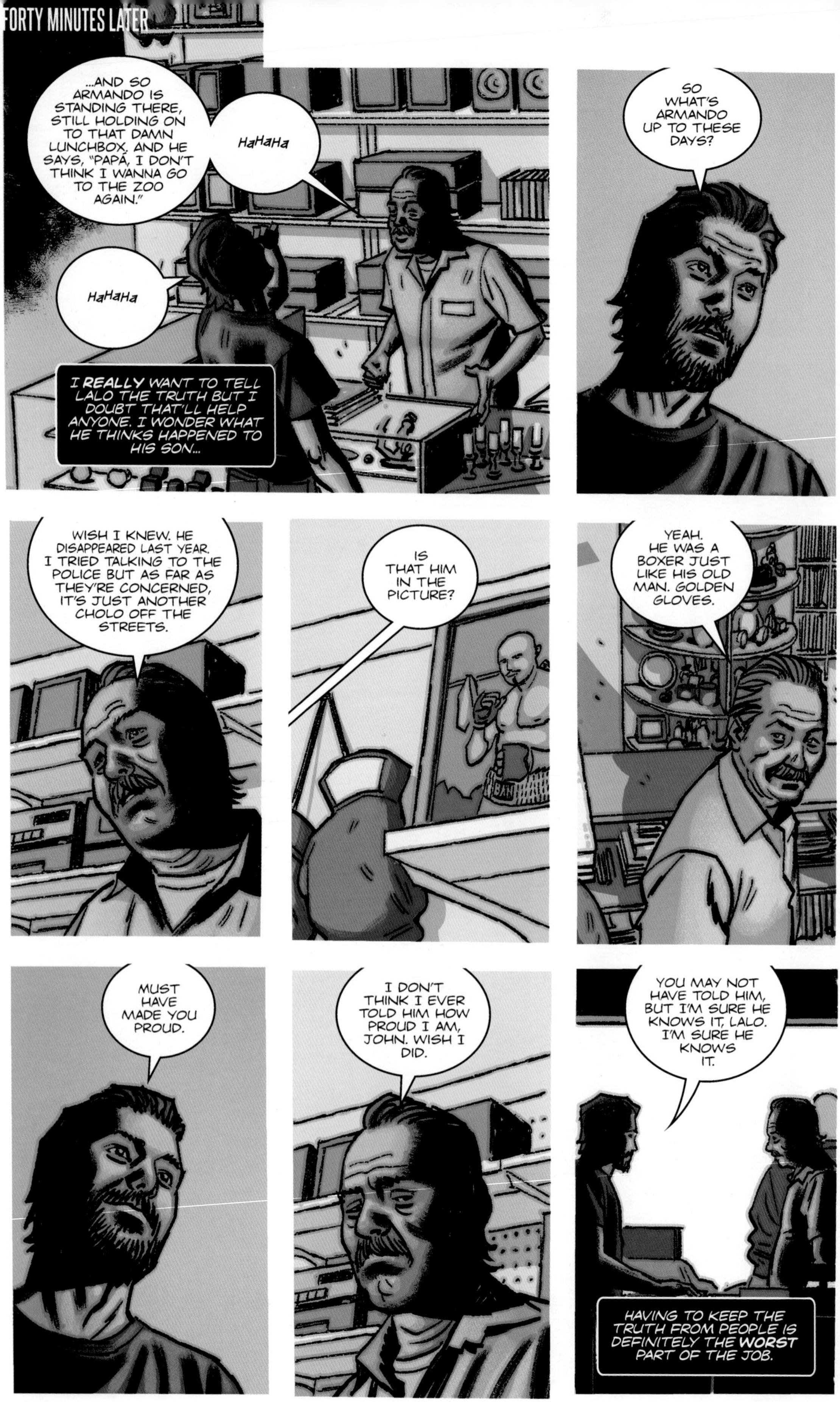
FORTY MINUTES LATER
...AND SO ARMANDO IS STANDING THERE, STILL HOLDING ON TO THAT DAMN LUNCHBOX. AND HE SAYS, "PAPÁ, I DON'T THINK I WANNA GO TO THE ZOO AGAIN."
HaHaHa
HaHaHa
I REALLY WANT TO TELL LALO THE TRUTH BUT I DOUBT THAT'LL HELP ANYONE. I WONDER WHAT HE THINKS HAPPENED TO HIS SON...
SO WHAT'S ARMANDO UP TO THESE DAYS?
WISH I KNEW. HE DISAPPEARED LAST YEAR. I TRIED TALKING TO THE POLICE BUT AS FAR AS THEY'RE CONCERNED, IT'S JUST ANOTHER CHOLO OFF THE STREETS.
IS THAT HIM IN THE PICTURE?
YEAH. HE WAS A BOXER JUST LIKE HIS OLD MAN. GOLDEN GLOVES.
MUST HAVE MADE YOU PROUD.
I DON'T THINK I EVER TOLD HIM HOW PROUD I AM, JOHN. WISH I DID.
YOU MAY NOT HAVE TOLD HIM, BUT I'M SURE HE KNOWS IT, LALO. I'M SURE HE KNOWS IT.
HAVING TO KEEP THE TRUTH FROM PEOPLE IS DEFINITELY THE WORST PART OF THE JOB.

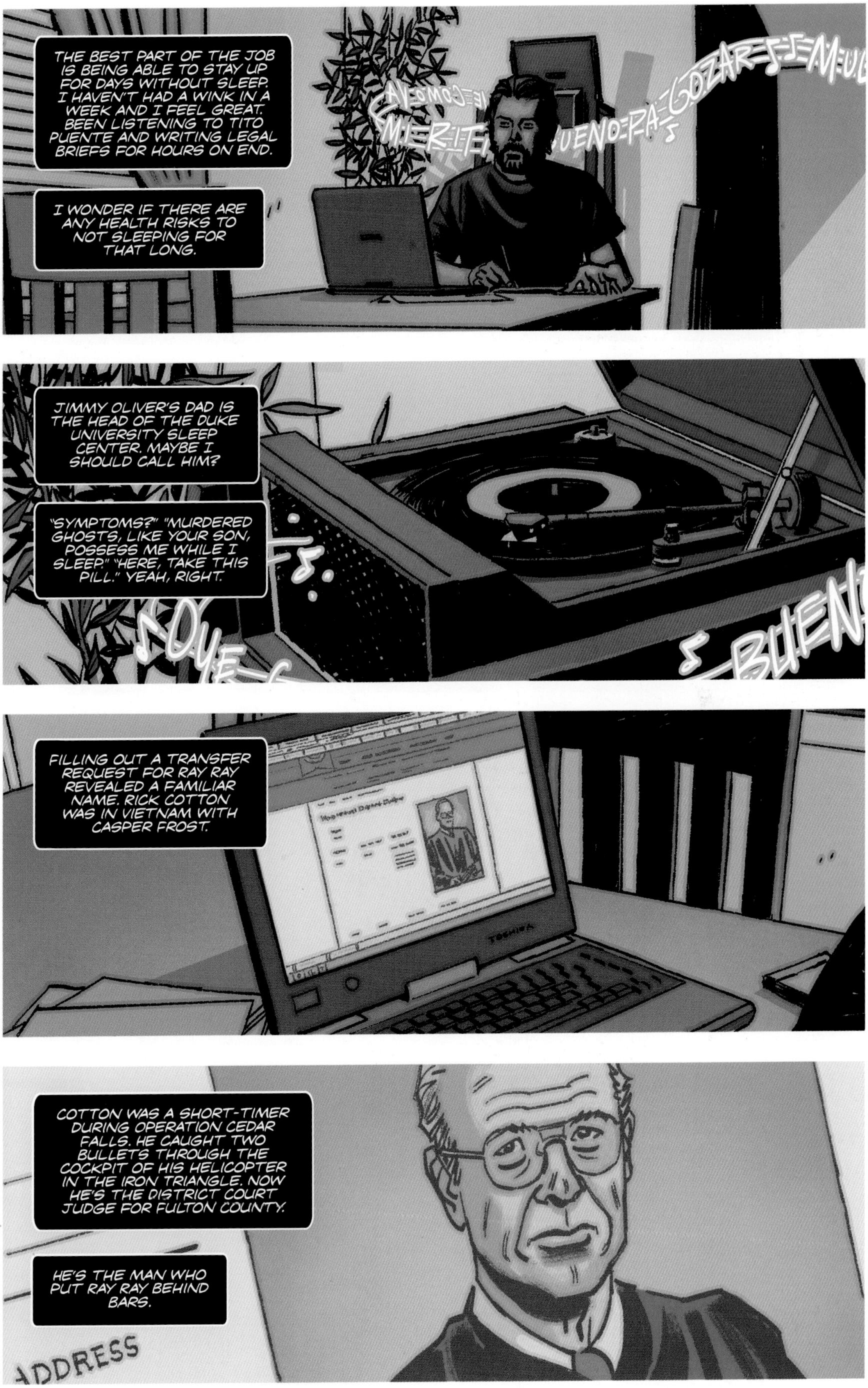
THE BEST PART OF THE JOB IS BEING ABLE TO STAY UP FOR DAYS WITHOUT SLEEP. I HAVEN'T HAD A WINK IN A WEEK AND I FEEL GREAT. BEEN LISTENING TO TITO PUENTE AND WRITING LEGAL BRIEFS FOR HOURS ON END.
I WONDER IF THERE ARE ANY HEALTH RISKS TO NOT SLEEPING FOR THAT LONG.
JIMMY OLIVER'S DAD IS THE HEAD OF THE DUKE UNIVERSITY SLEEP CENTER. MAYBE I SHOULD CALL HIM?
"SYMPTOMS?" "MURDERED GHOSTS, LIKE YOUR SON, POSSESS ME WHILE I SLEEP." "HERE, TAKE THIS PILL." YEAH, RIGHT.
FILLING OUT A TRANSFER REQUEST FOR RAY RAY REVEALED A FAMILIAR NAME. RICK COTTON WAS IN VIETNAM WITH CASPER FROST.
COTTON WAS A SHORT-TIMER DURING OPERATION CEDAR FALLS. HE CAUGHT TWO BULLETS THROUGH THE COCKPIT OF HIS HELICOPTER IN THE IRON TRIANGLE. NOW HE'S THE DISTRICT COURT JUDGE FOR FULTON COUNTY.
HE'S THE MAN WHO PUT RAY RAY BEHIND BARS.
ADDRESS

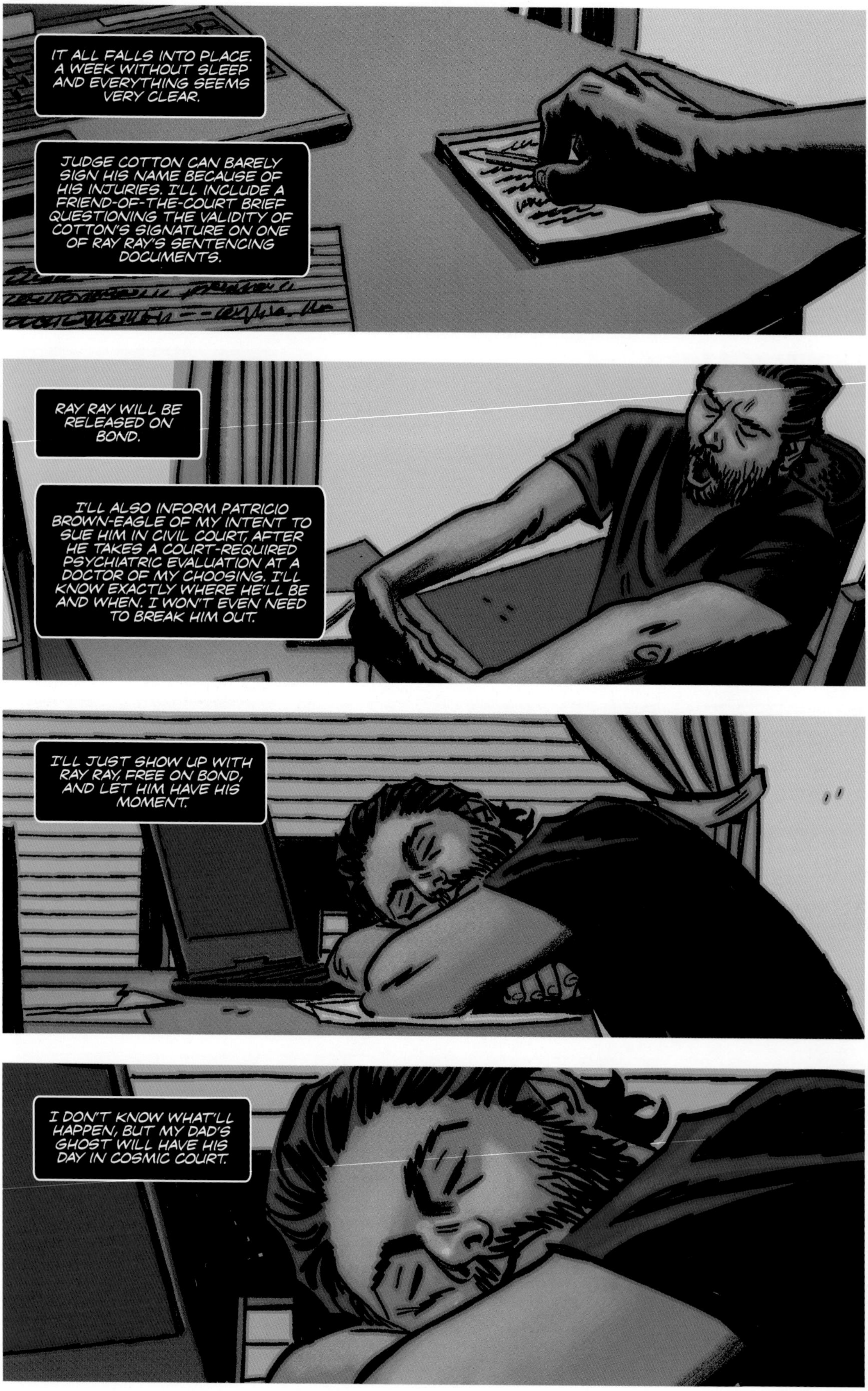
IT ALL FALLS INTO PLACE. A WEEK WITHOUT SLEEP AND EVERYTHING SEEMS VERY CLEAR.
JUDGE COTTON CAN BARELY SIGN HIS NAME BECAUSE OF HIS INJURIES. I'LL INCLUDE A FRIEND-OF-THE-COURT BRIEF QUESTIONING THE VALIDITY OF COTTON'S SIGNATURE ON ONE OF RAY RAY'S SENTENCING DOCUMENTS.
RAY RAY WILL BE RELEASED ON BOND.
I'LL ALSO INFORM PATRICIO BROWN-EAGLE OF MY INTENT TO SUE HIM IN CIVIL COURT, AFTER HE TAKES A COURT-REQUIRED PSYCHIATRIC EVALUATION AT A DOCTOR OF MY CHOOSING. I'LL KNOW EXACTLY WHERE HE'LL BE AND WHEN. I WON'T EVEN NEED TO BREAK HIM OUT.
I'LL JUST SHOW UP WITH RAY RAY, FREE ON BOND, AND LET HIM HAVE HIS MOMENT.
I DON'T KNOW WHAT'LL HAPPEN, BUT MY DAD'S GHOST WILL HAVE HIS DAY IN COSMIC COURT.

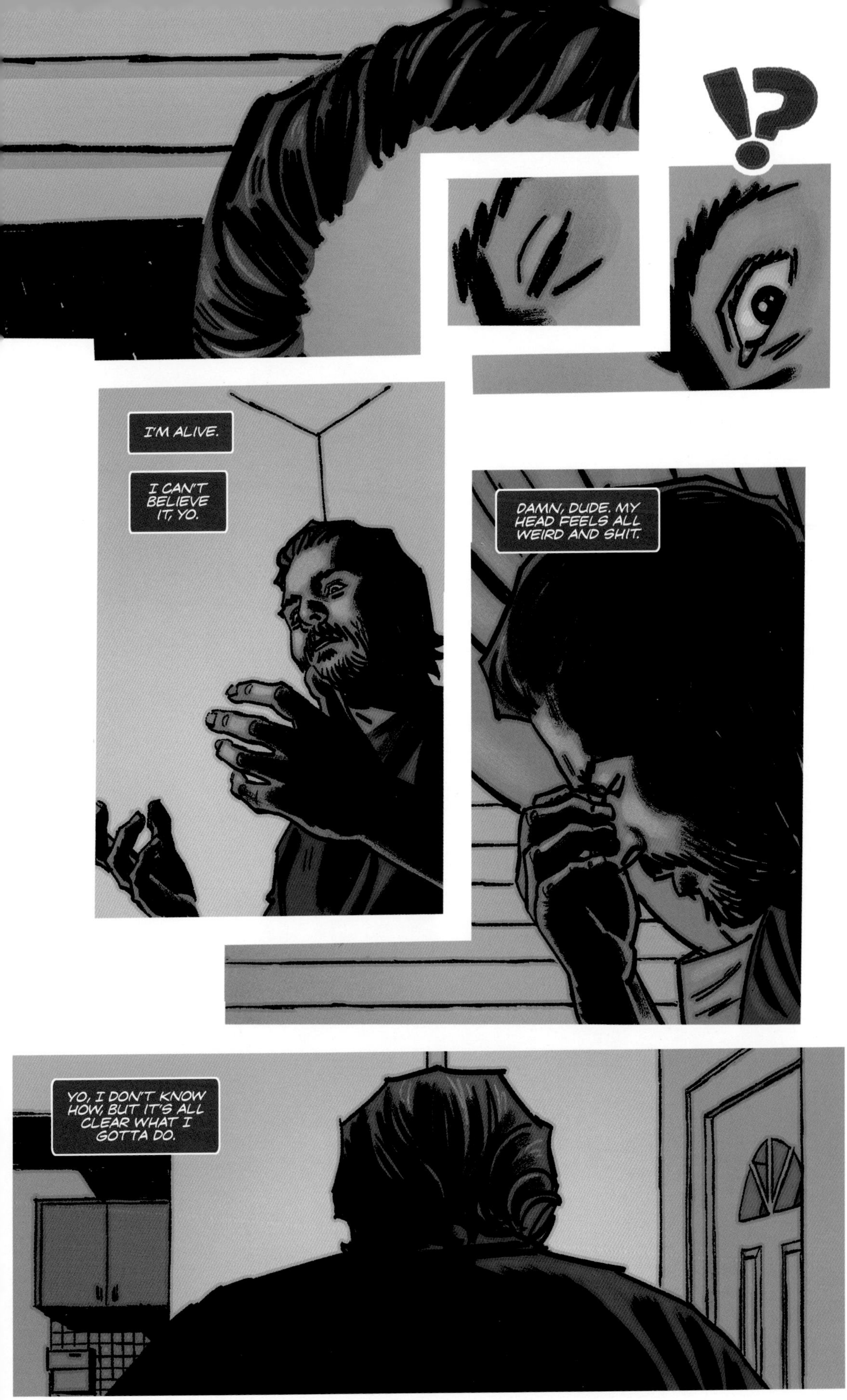
!?
I'M ALIVE.
I CAN'T BELIEVE IT, YO.
DAMN, DUDE. MY HEAD FEELS ALL WEIRD AND SHIT.
YO, I DON'T KNOW HOW, BUT IT'S ALL CLEAR WHAT I GOTTA DO.

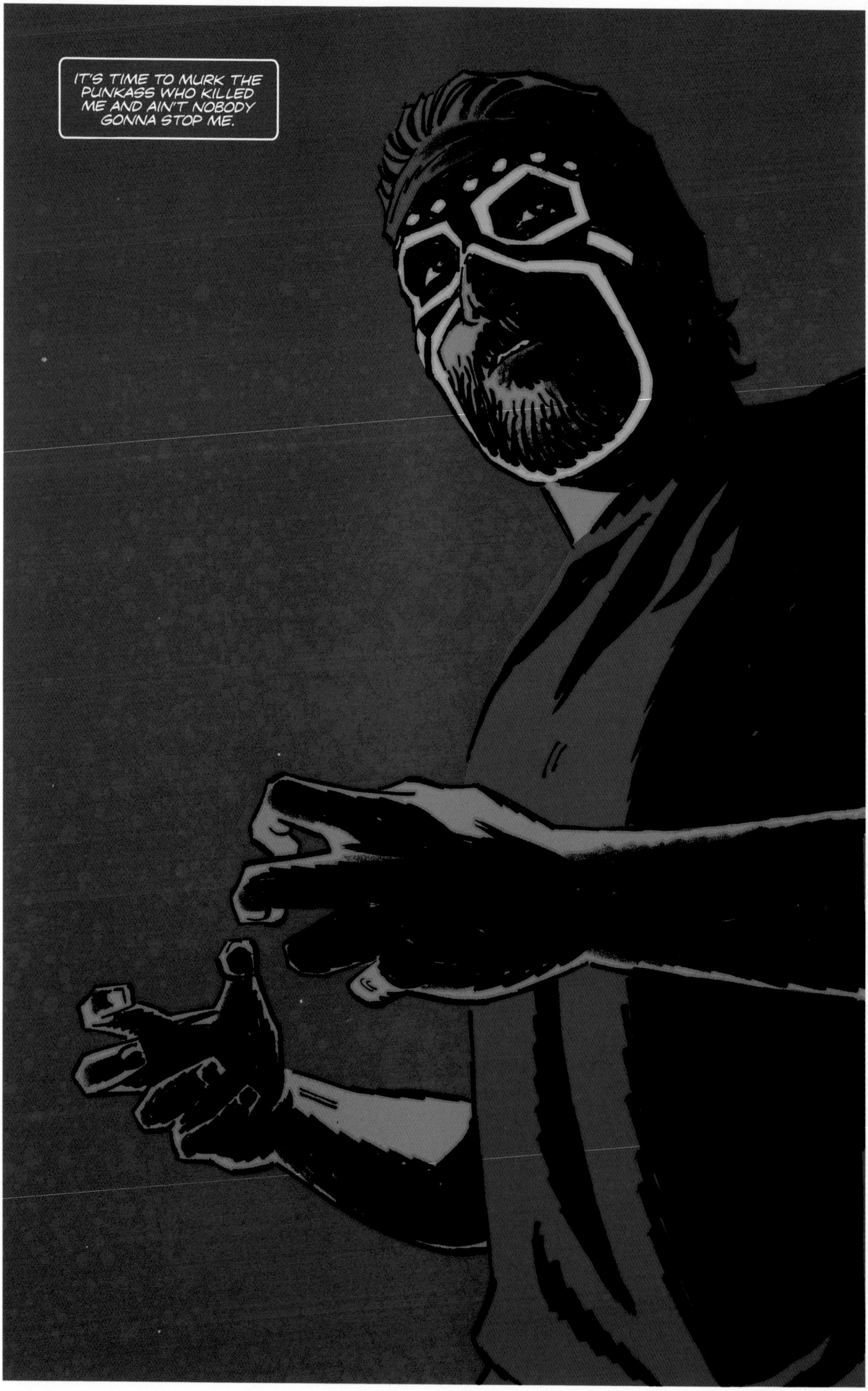
IT'S TIME TO MURK THE PUNKASS WHO KILLED ME AND AIN'T NOBODY GONNA STOP ME.

CHAPTER 3

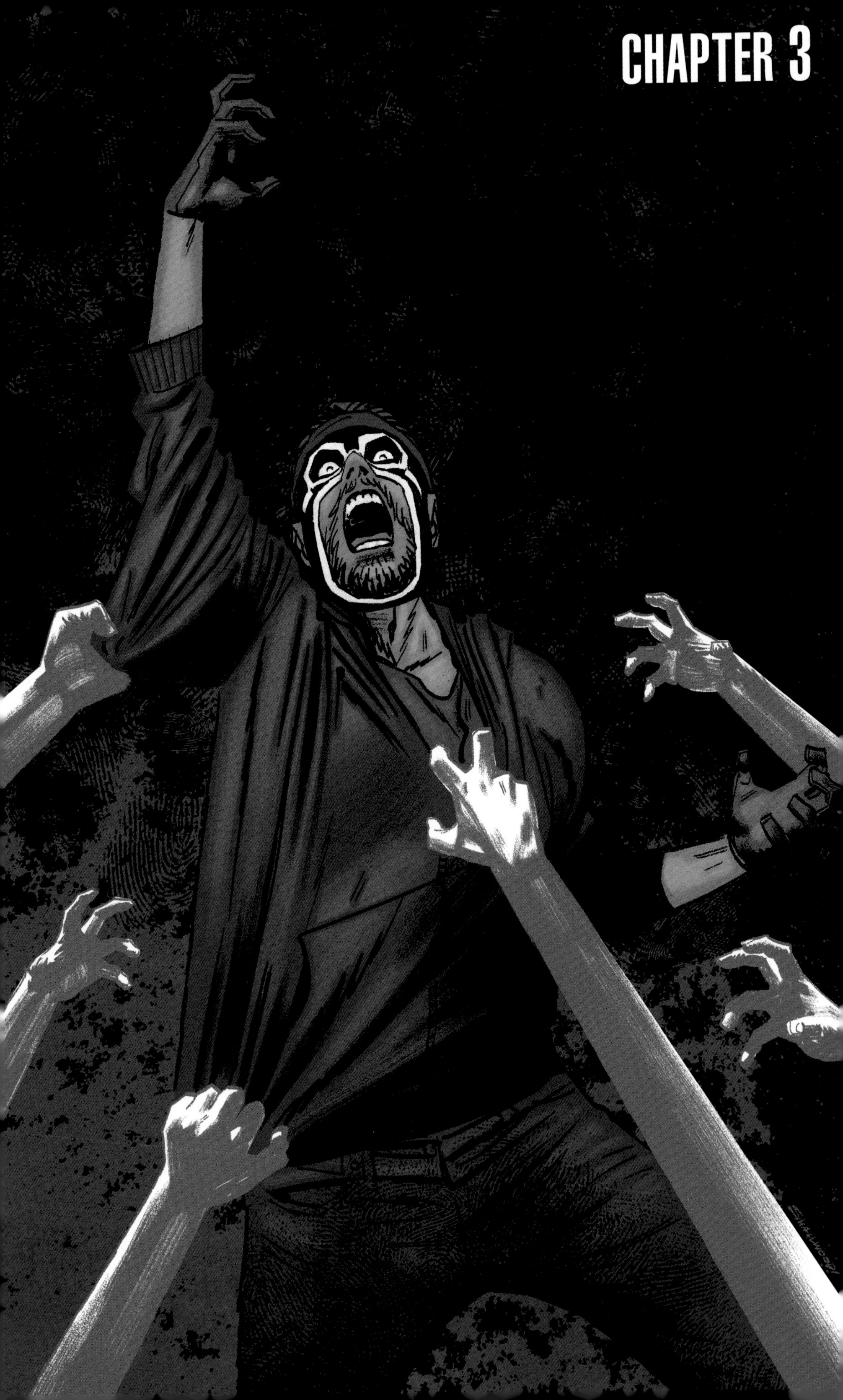

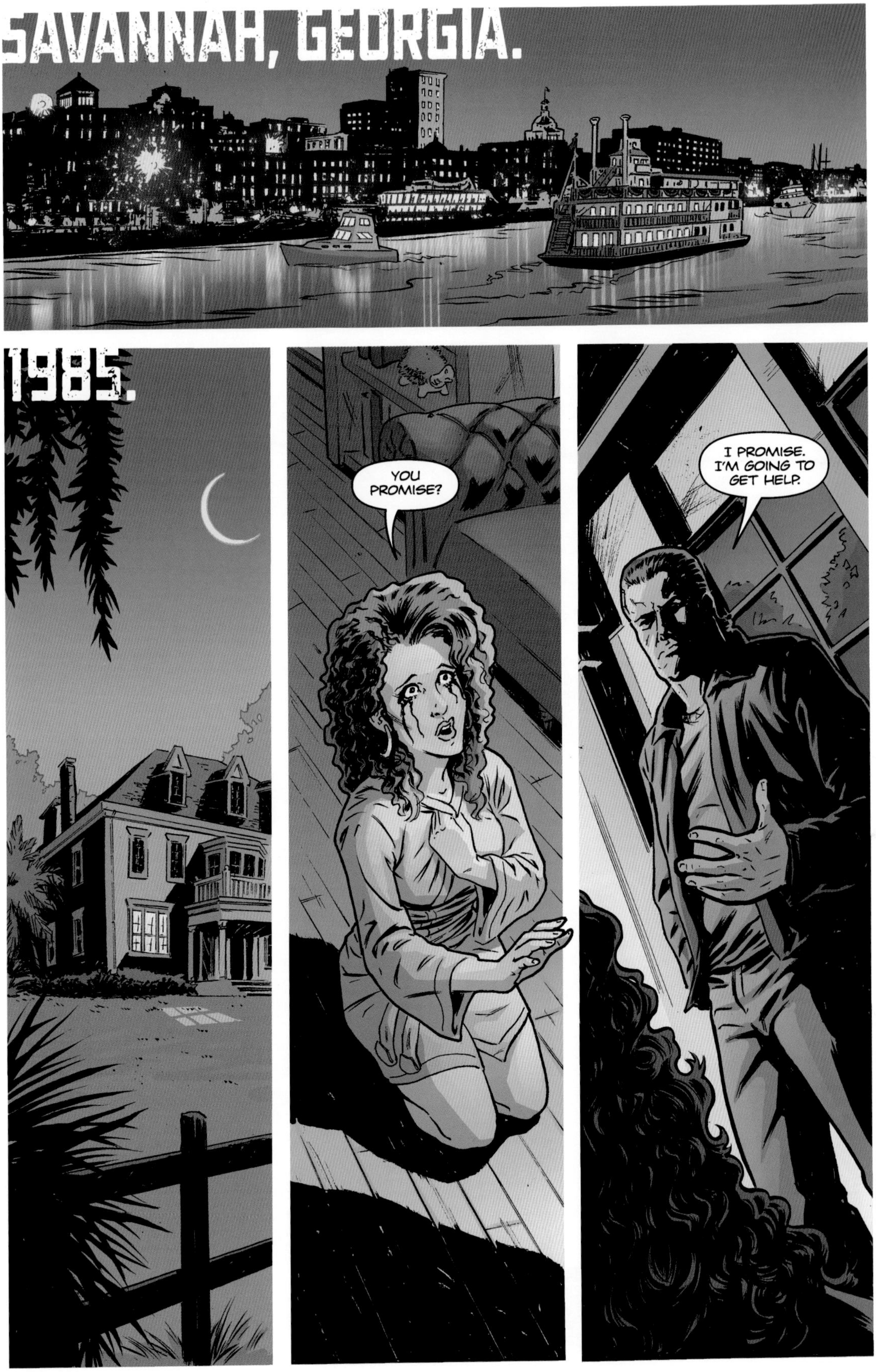
SAVANNAH, GEORGIA.
1985.
YOU PROMISE?
I PROMISE. I'M GOING TO GET HELP.

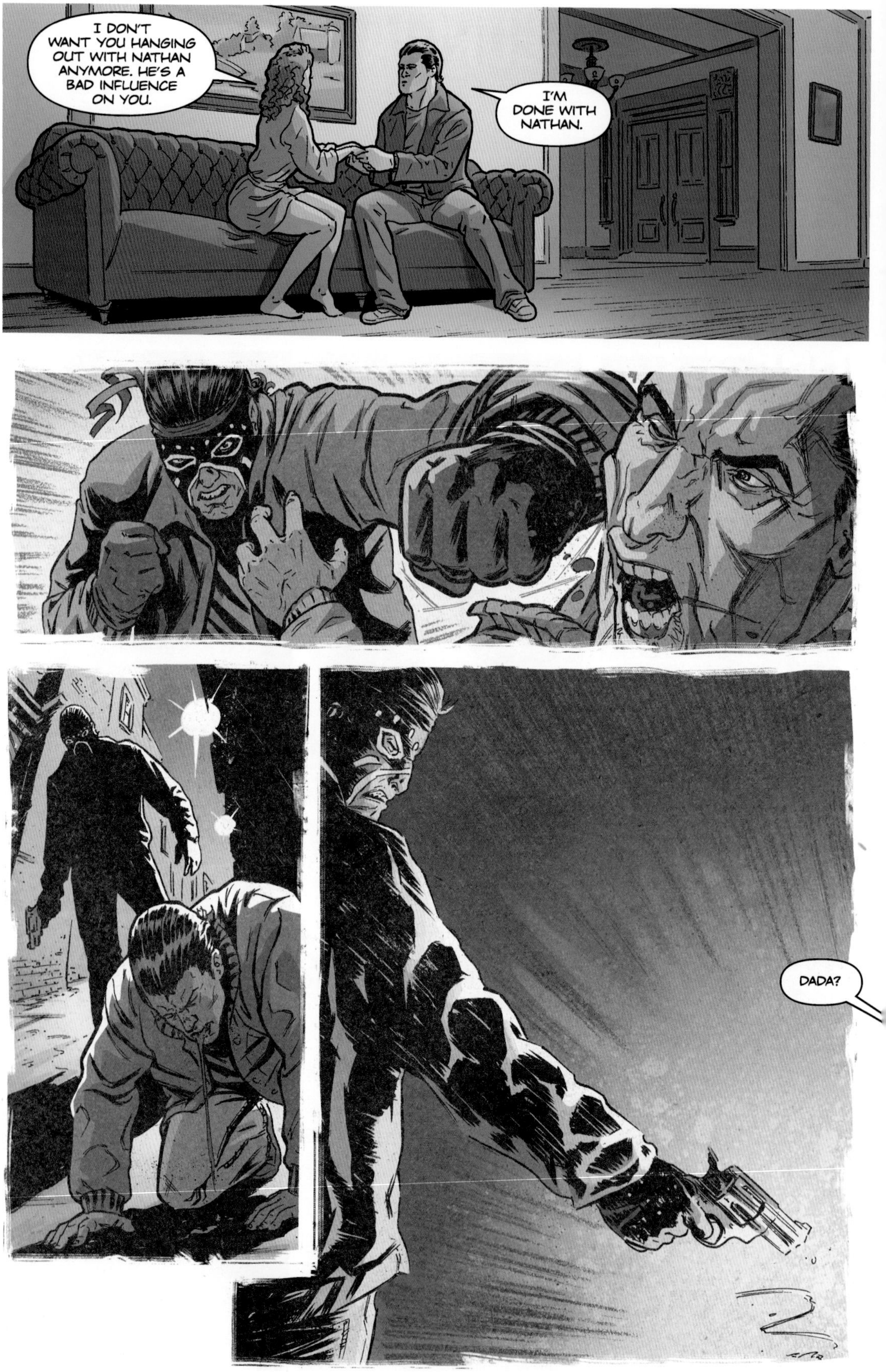
I DON'T WANT YOU HANGING OUT WITH NATHAN ANYMORE. HE'S A BAD INFLUENCE ON YOU.
I'M DONE WITH NATHAN.
DADA?

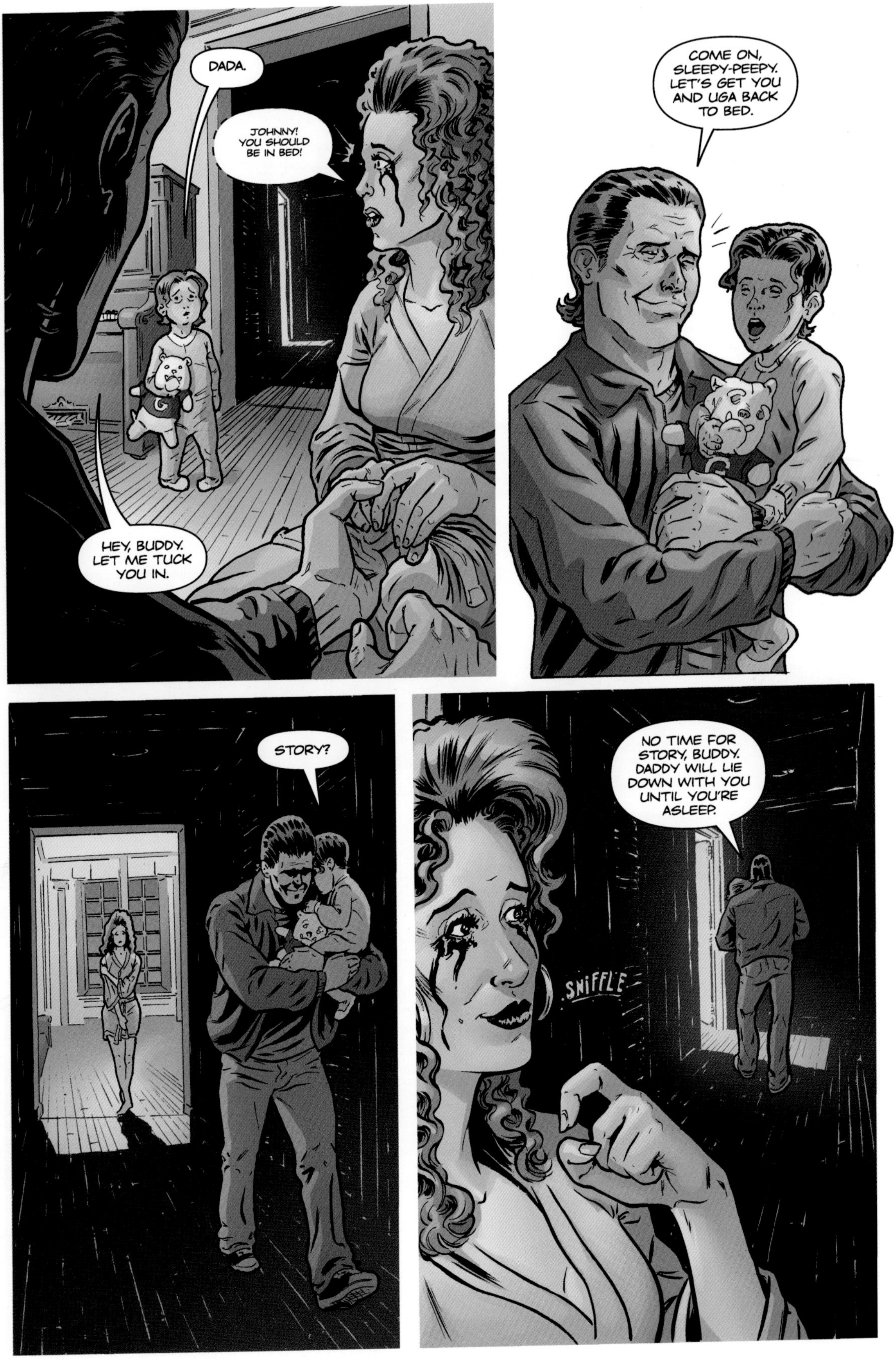
DADA.
JOHNNY! YOU SHOULD BE IN BED!
HEY, BUDDY. LET ME TUCK YOU IN.
COME ON, SLEEPY-PEEPY. LET'S GET YOU AND UGA BACK TO BED.
STORY?
NO TIME FOR STORY, BUDDY. DADDY WILL LIE DOWN WITH YOU UNTIL YOU'RE ASLEEP.
SNIFFLE

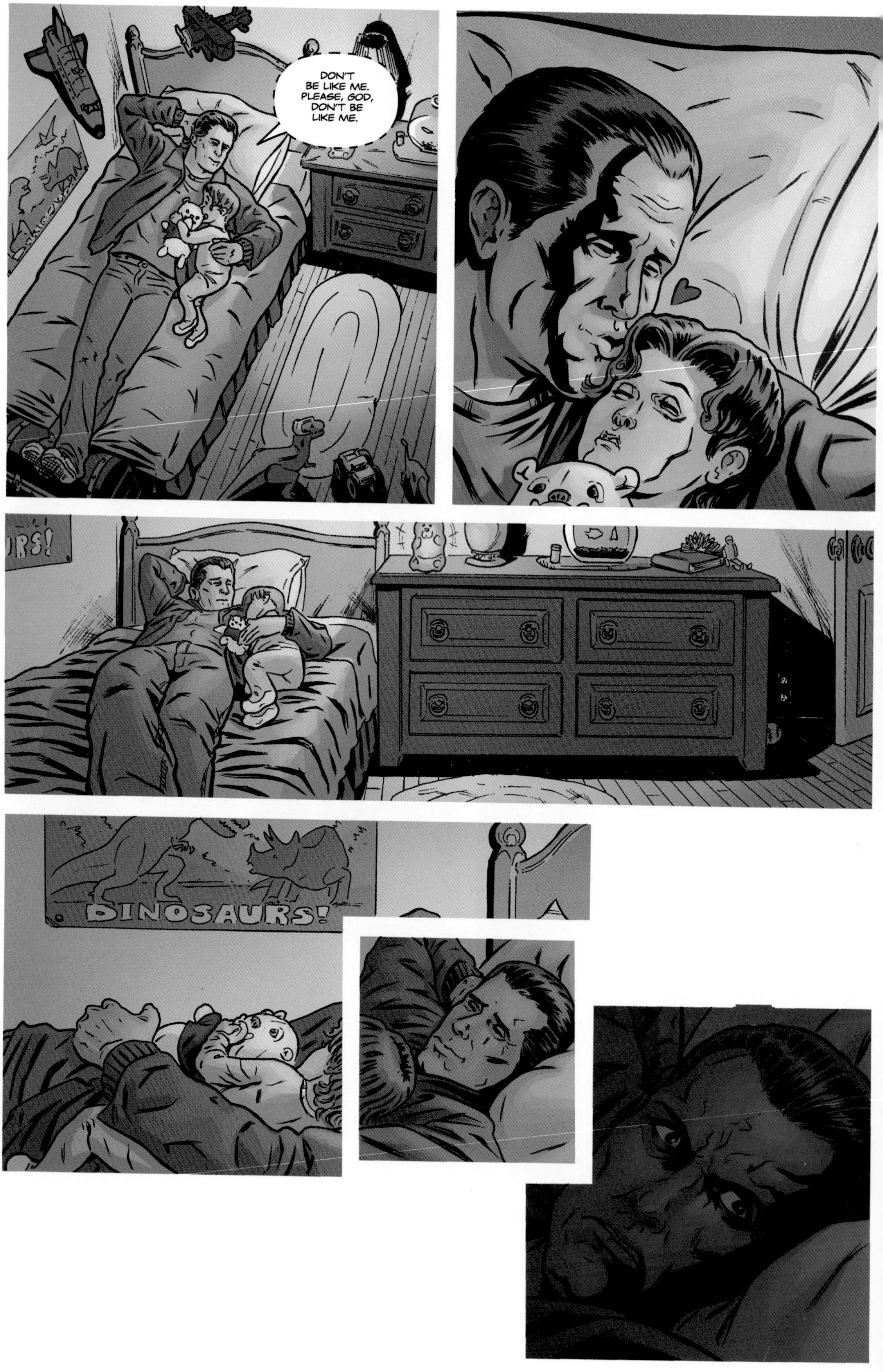
DON'T BE LIKE ME. PLEASE, GOD, DON'T BE LIKE ME.
DINOSAURS!

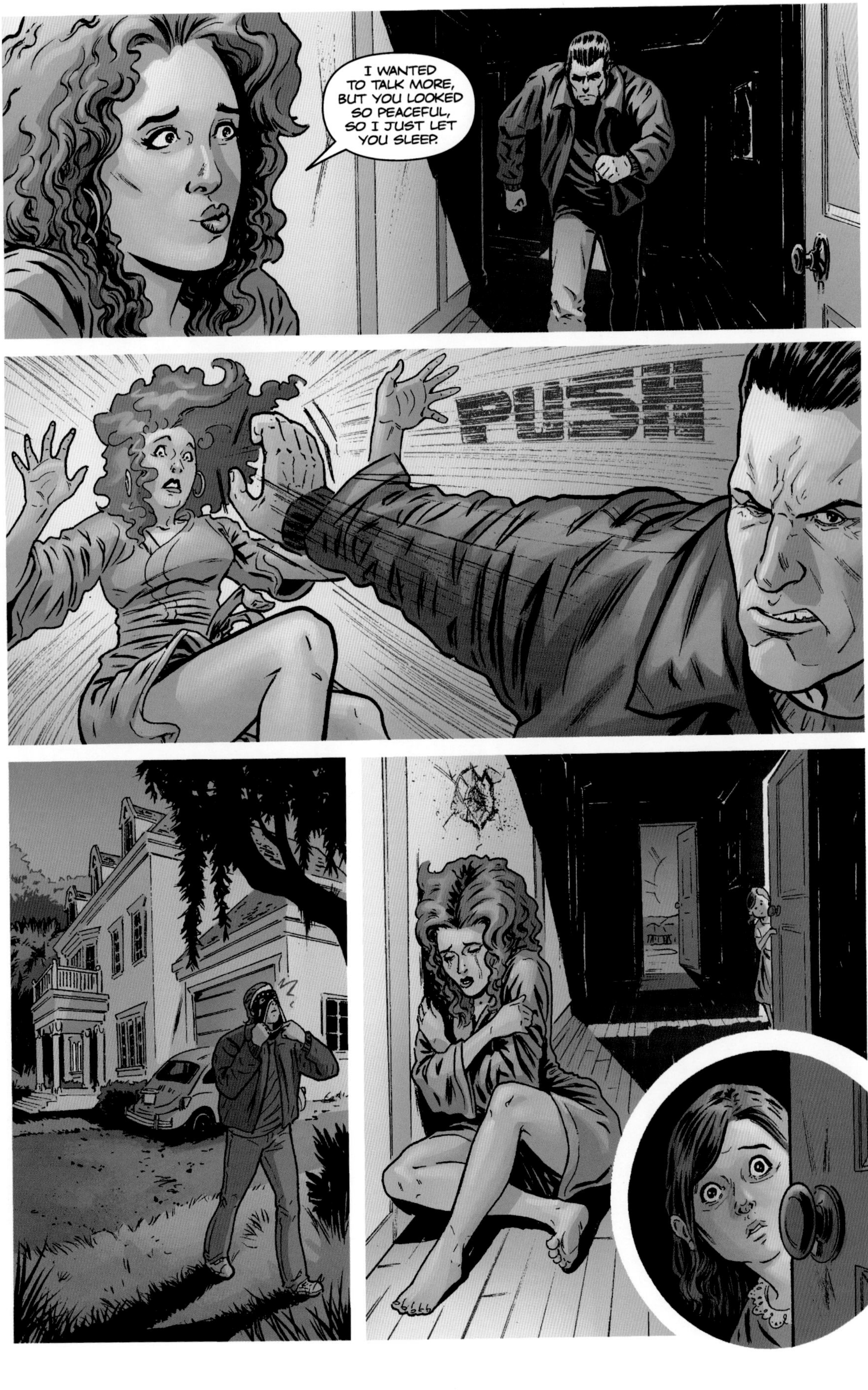
I WANTED TO TALK MORE, BUT YOU LOOKED SO PEACEFUL, SO I JUST LET YOU SLEEP.
PUSH

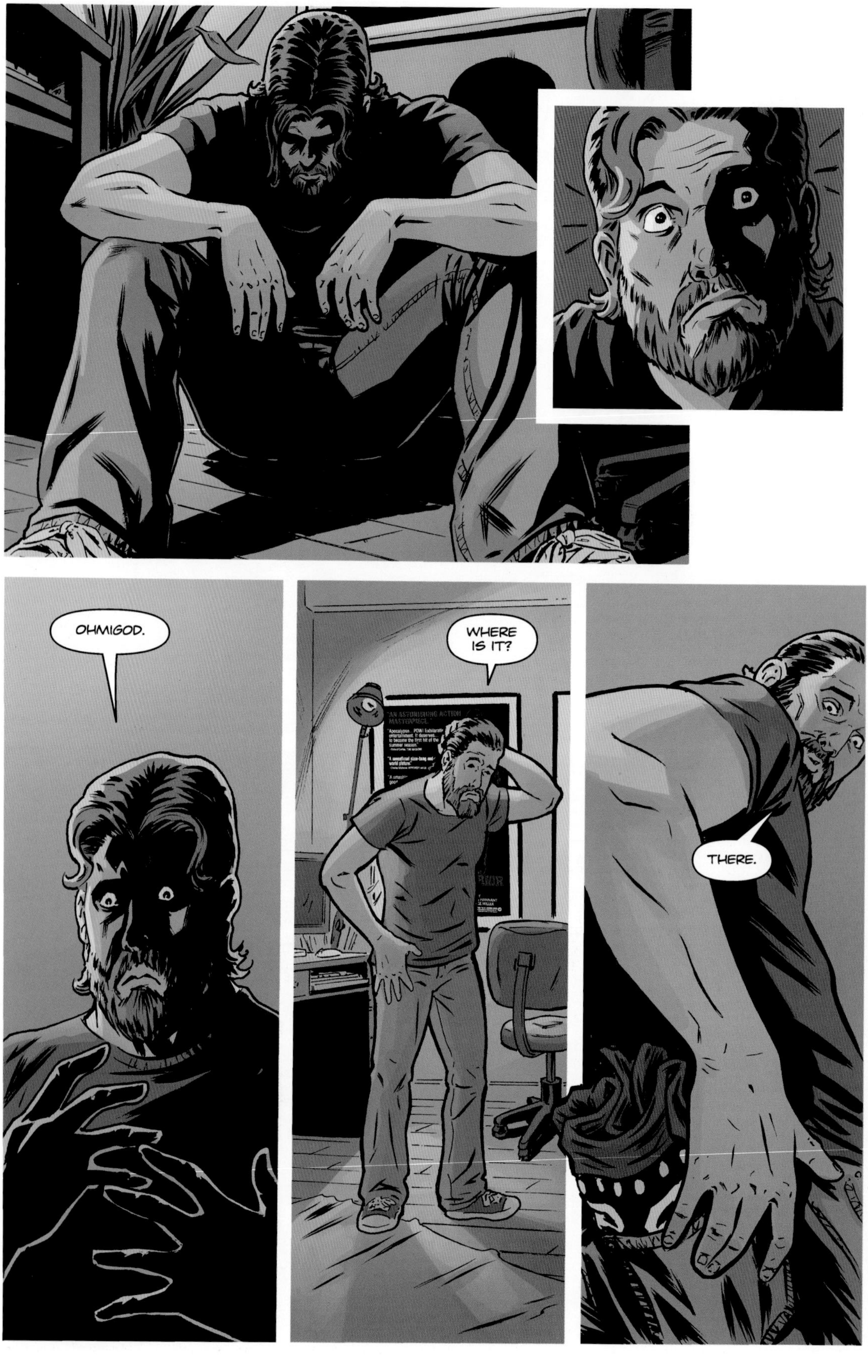
OHMIGOD.
WHERE IS IT?
THERE.

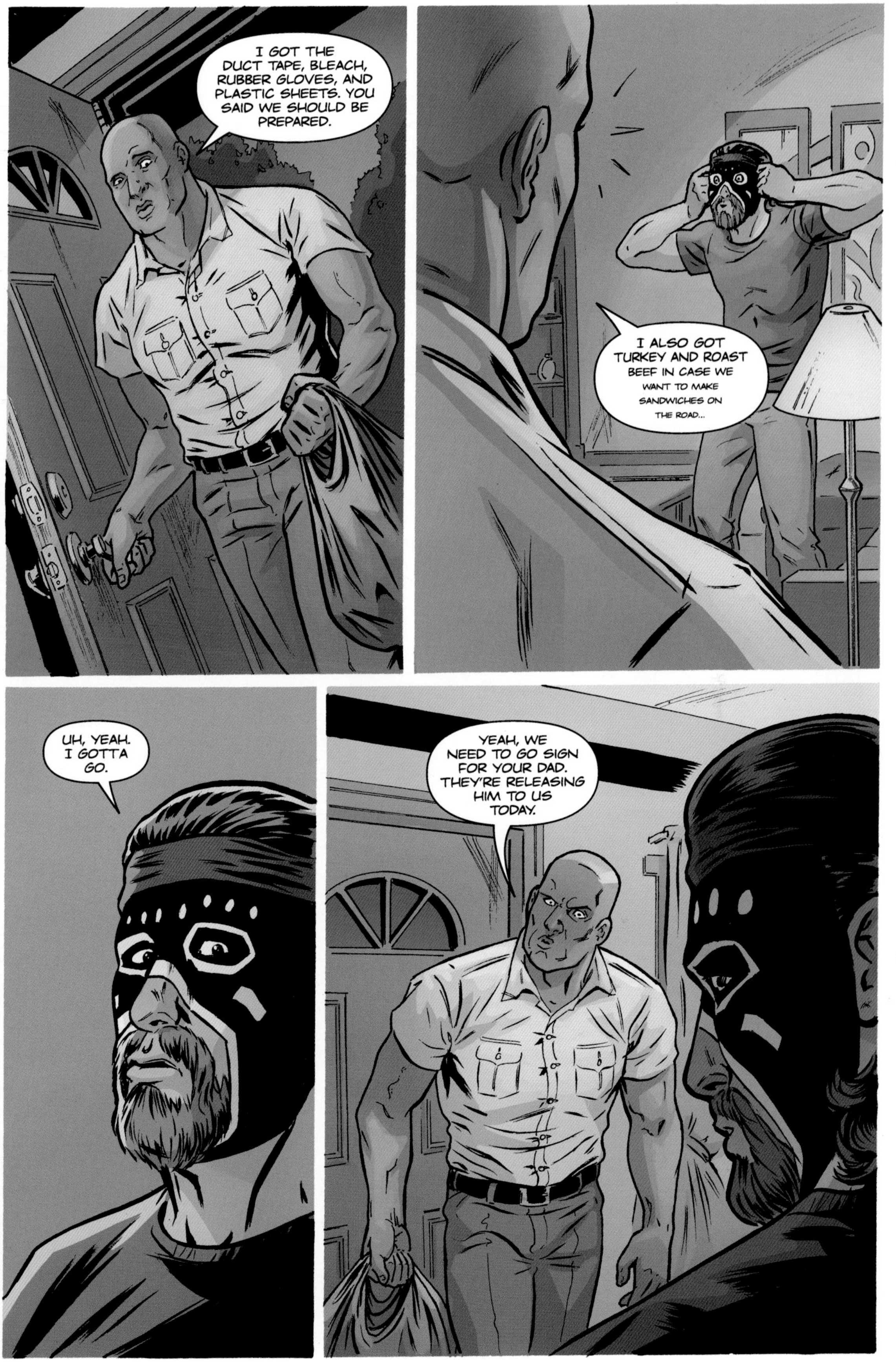

I GOT THE DUCT TAPE, BLEACH, RUBBER GLOVES, AND PLASTIC SHEETS. YOU SAID WE SHOULD BE PREPARED.
I ALSO GOT TURKEY AND ROAST BEEF IN CASE WE WANT TO MAKE SANDWICHES ON THE ROAD...
UH, YEAH. I GOTTA GO.
YEAH, WE NEED TO GO SIGN FOR YOUR DAD. THEY'RE RELEASING HIM TO US TODAY.

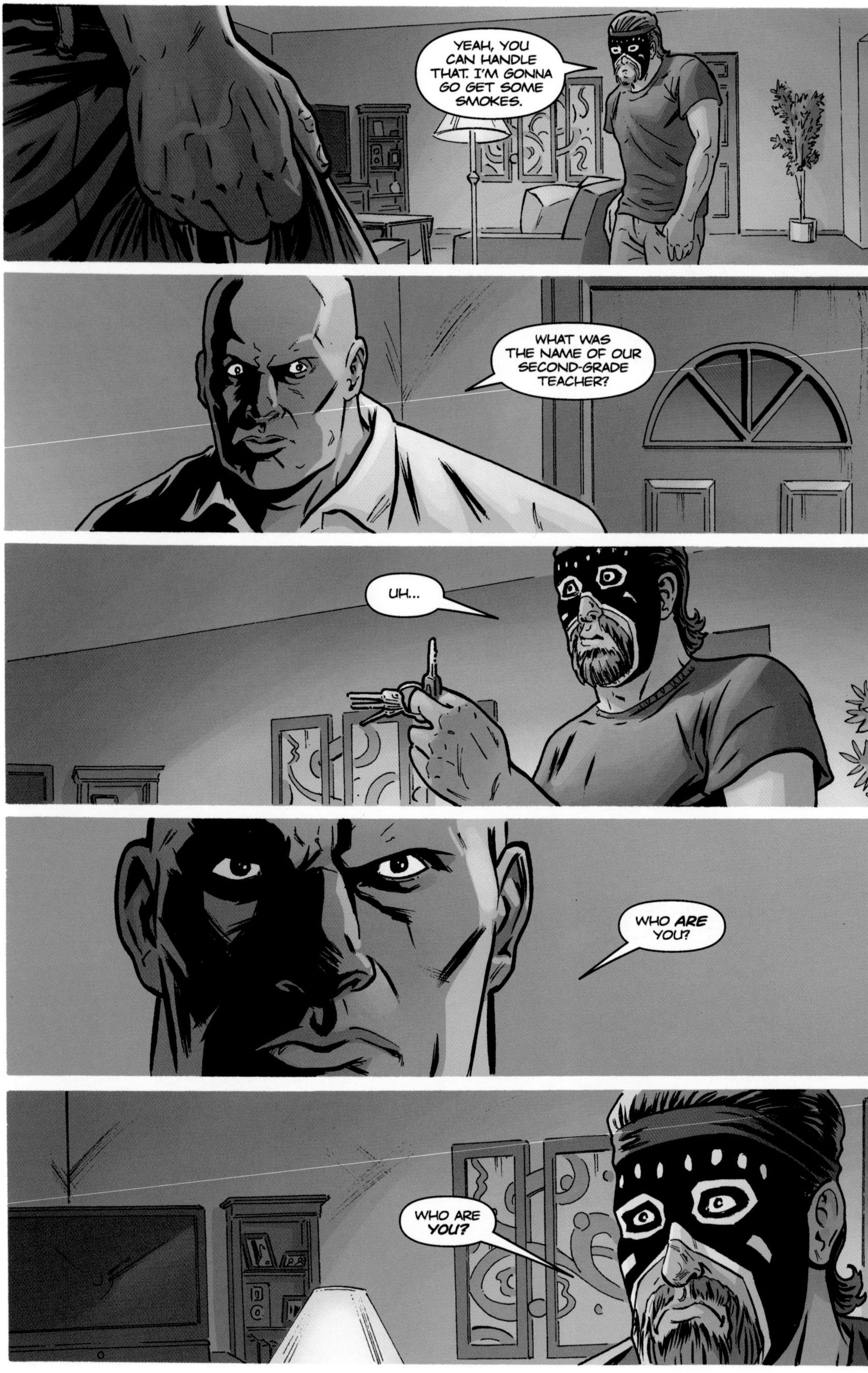
YEAH, YOU CAN HANDLE THAT. I'M GONNA GO GET SOME SMOKES.
WHAT WAS THE NAME OF OUR SECOND-GRADE TEACHER?
UH...
WHO *ARE* YOU?
WHO ARE *YOU?*

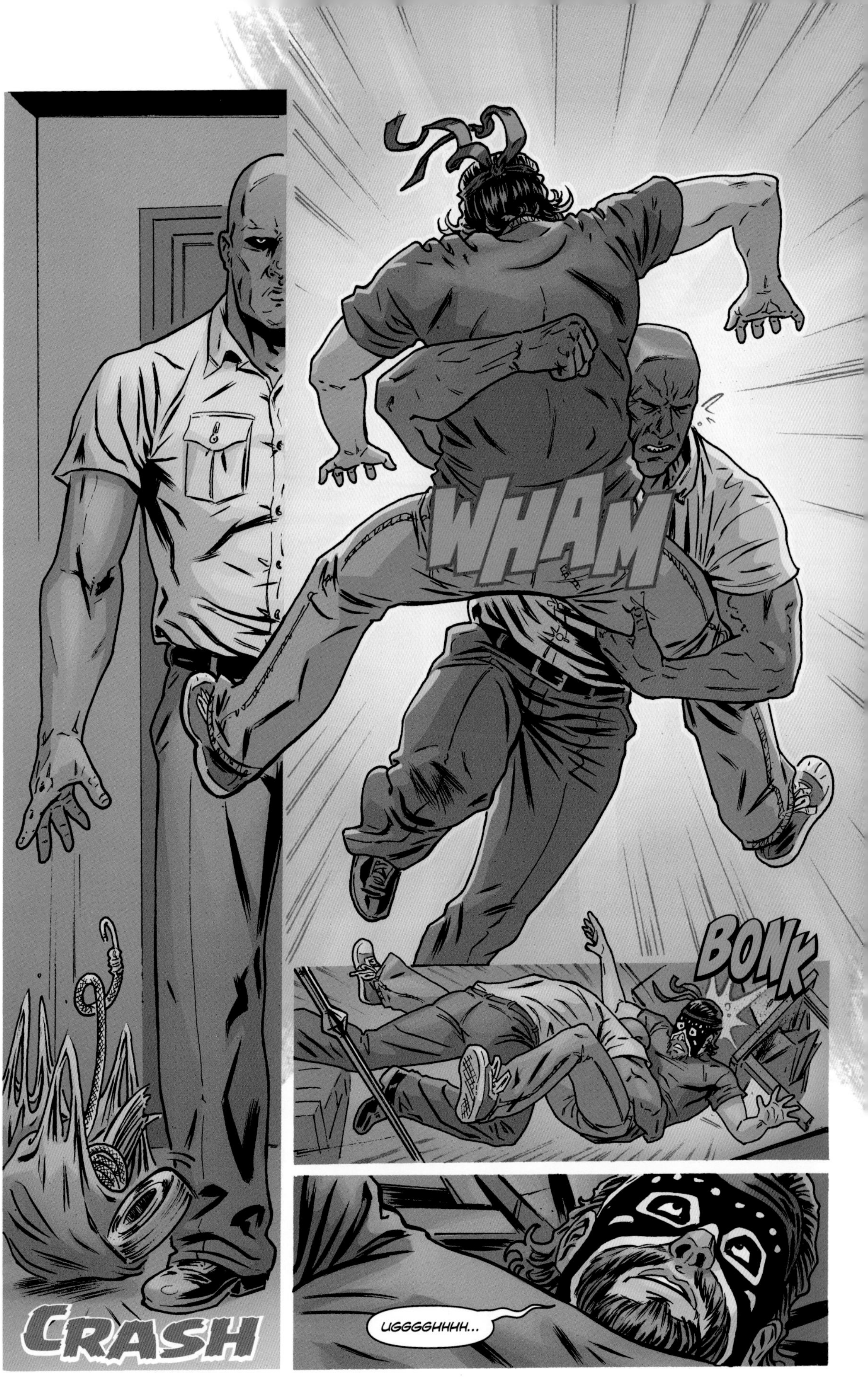
CRASH
WHAM
BONK
UGGGGHHHH...

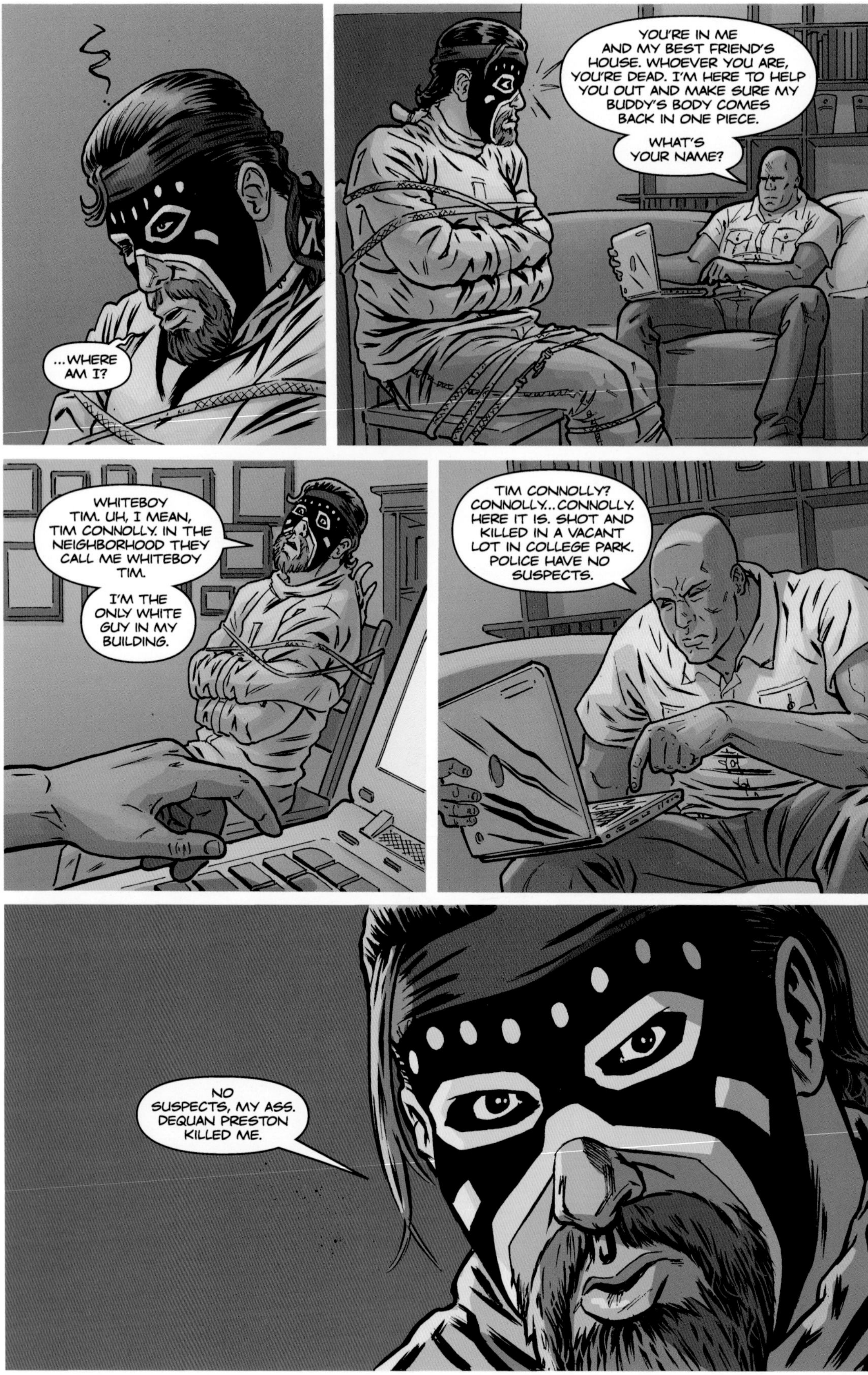
...WHERE AM I?
YOU'RE IN ME AND MY BEST FRIEND'S HOUSE. WHOEVER YOU ARE, YOU'RE DEAD. I'M HERE TO HELP YOU OUT AND MAKE SURE MY BUDDY'S BODY COMES BACK IN ONE PIECE.
WHAT'S YOUR NAME?
WHITEBOY TIM. UH, I MEAN, TIM CONNOLLY. IN THE NEIGHBORHOOD THEY CALL ME WHITEBOY TIM.
I'M THE ONLY WHITE GUY IN MY BUILDING.
TIM CONNOLLY? CONNOLLY...CONNOLLY. HERE IT IS. SHOT AND KILLED IN A VACANT LOT IN COLLEGE PARK. POLICE HAVE NO SUSPECTS.
NO SUSPECTS, MY ASS. DEQUAN PRESTON KILLED ME.

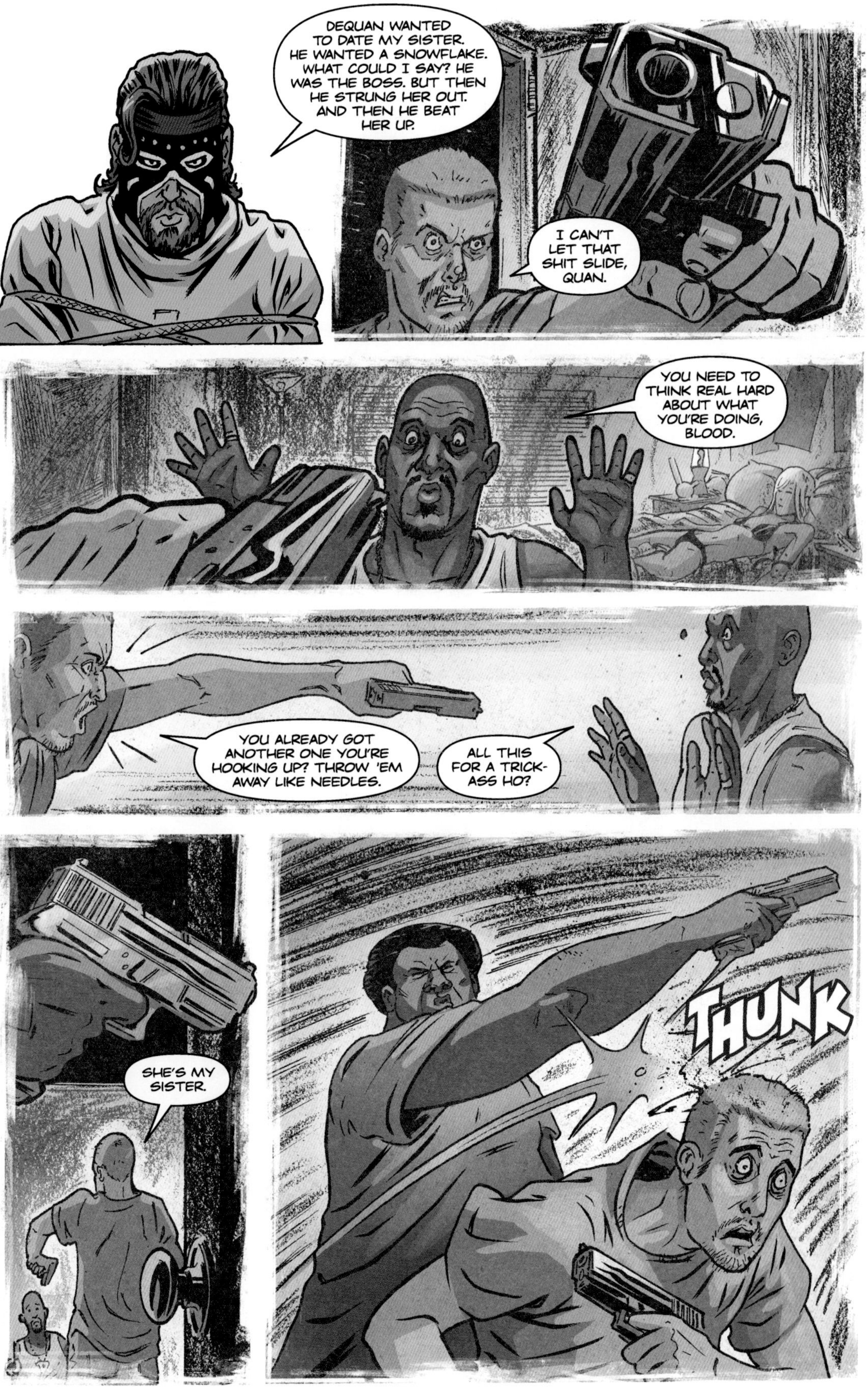
DEQUAN WANTED TO DATE MY SISTER. HE WANTED A SNOWFLAKE. WHAT COULD I SAY? HE WAS THE BOSS. BUT THEN HE STRUNG HER OUT. AND THEN HE BEAT HER UP.
I CAN'T LET THAT SHIT SLIDE, QUAN.
YOU NEED TO THINK REAL HARD ABOUT WHAT YOU'RE DOING, BLOOD.
YOU ALREADY GOT ANOTHER ONE YOU'RE HOOKING UP? THROW 'EM AWAY LIKE NEEDLES.
ALL THIS FOR A TRICK-ASS HO?
SHE'S MY SISTER.
THUNK

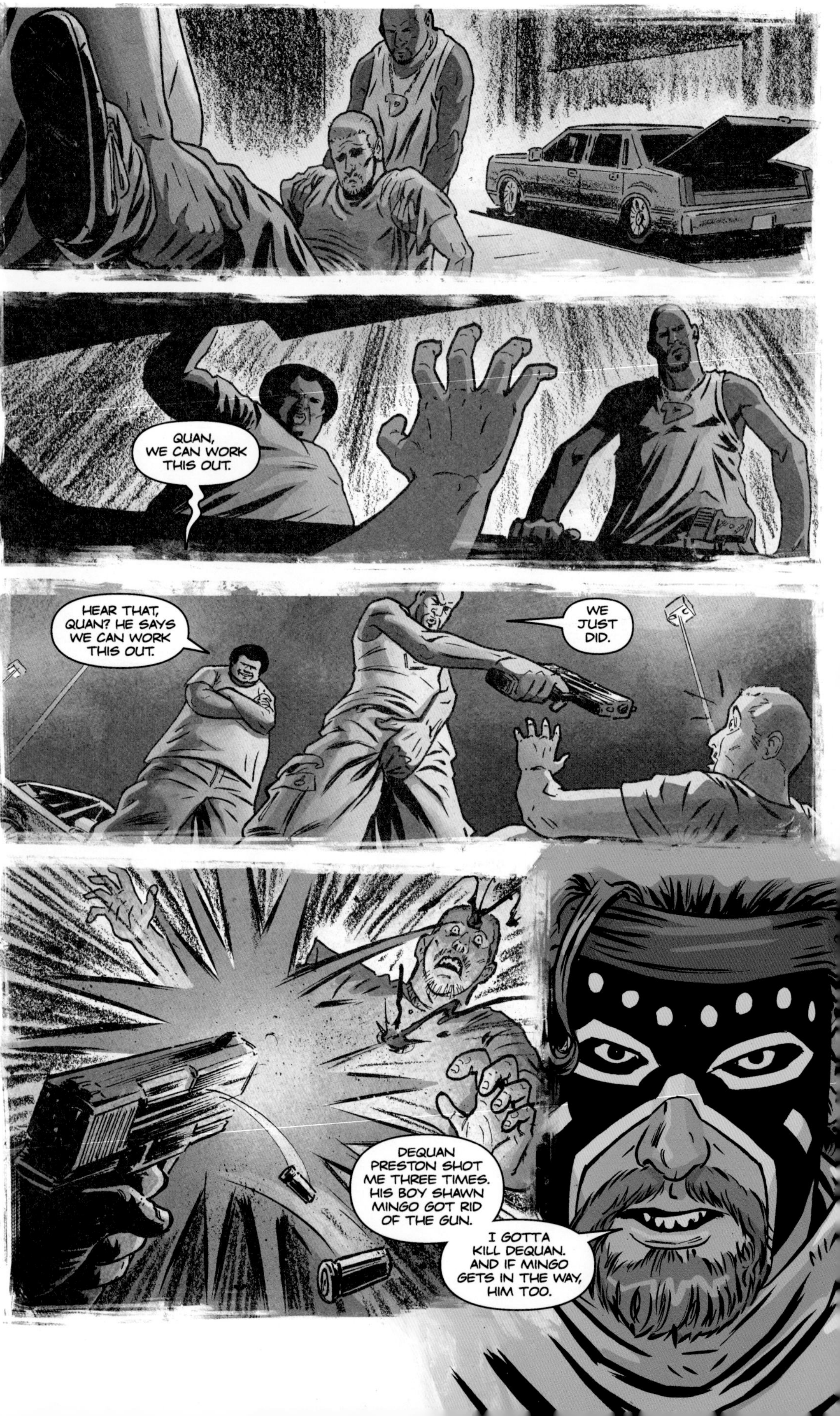
QUAN, WE CAN WORK THIS OUT.
HEAR THAT, QUAN? HE SAYS WE CAN WORK THIS OUT.
WE JUST DID.
DEQUAN PRESTON SHOT ME THREE TIMES. HIS BOY SHAWN MINGO GOT RID OF THE GUN.
I GOTTA KILL DEQUAN. AND IF MINGO GETS IN THE WAY, HIM TOO.

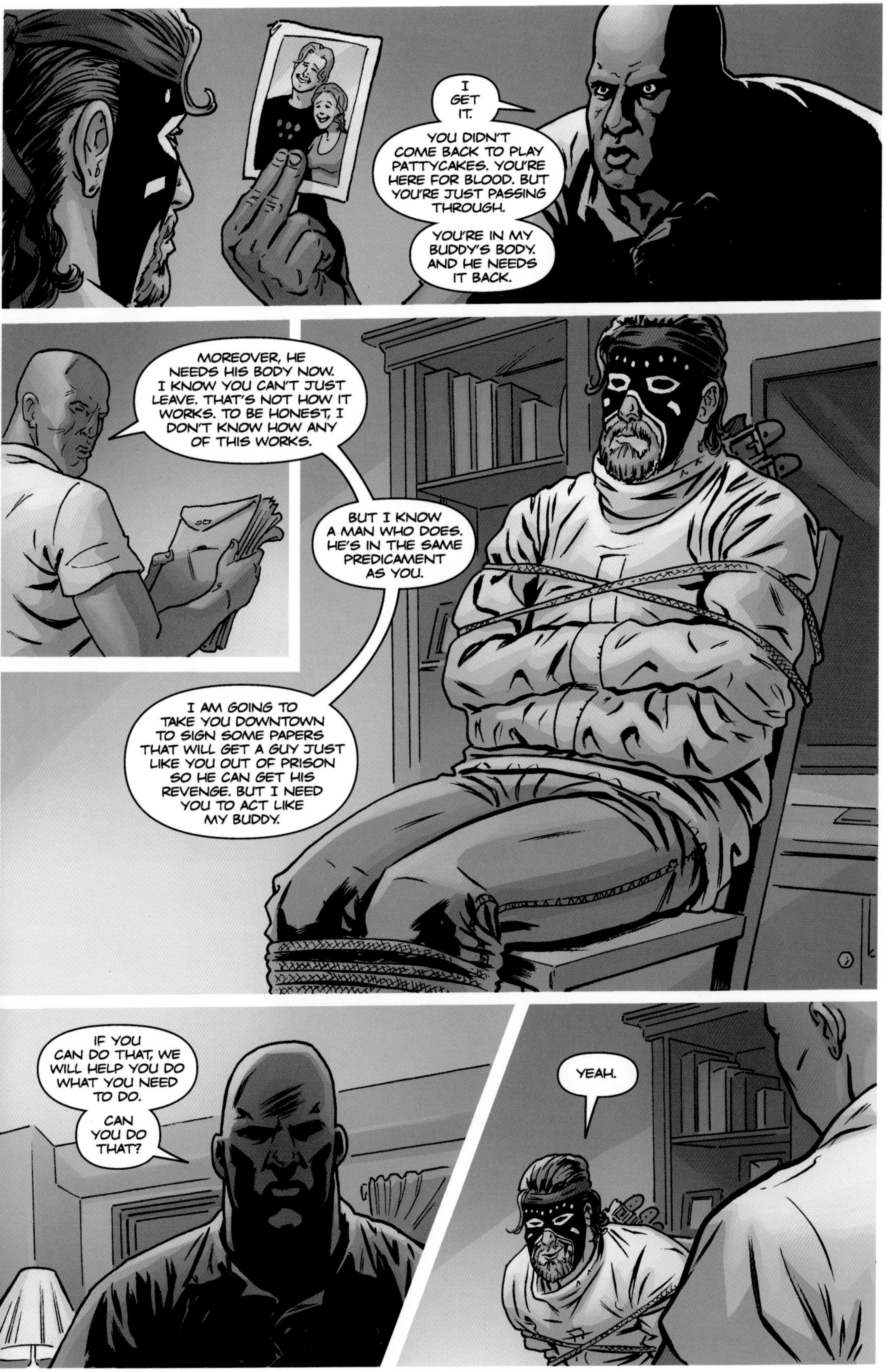
I GET IT.
YOU DIDN'T COME BACK TO PLAY PATTYCAKES. YOU'RE HERE FOR BLOOD. BUT YOU'RE JUST PASSING THROUGH.
YOU'RE IN MY BUDDY'S BODY. AND HE NEEDS IT BACK.
MOREOVER, HE NEEDS HIS BODY NOW. I KNOW YOU CAN'T JUST LEAVE. THAT'S NOT HOW IT WORKS. TO BE HONEST, I DON'T KNOW HOW ANY OF THIS WORKS.
BUT I KNOW A MAN WHO DOES. HE'S IN THE SAME PREDICAMENT AS YOU.
I AM GOING TO TAKE YOU DOWNTOWN TO SIGN SOME PAPERS THAT WILL GET A GUY JUST LIKE YOU OUT OF PRISON SO HE CAN GET HIS REVENGE. BUT I NEED YOU TO ACT LIKE MY BUDDY.
IF YOU CAN DO THAT, WE WILL HELP YOU DO WHAT YOU NEED TO DO.
CAN YOU DO THAT?
YEAH.

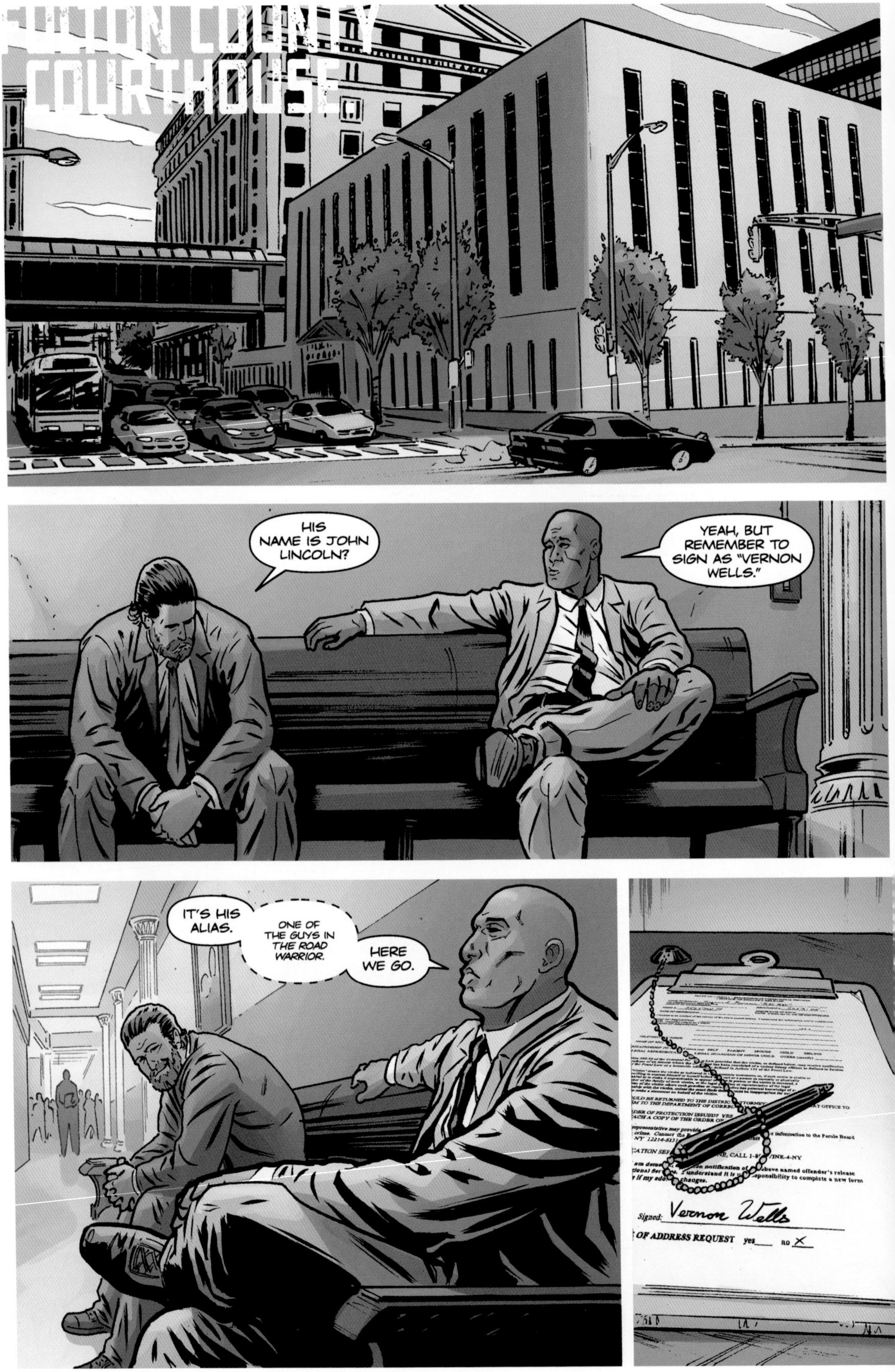
FULTON COUNTY COURTHOUSE.
HIS NAME IS JOHN LINCOLN?
YEAH, BUT REMEMBER TO SIGN AS "VERNON WELLS."
IT'S HIS ALIAS.
ONE OF THE GUYS IN THE ROAD WARRIOR.
HERE WE GO.
Signed: Vernon Wells
OF ADDRESS REQUEST yes___ no X

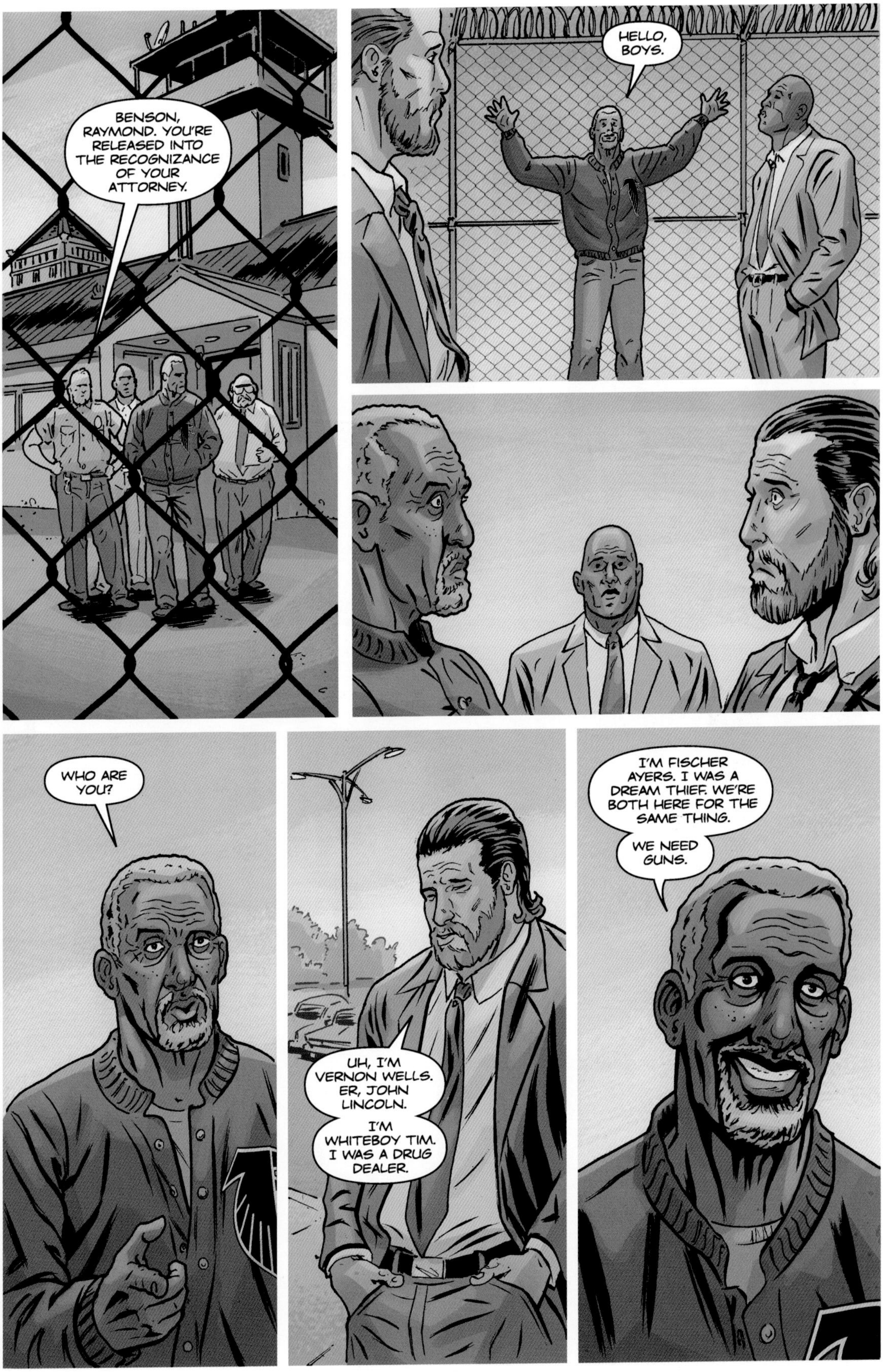
BENSON, RAYMOND. YOU'RE RELEASED INTO THE RECOGNIZANCE OF YOUR ATTORNEY.
HELLO, BOYS.
WHO ARE YOU?
UH, I'M VERNON WELLS. ER, JOHN LINCOLN.
I'M WHITEBOY TIM. I WAS A DRUG DEALER.
I'M FISCHER AYERS. I WAS A DREAM THIEF. WE'RE BOTH HERE FOR THE SAME THING.
WE NEED GUNS.

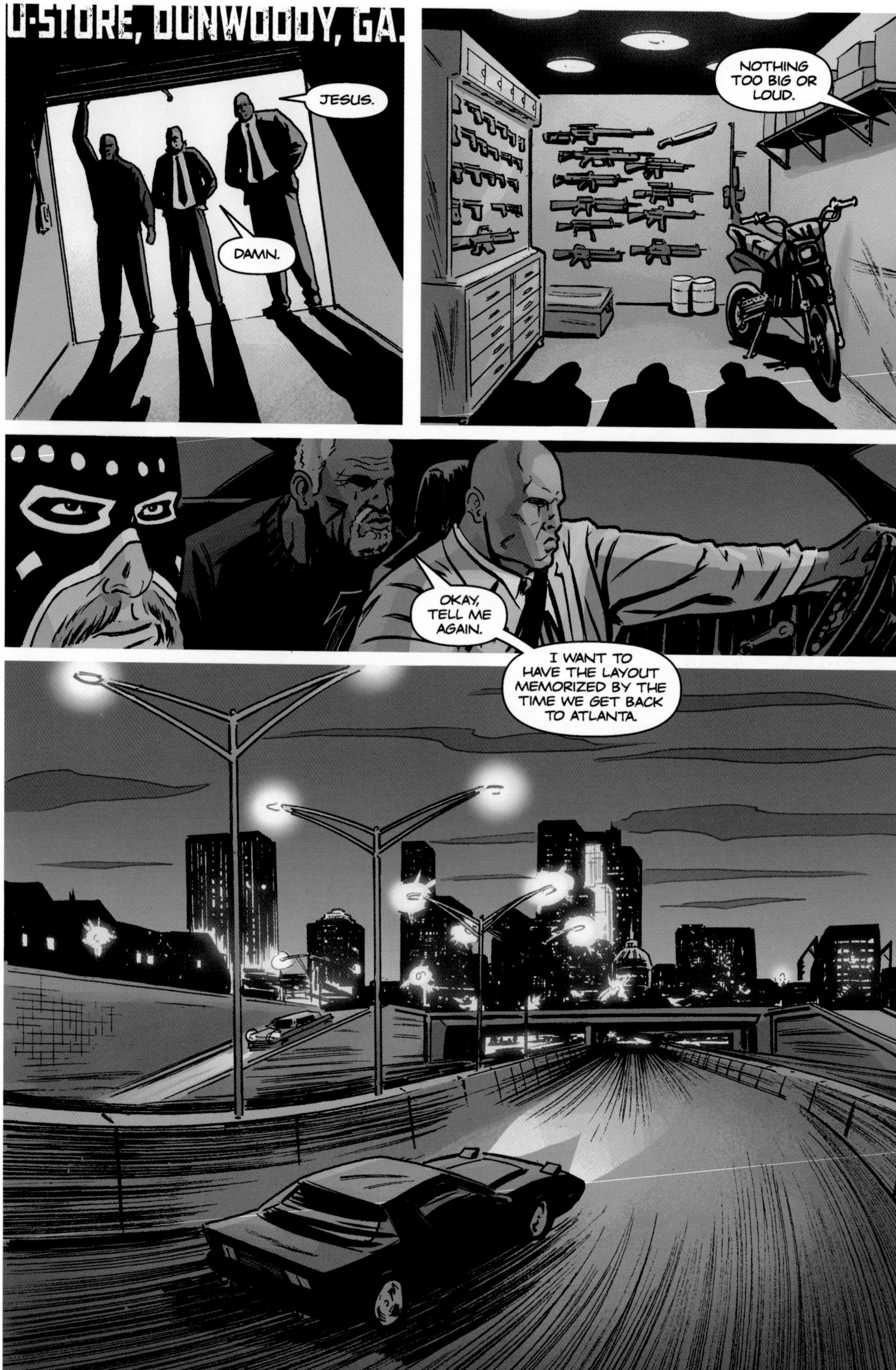
U-STORE, DUNWOODY, GA.
JESUS.
DAMN.
NOTHING TOO BIG OR LOUD.
OKAY, TELL ME AGAIN.
I WANT TO HAVE THE LAYOUT MEMORIZED BY THE TIME WE GET BACK TO ATLANTA.

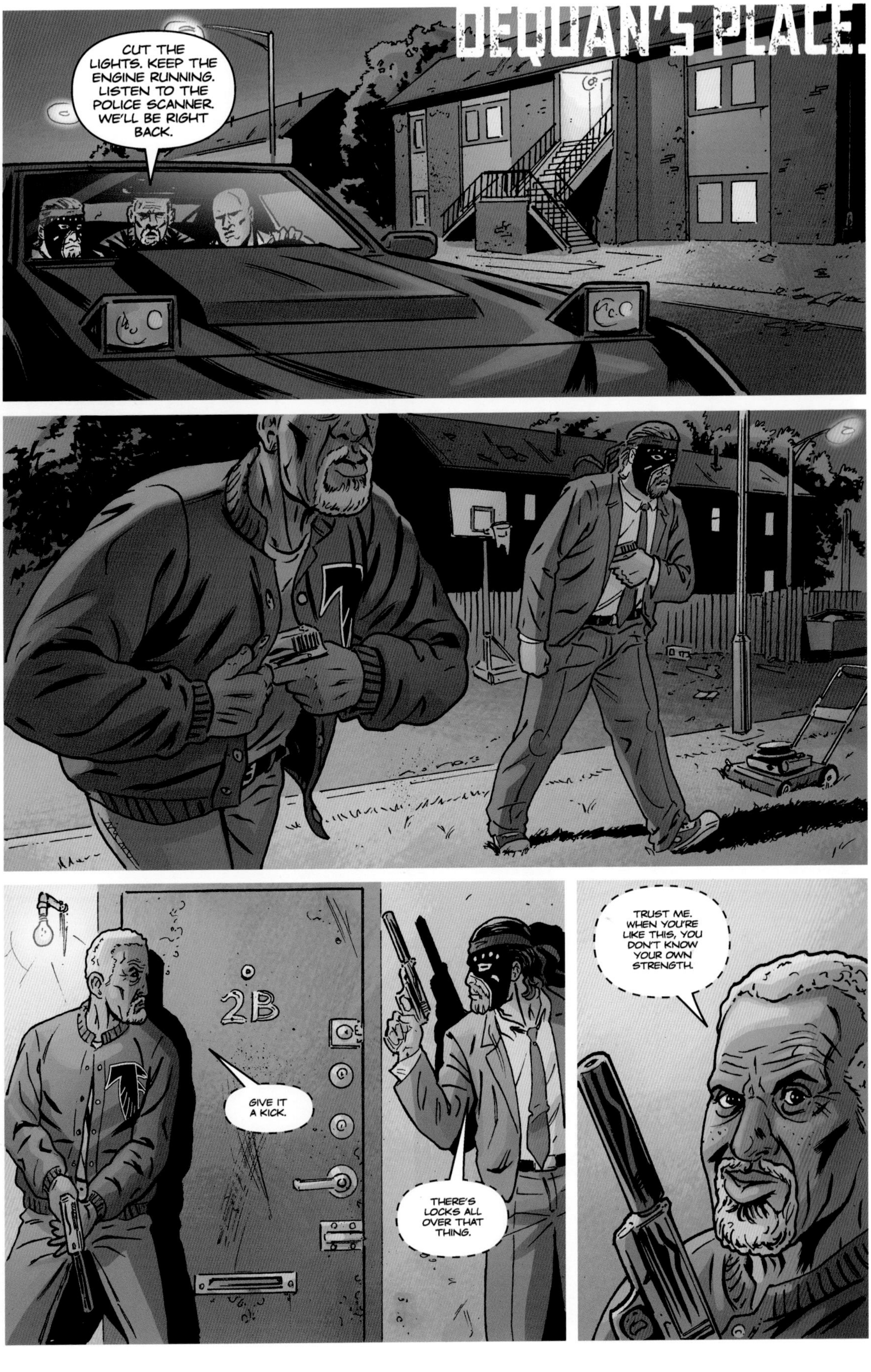
DEQUAN'S PLACE.
CUT THE LIGHTS. KEEP THE ENGINE RUNNING. LISTEN TO THE POLICE SCANNER. WE'LL BE RIGHT BACK.
2B
GIVE IT A KICK.
THERE'S LOCKS ALL OVER THAT THING.
TRUST ME. WHEN YOU'RE LIKE THIS, YOU DON'T KNOW YOUR OWN STRENGTH.

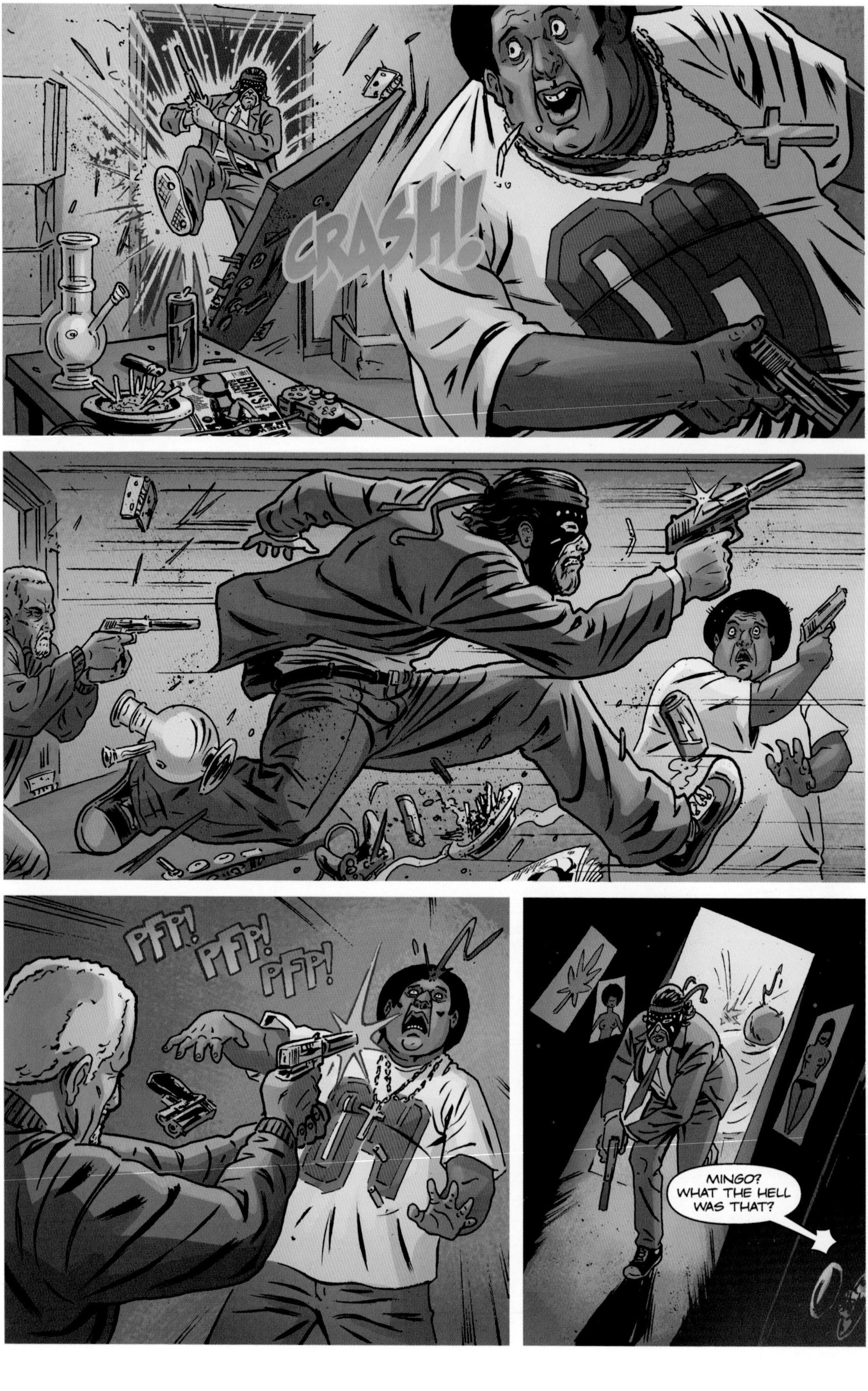
CRASH!
PFP! PFP! PFP!
MINGO? WHAT THE HELL WAS THAT?

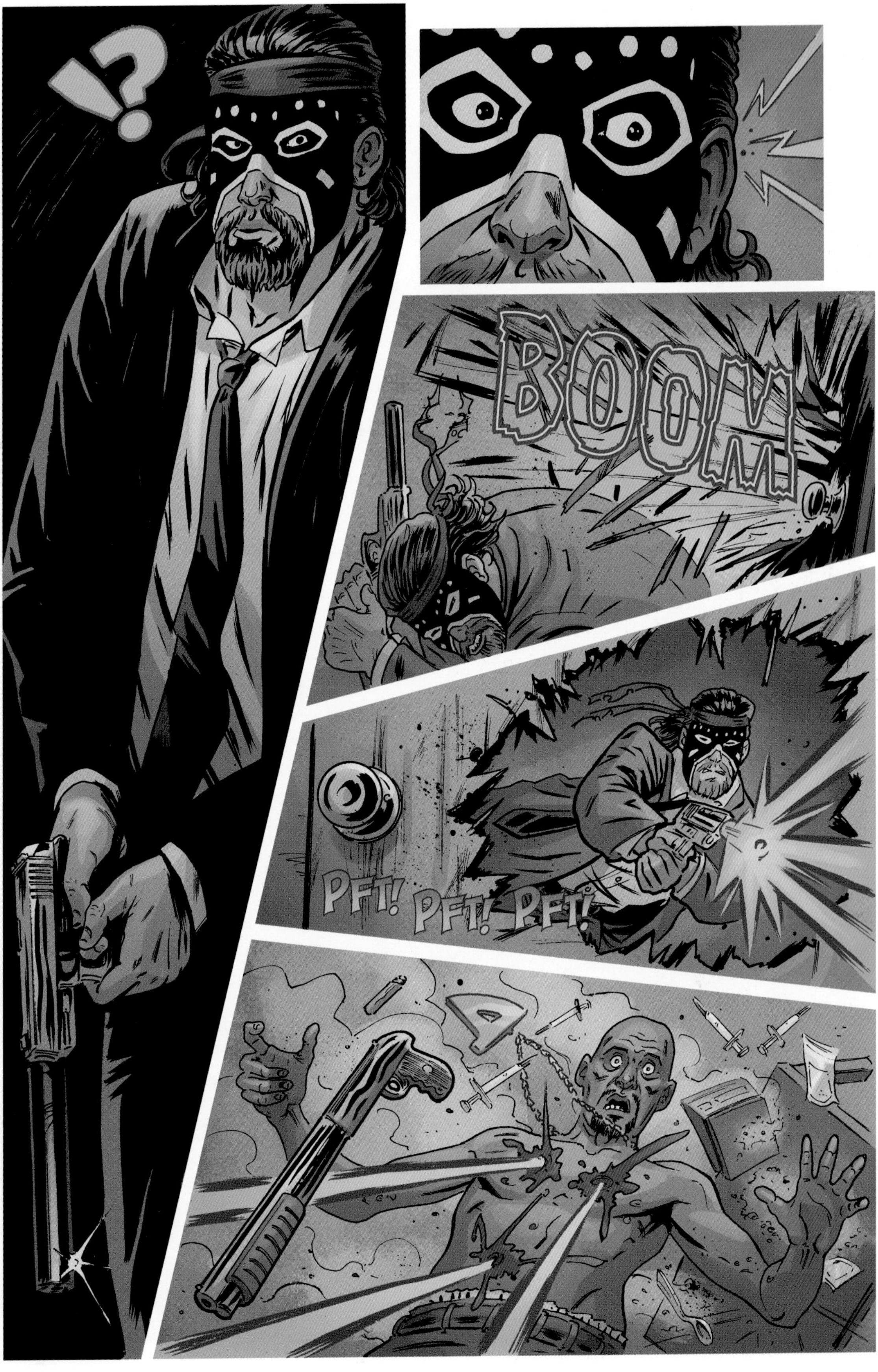
!?
BOOM
PFT! PFT! PFT!

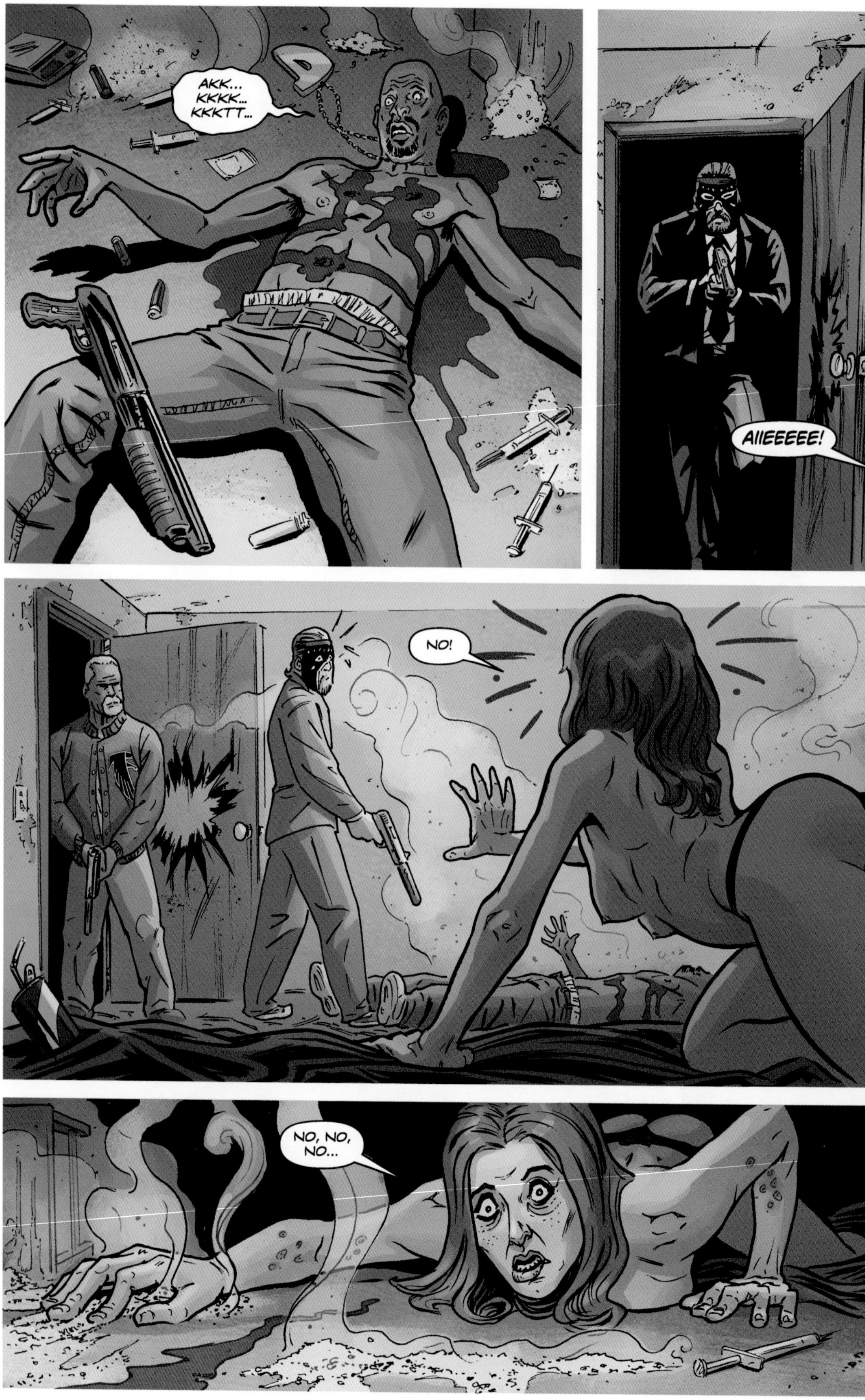
AKK... KKKK... KKKTT...
AIIEEEEE!
NO!
NO, NO, NO...

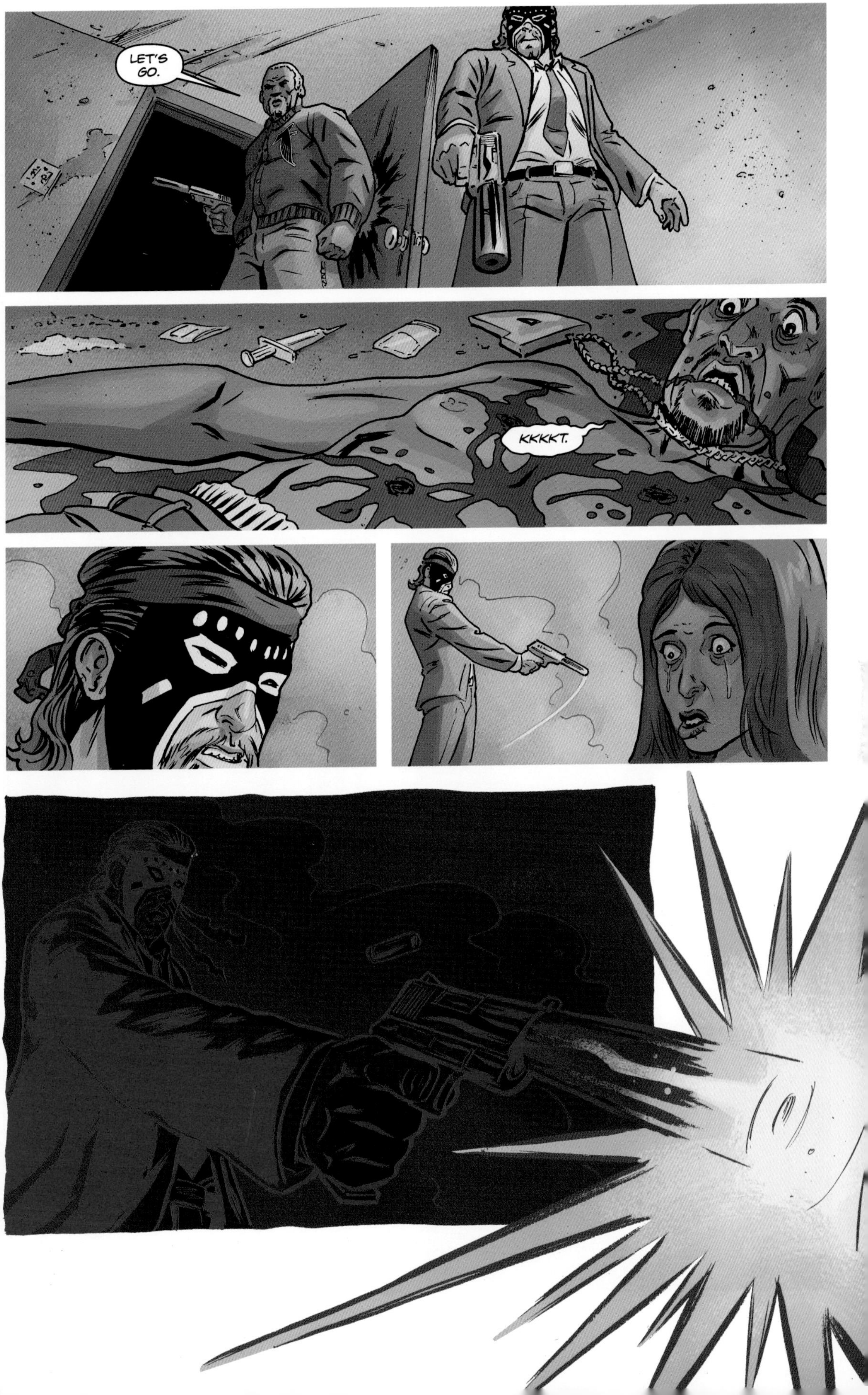
LET'S GO.
KKKKT.

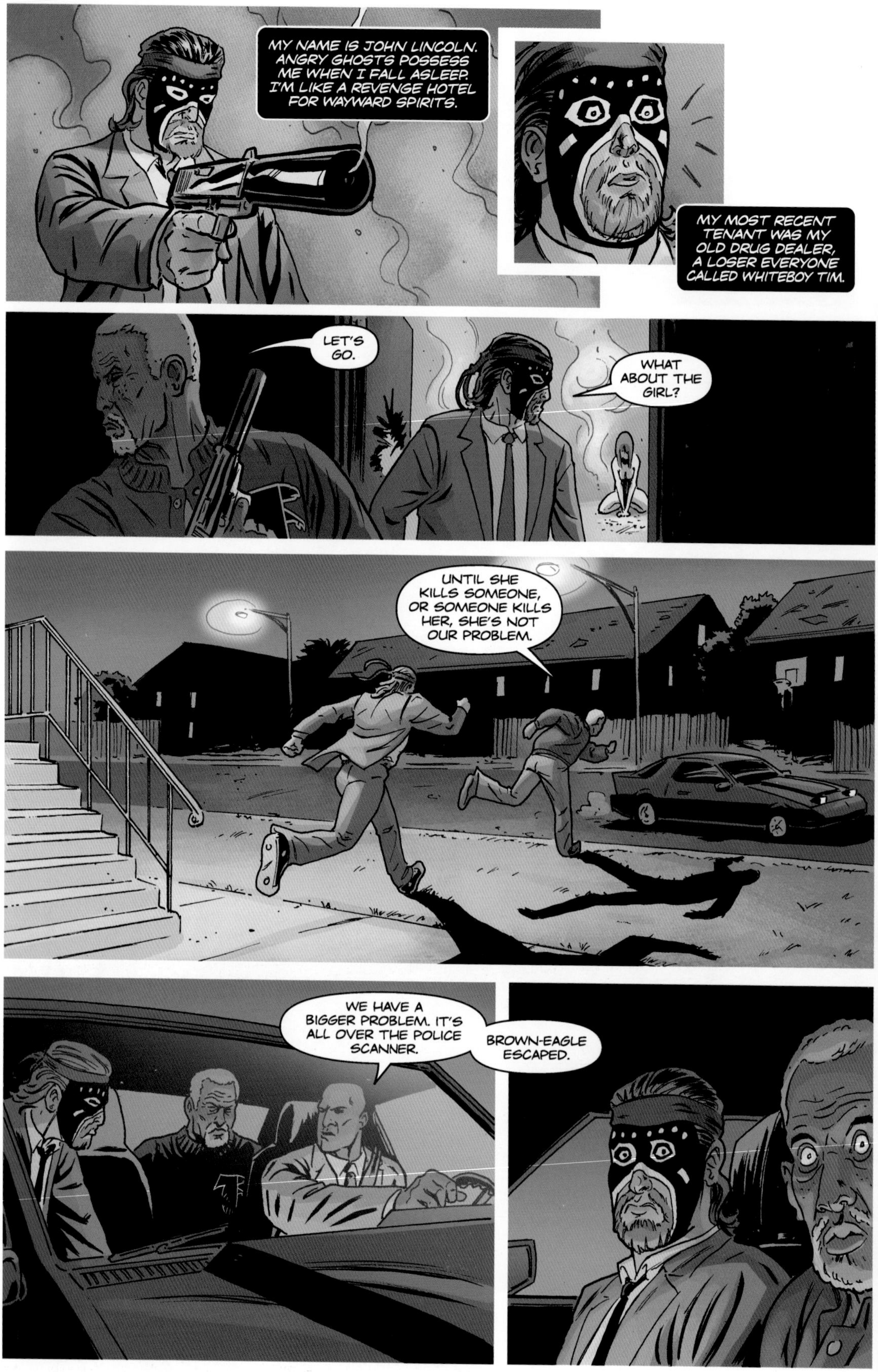
MY NAME IS JOHN LINCOLN. ANGRY GHOSTS POSSESS ME WHEN I FALL ASLEEP. I'M LIKE A REVENGE HOTEL FOR WAYWARD SPIRITS.
MY MOST RECENT TENANT WAS MY OLD DRUG DEALER, A LOSER EVERYONE CALLED WHITEBOY TIM.
LET'S GO.
WHAT ABOUT THE GIRL?
UNTIL SHE KILLS SOMEONE, OR SOMEONE KILLS HER, SHE'S NOT OUR PROBLEM.
WE HAVE A BIGGER PROBLEM. IT'S ALL OVER THE POLICE SCANNER.
BROWN-EAGLE ESCAPED.

CHAPTER 4

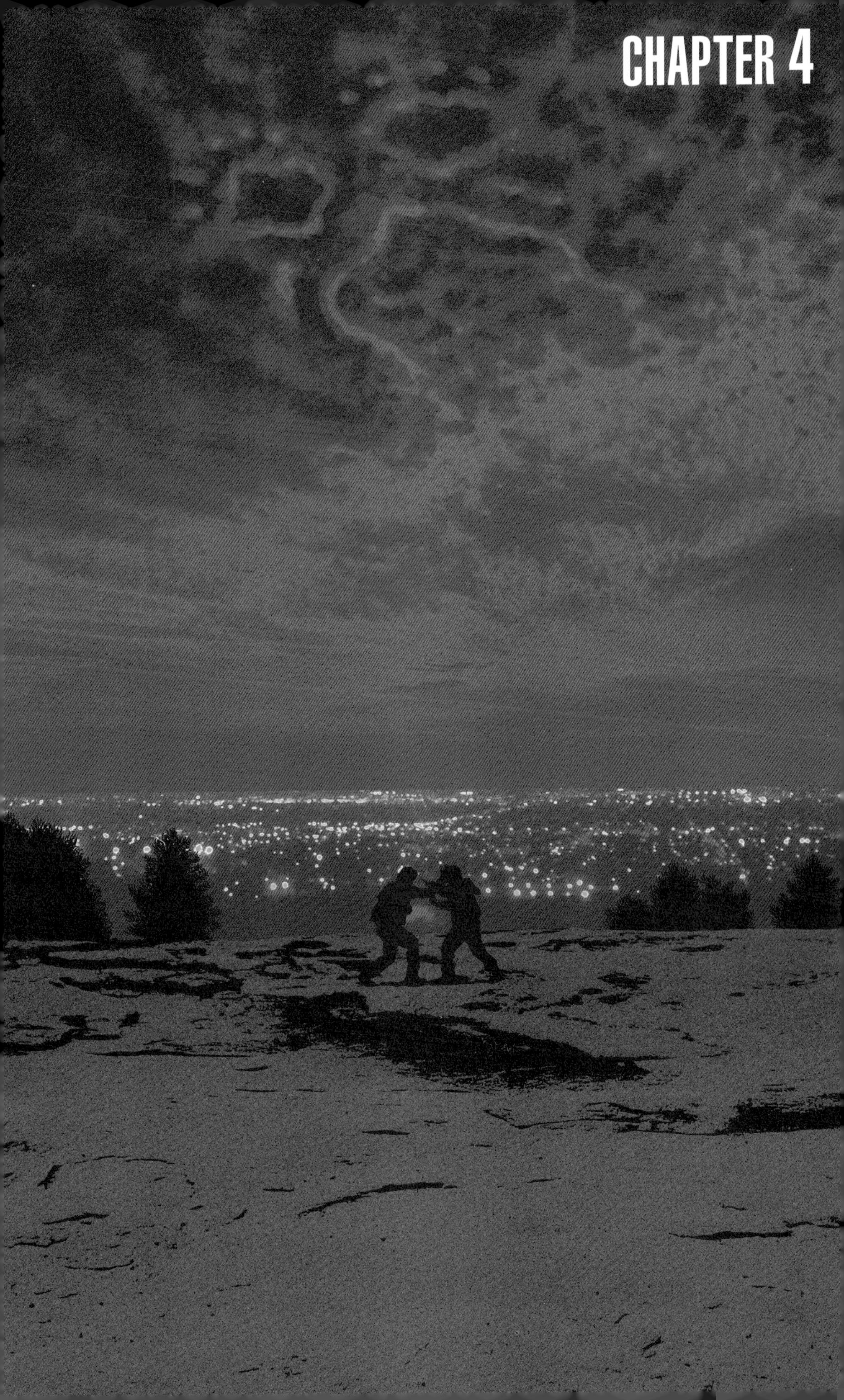

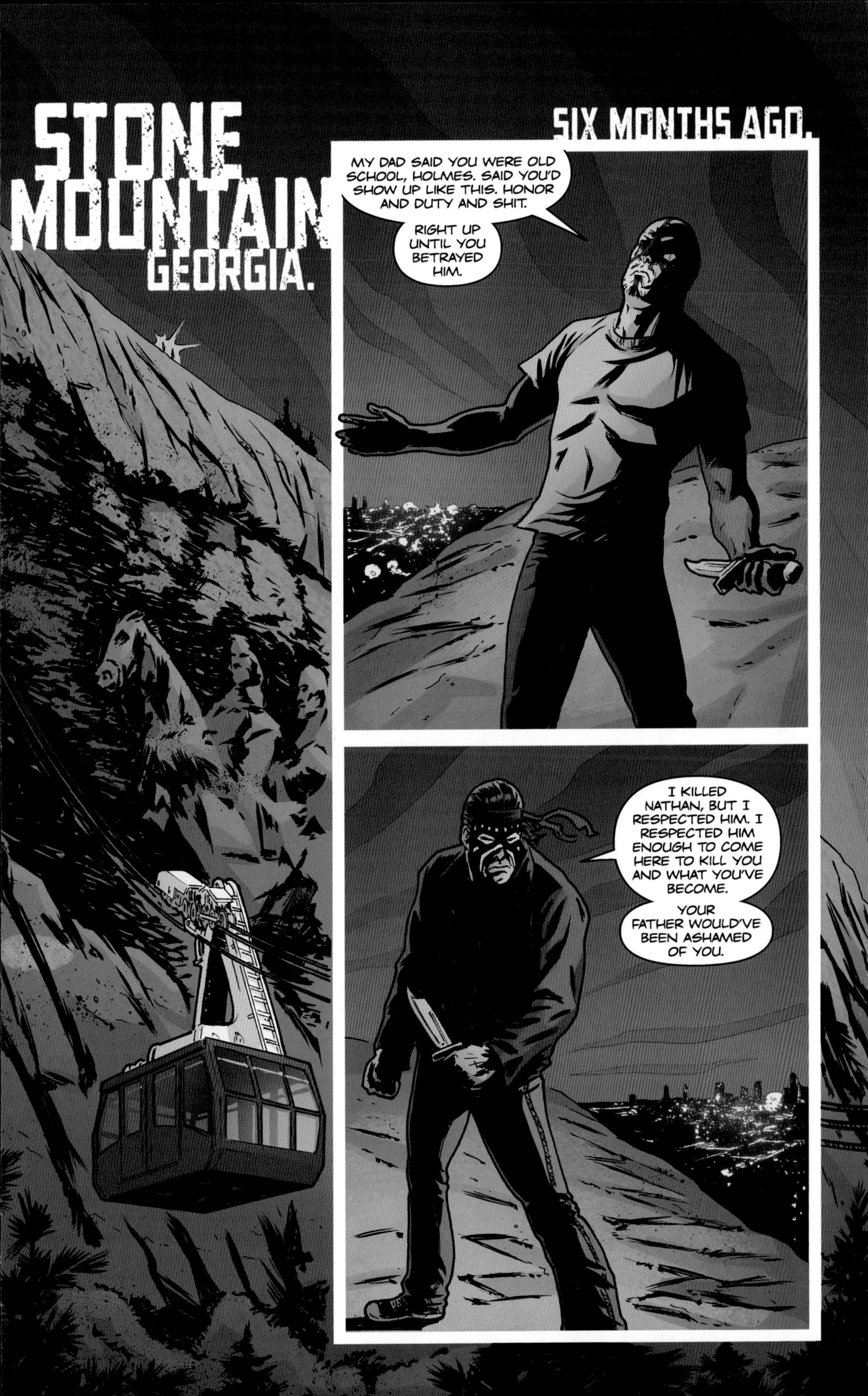
STONE MOUNTAIN GEORGIA.
SIX MONTHS AGO.
MY DAD SAID YOU WERE OLD SCHOOL, HOLMES. SAID YOU'D SHOW UP LIKE THIS. HONOR AND DUTY AND SHIT.
RIGHT UP UNTIL YOU BETRAYED HIM.
I KILLED NATHAN, BUT I RESPECTED HIM. I RESPECTED HIM ENOUGH TO COME HERE TO KILL YOU AND WHAT YOU'VE BECOME.
YOUR FATHER WOULD'VE BEEN ASHAMED OF YOU.

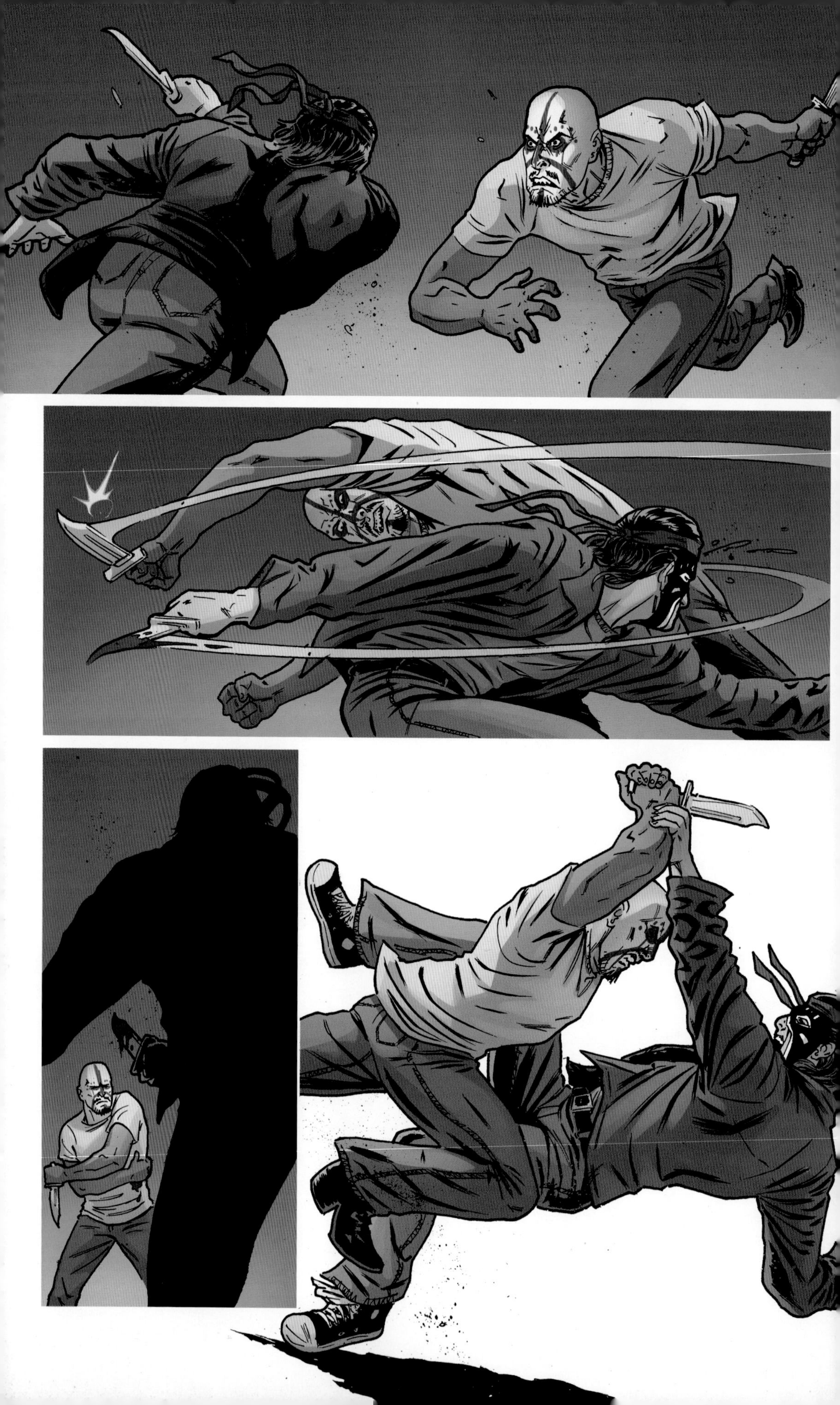

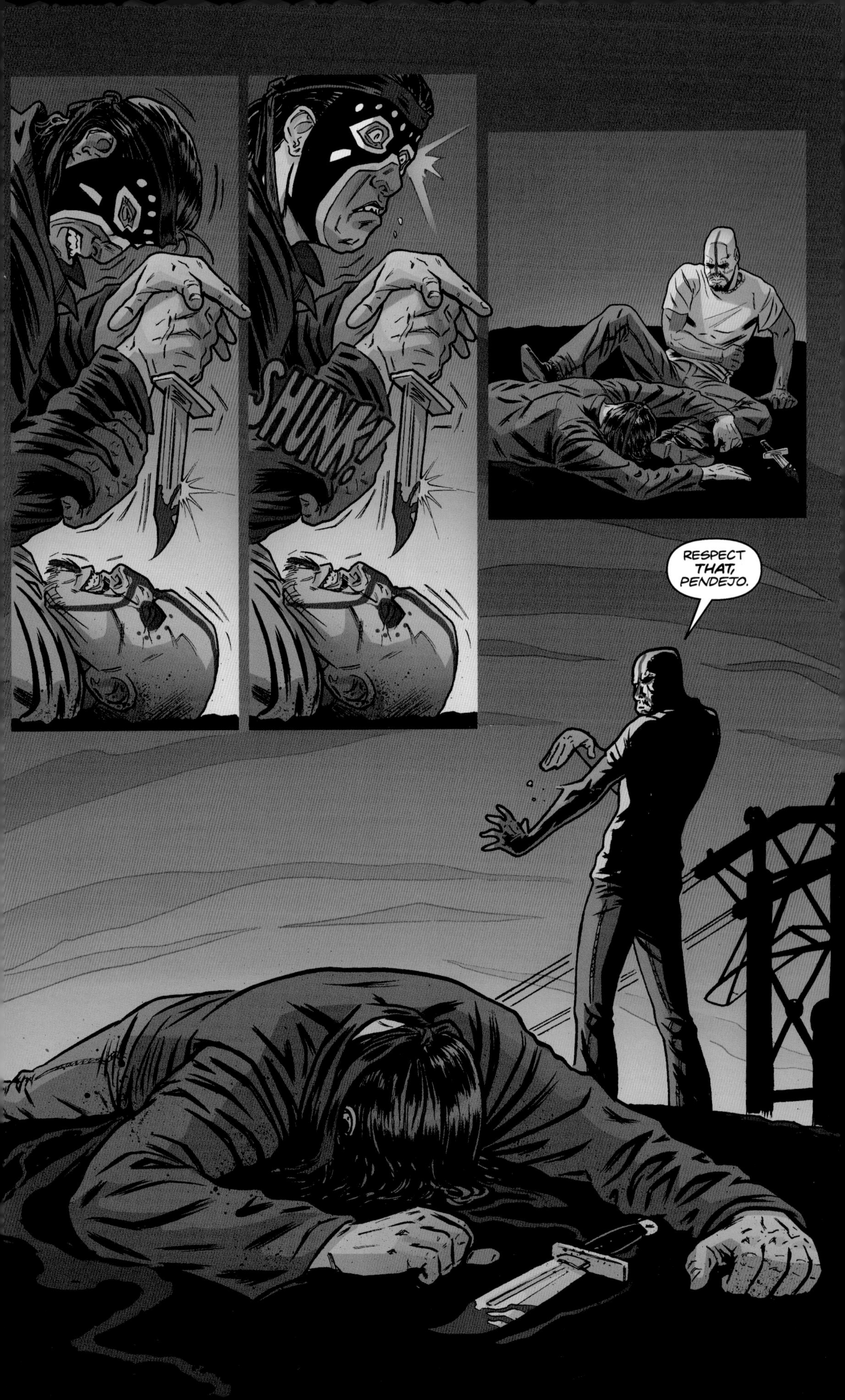
SHUNK!
RESPECT THAT, PENDEJO.

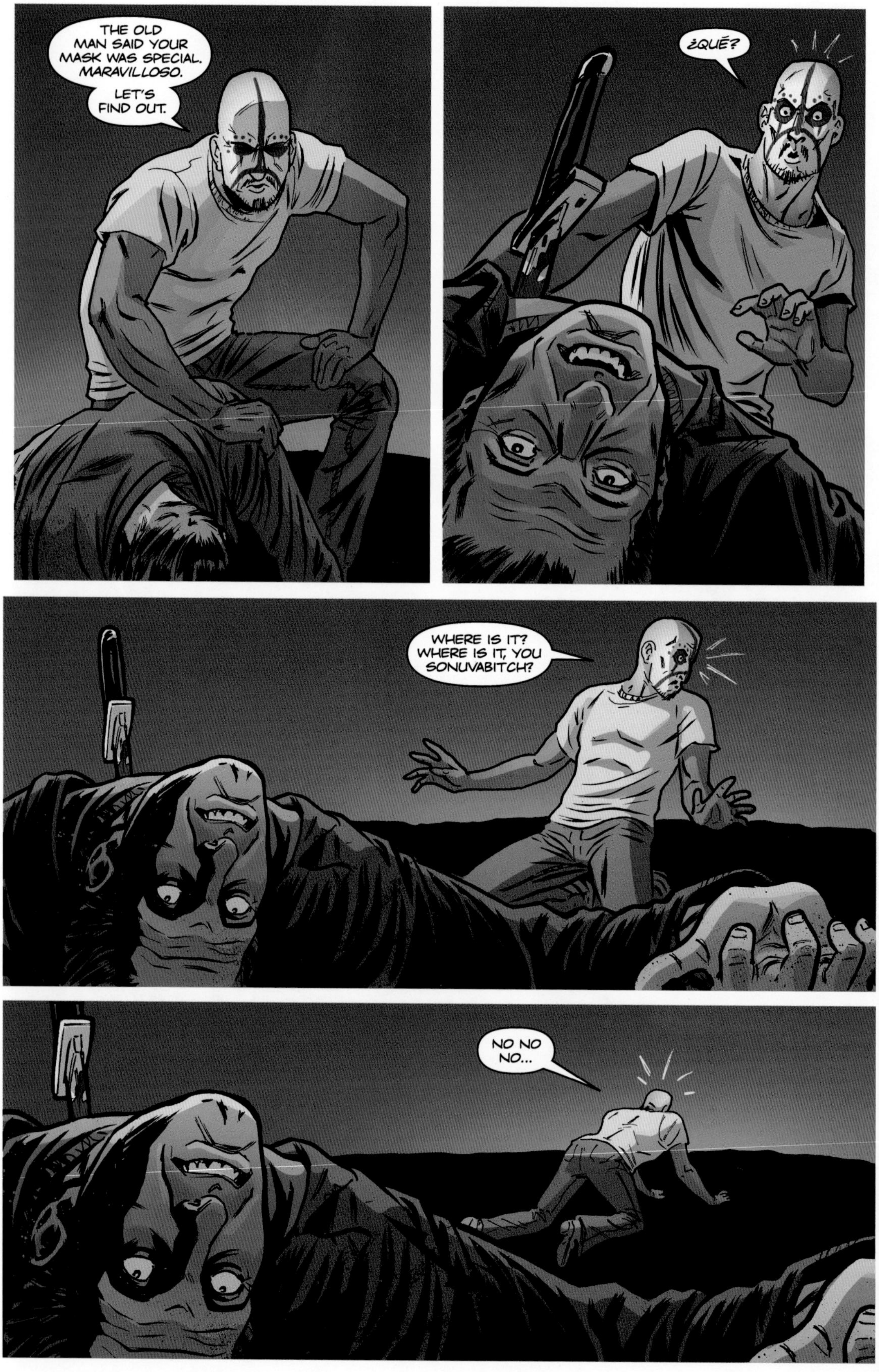
THE OLD MAN SAID YOUR MASK WAS SPECIAL. MARAVILLOSO.
LET'S FIND OUT.
¿QUÉ?
WHERE IS IT? WHERE IS IT, YOU SONUVABITCH?
NO NO NO...

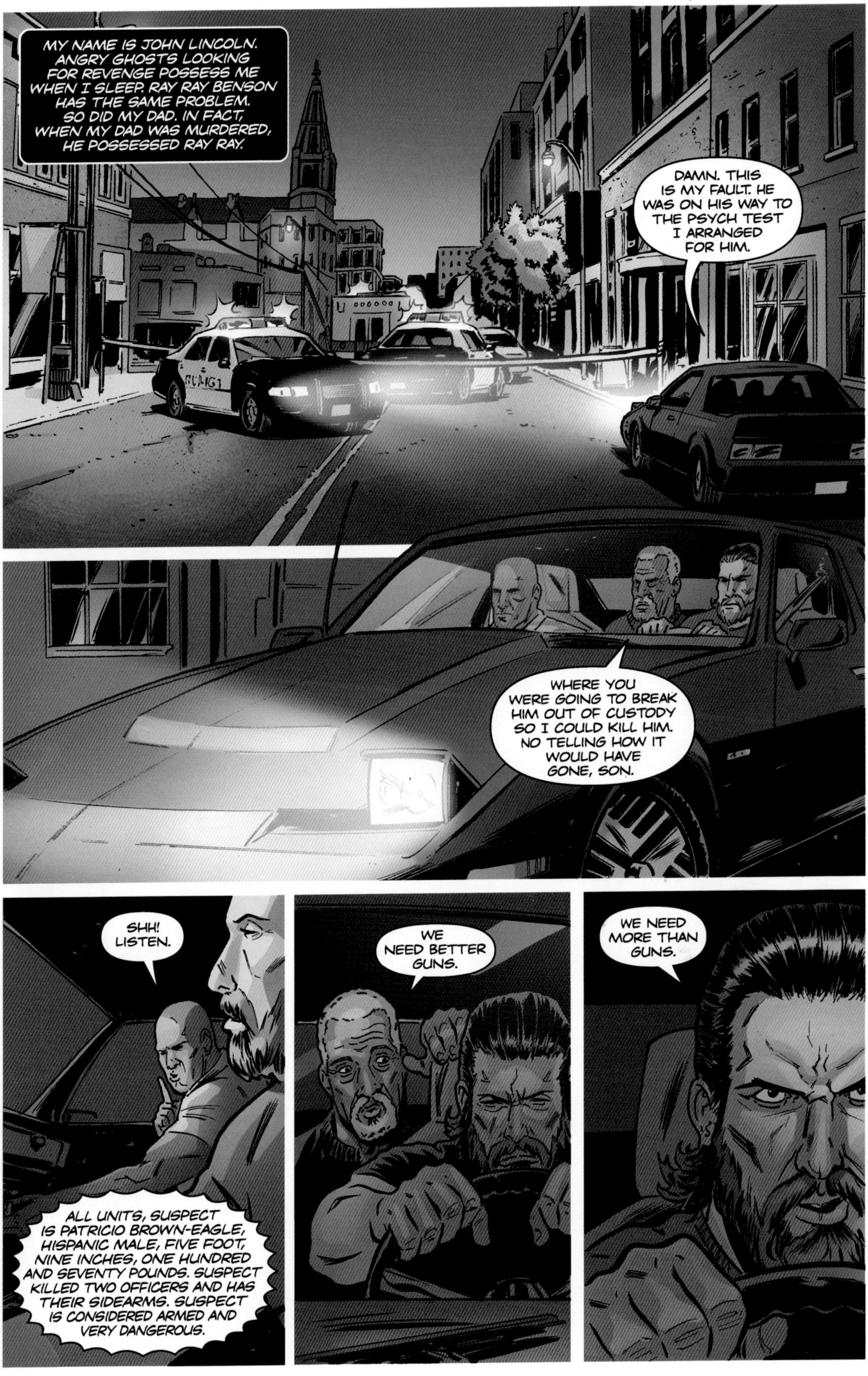
MY NAME IS JOHN LINCOLN. ANGRY GHOSTS LOOKING FOR REVENGE POSSESS ME WHEN I SLEEP. RAY RAY BENSON HAS THE SAME PROBLEM. SO DID MY DAD. IN FACT, WHEN MY DAD WAS MURDERED, HE POSSESSED RAY RAY.
DAMN. THIS IS MY FAULT. HE WAS ON HIS WAY TO THE PSYCH TEST I ARRANGED FOR HIM.
WHERE YOU WERE GOING TO BREAK HIM OUT OF CUSTODY SO I COULD KILL HIM. NO TELLING HOW IT WOULD HAVE GONE, SON.
SHH! LISTEN.
ALL UNITS, SUSPECT IS PATRICIO BROWN-EAGLE, HISPANIC MALE, FIVE FOOT, NINE INCHES, ONE HUNDRED AND SEVENTY POUNDS. SUSPECT KILLED TWO OFFICERS AND HAS THEIR SIDEARMS. SUSPECT IS CONSIDERED ARMED AND VERY DANGEROUS.
WE NEED BETTER GUNS.
WE NEED MORE THAN GUNS.

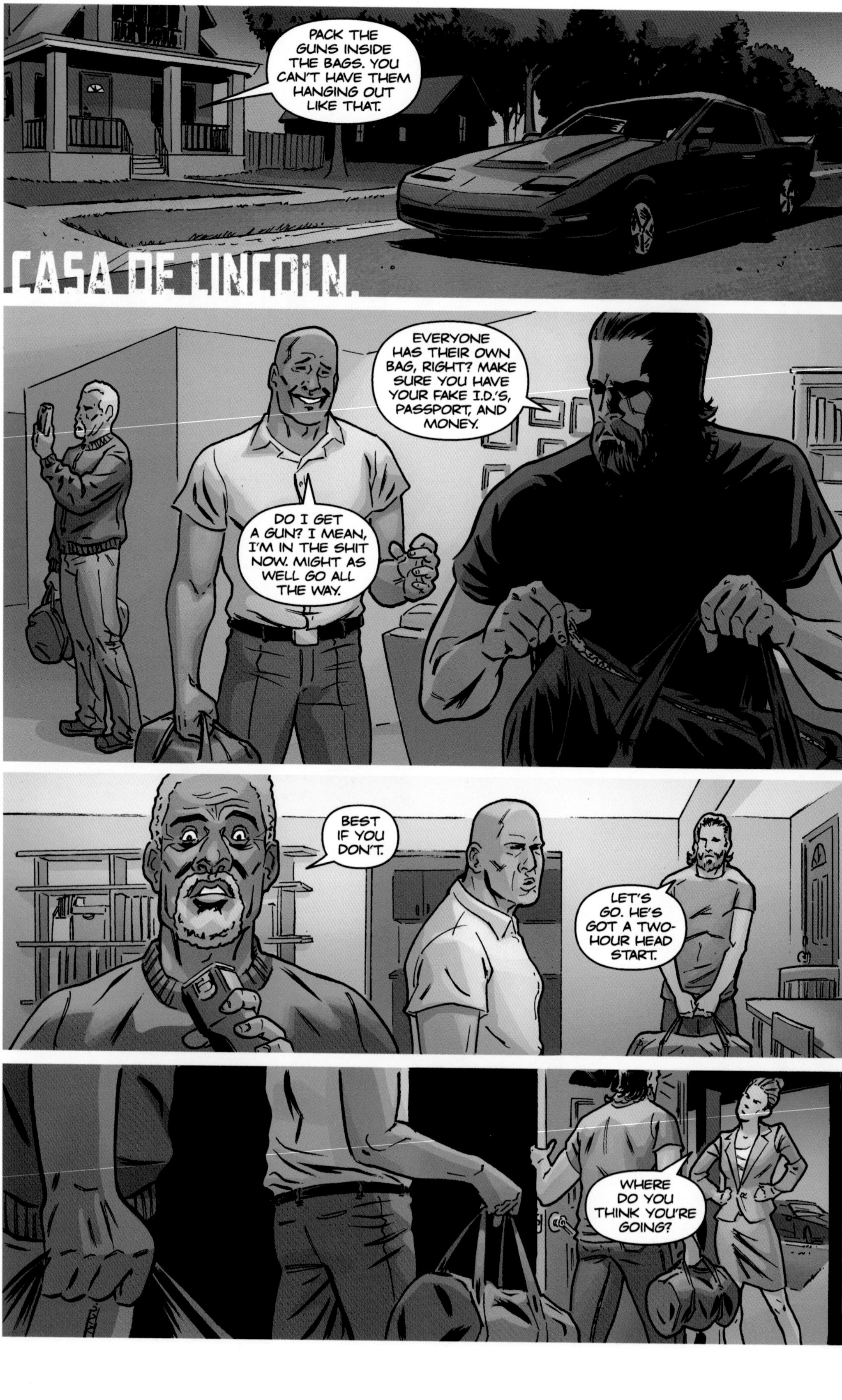
PACK THE GUNS INSIDE THE BAGS. YOU CAN'T HAVE THEM HANGING OUT LIKE THAT.
CASA DE LINCOLN.
EVERYONE HAS THEIR OWN BAG, RIGHT? MAKE SURE YOU HAVE YOUR FAKE I.D.'S, PASSPORT, AND MONEY.
DO I GET A GUN? I MEAN, I'M IN THE SHIT NOW. MIGHT AS WELL GO ALL THE WAY.
BEST IF YOU DON'T.
LET'S GO. HE'S GOT A TWO-HOUR HEAD START.
WHERE DO YOU THINK YOU'RE GOING?

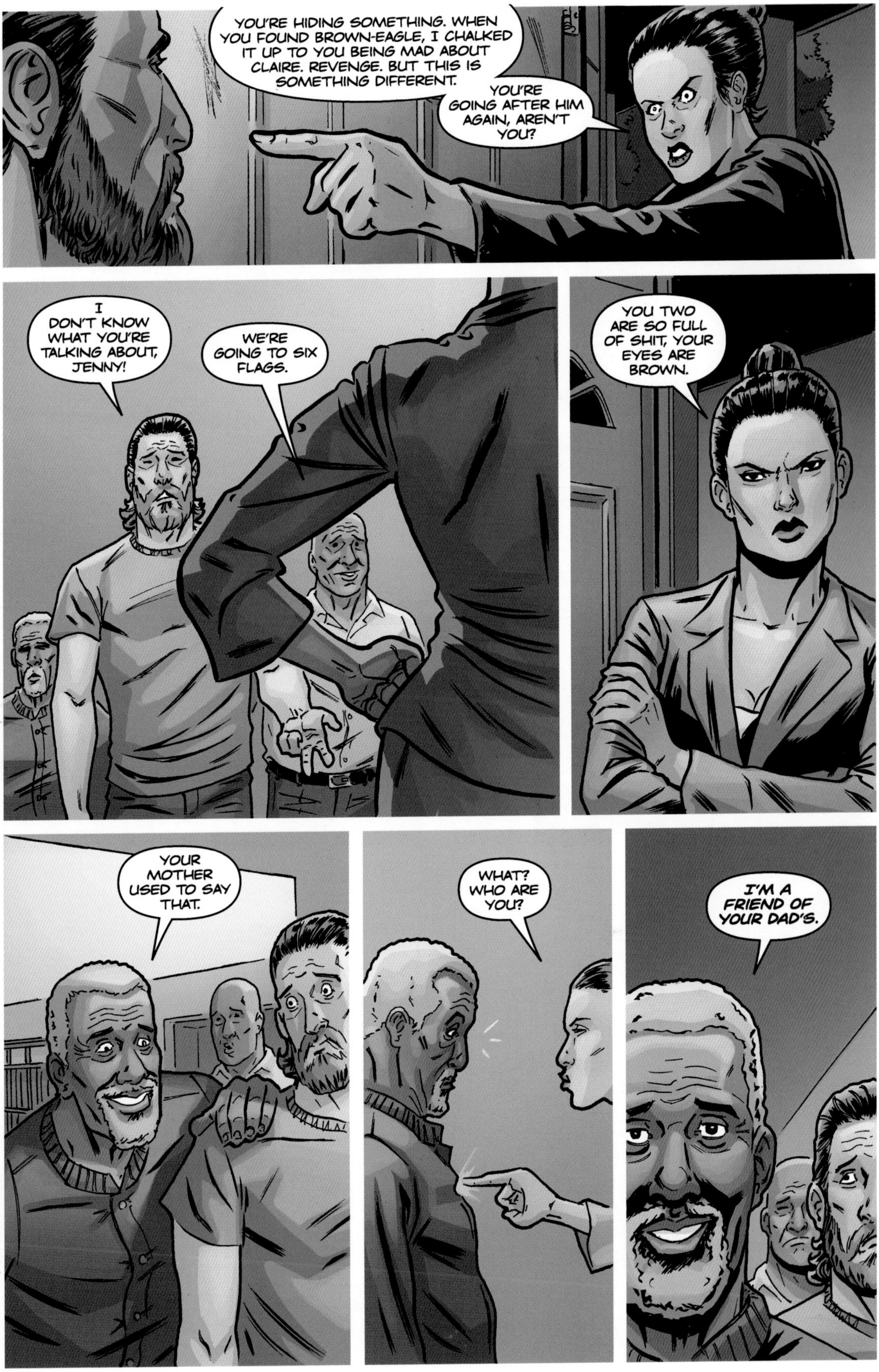
YOU'RE HIDING SOMETHING. WHEN YOU FOUND BROWN-EAGLE, I CHALKED IT UP TO YOU BEING MAD ABOUT CLAIRE. REVENGE. BUT THIS IS SOMETHING DIFFERENT.
YOU'RE GOING AFTER HIM AGAIN, AREN'T YOU?
I DON'T KNOW WHAT YOU'RE TALKING ABOUT, JENNY!
WE'RE GOING TO SIX FLAGS.
YOU TWO ARE SO FULL OF SHIT, YOUR EYES ARE BROWN.
YOUR MOTHER USED TO SAY THAT.
WHAT? WHO ARE YOU?
I'M A FRIEND OF YOUR DAD'S.

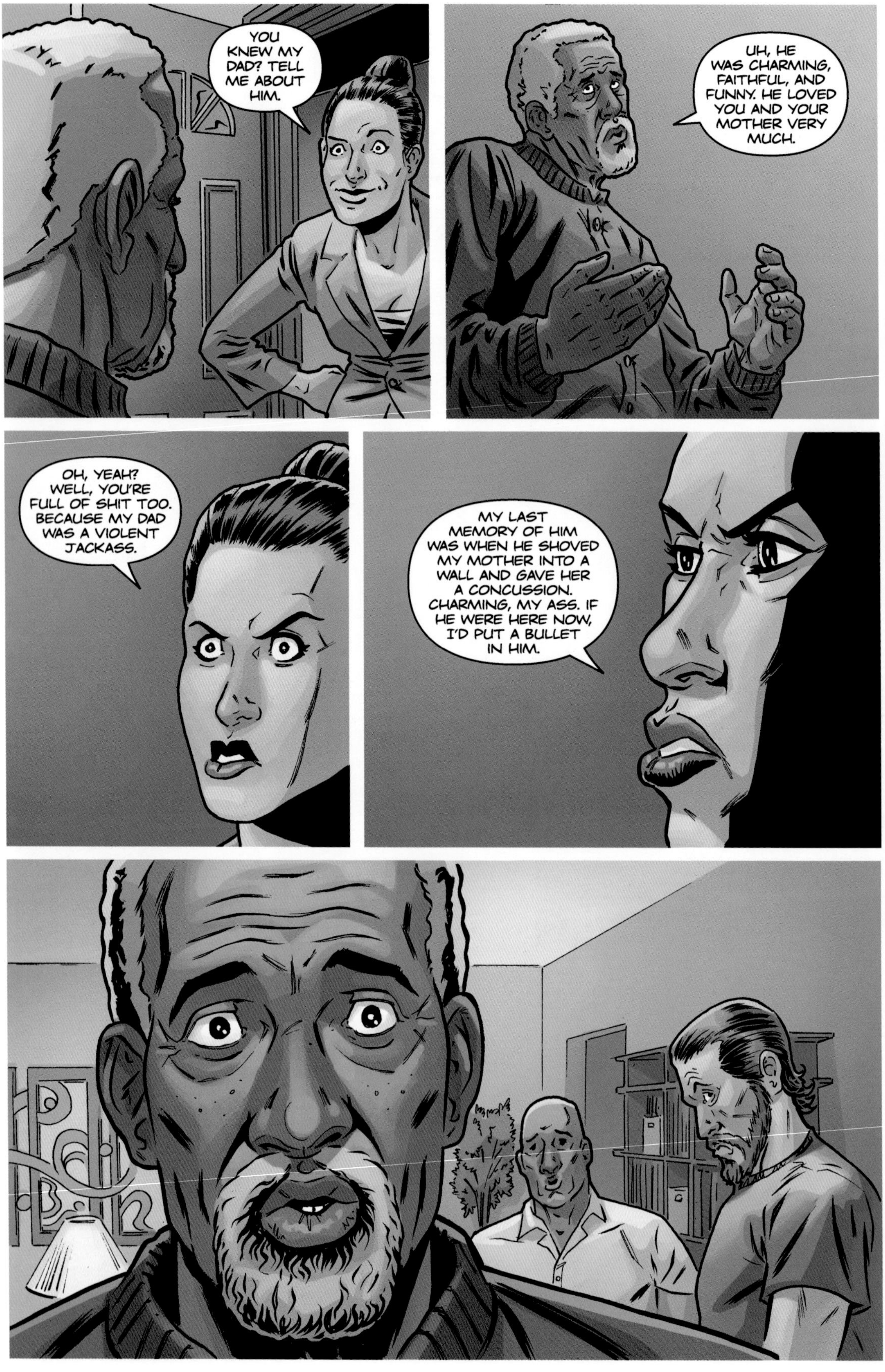
YOU KNEW MY DAD? TELL ME ABOUT HIM.
UH, HE WAS CHARMING, FAITHFUL, AND FUNNY. HE LOVED YOU AND YOUR MOTHER VERY MUCH.
OH, YEAH? WELL, YOU'RE FULL OF SHIT TOO. BECAUSE MY DAD WAS A VIOLENT JACKASS.
MY LAST MEMORY OF HIM WAS WHEN HE SHOVED MY MOTHER INTO A WALL AND GAVE HER A CONCUSSION. CHARMING, MY ASS. IF HE WERE HERE NOW, I'D PUT A BULLET IN HIM.

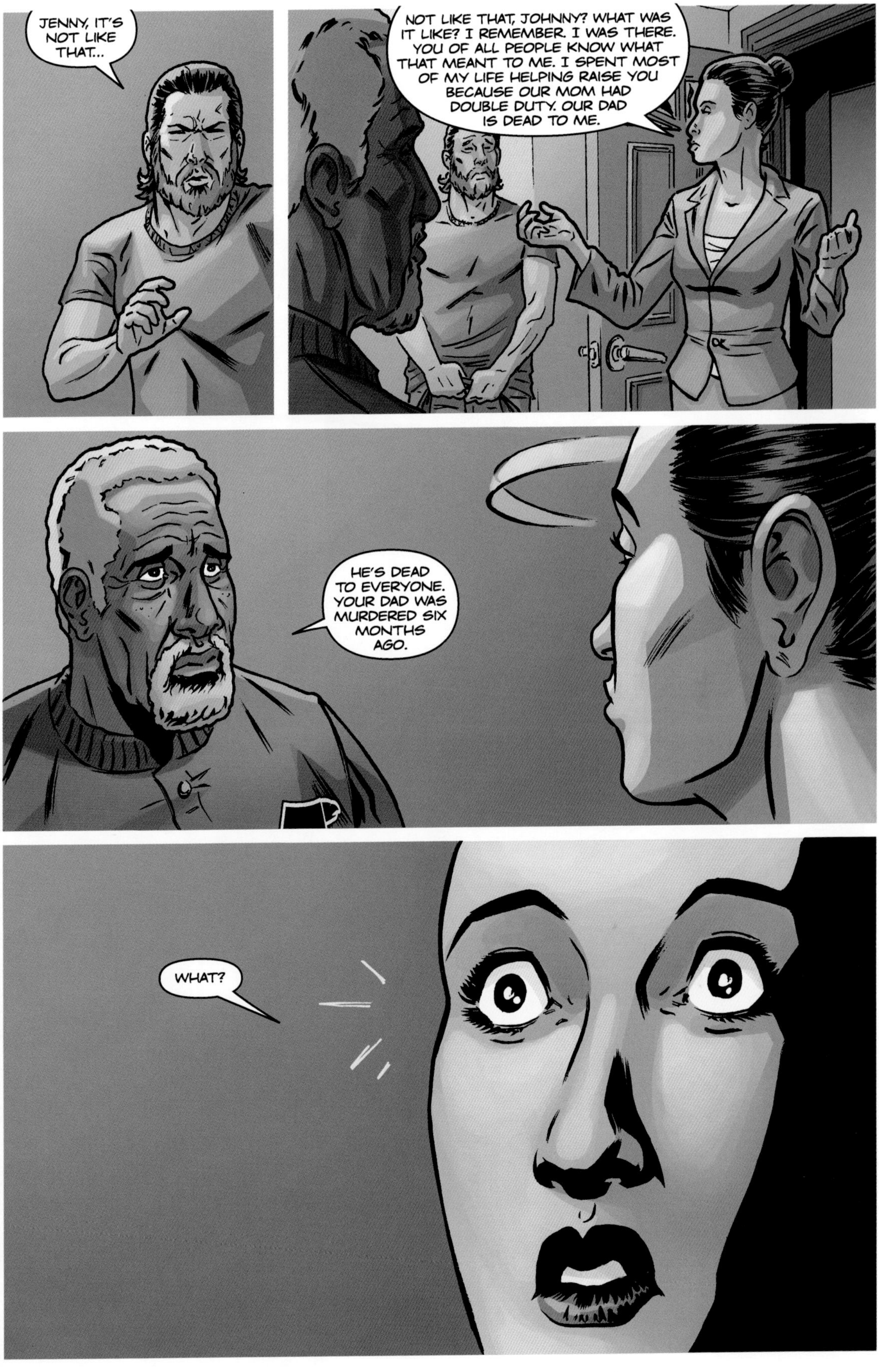
JENNY, IT'S NOT LIKE THAT...
NOT LIKE THAT, JOHNNY? WHAT WAS IT LIKE? I REMEMBER. I WAS THERE. YOU OF ALL PEOPLE KNOW WHAT THAT MEANT TO ME. I SPENT MOST OF MY LIFE HELPING RAISE YOU BECAUSE OUR MOM HAD DOUBLE DUTY. OUR DAD IS DEAD TO ME.
HE'S DEAD TO EVERYONE. YOUR DAD WAS MURDERED SIX MONTHS AGO.
WHAT?

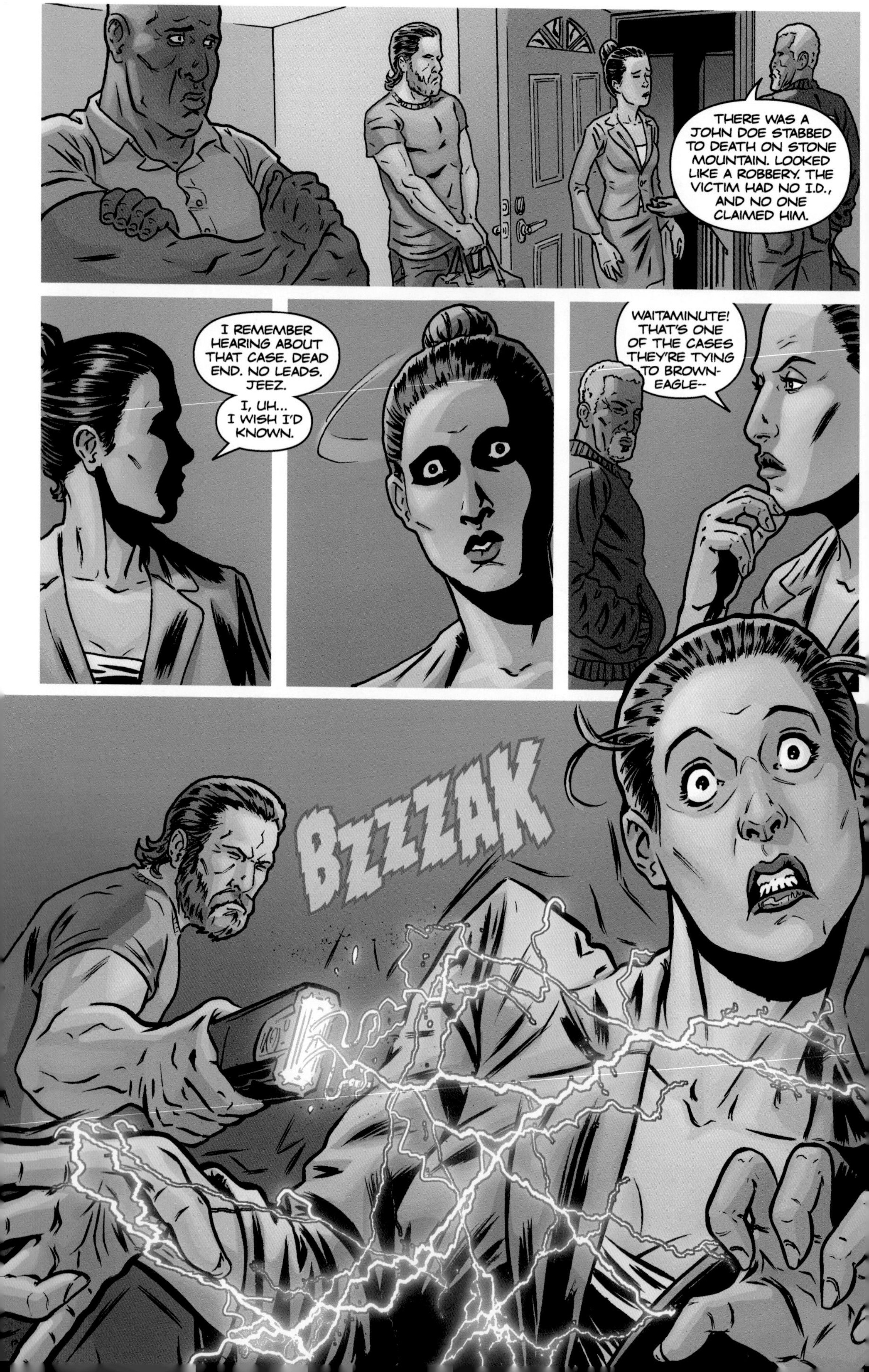
THERE WAS A JOHN DOE STABBED TO DEATH ON STONE MOUNTAIN. LOOKED LIKE A ROBBERY. THE VICTIM HAD NO I.D., AND NO ONE CLAIMED HIM.
I REMEMBER HEARING ABOUT THAT CASE. DEAD END. NO LEADS. JEEZ.
I, UH... I WISH I'D KNOWN.
WAITAMINUTE! THAT'S ONE OF THE CASES THEY'RE TYING TO BROWN-EAGLE--
BZZZAK

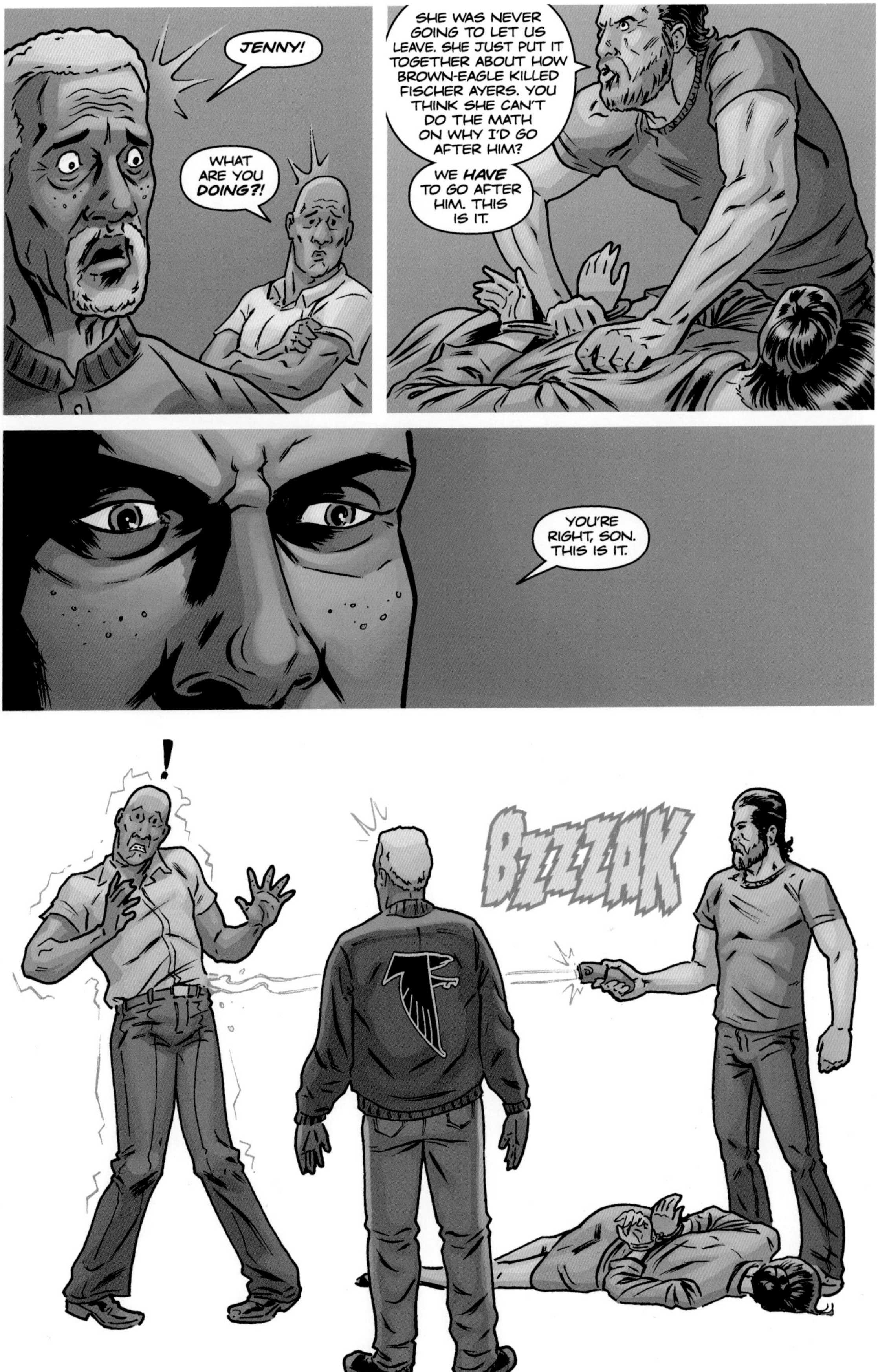
JENNY!
WHAT ARE YOU DOING?!
SHE WAS NEVER GOING TO LET US LEAVE. SHE JUST PUT IT TOGETHER ABOUT HOW BROWN-EAGLE KILLED FISCHER AYERS. YOU THINK SHE CAN'T DO THE MATH ON WHY I'D GO AFTER HIM?
WE HAVE TO GO AFTER HIM. THIS IS IT.
YOU'RE RIGHT, SON. THIS IS IT.
!
BZZZAK

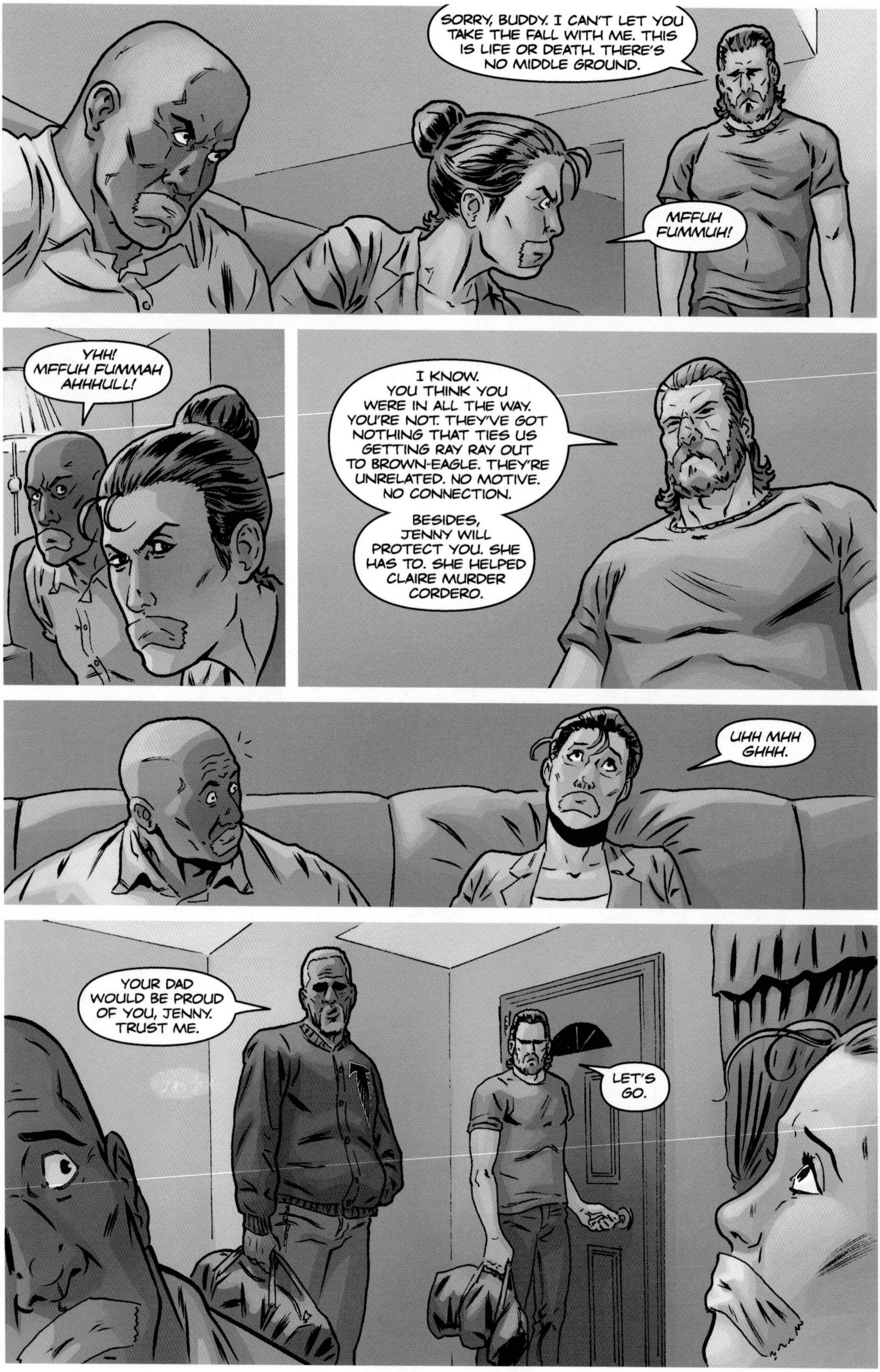
SORRY, BUDDY. I CAN'T LET YOU TAKE THE FALL WITH ME. THIS IS LIFE OR DEATH. THERE'S NO MIDDLE GROUND.
MFFUH FUMMUH!
YHH! MFFUH FUMMAH AHHHULL!
I KNOW. YOU THINK YOU WERE IN ALL THE WAY. YOU'RE NOT. THEY'VE GOT NOTHING THAT TIES US GETTING RAY RAY OUT TO BROWN-EAGLE. THEY'RE UNRELATED. NO MOTIVE. NO CONNECTION.
BESIDES, JENNY WILL PROTECT YOU. SHE HAS TO. SHE HELPED CLAIRE MURDER CORDERO.
UHH MHH GHHH.
YOUR DAD WOULD BE PROUD OF YOU, JENNY. TRUST ME.
LET'S GO.

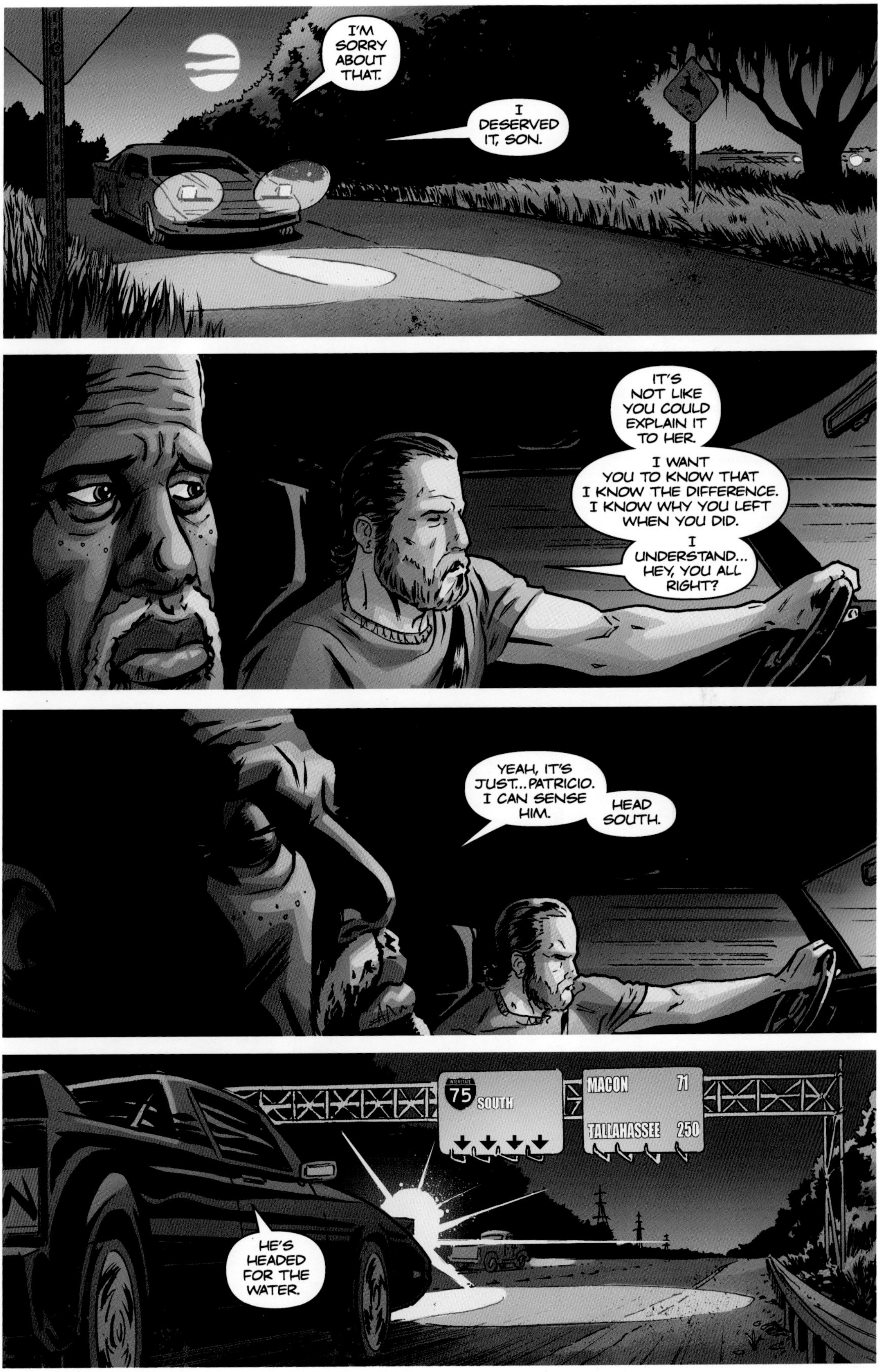
I'M SORRY ABOUT THAT.
I DESERVED IT, SON.
IT'S NOT LIKE YOU COULD EXPLAIN IT TO HER.
I WANT YOU TO KNOW THAT I KNOW THE DIFFERENCE. I KNOW WHY YOU LEFT WHEN YOU DID.
I UNDERSTAND... HEY, YOU ALL RIGHT?
YEAH, IT'S JUST...PATRICIO. I CAN SENSE HIM.
HEAD SOUTH.
INTERSTATE 75 SOUTH
MACON 71
TALLAHASSEE 250
HE'S HEADED FOR THE WATER.

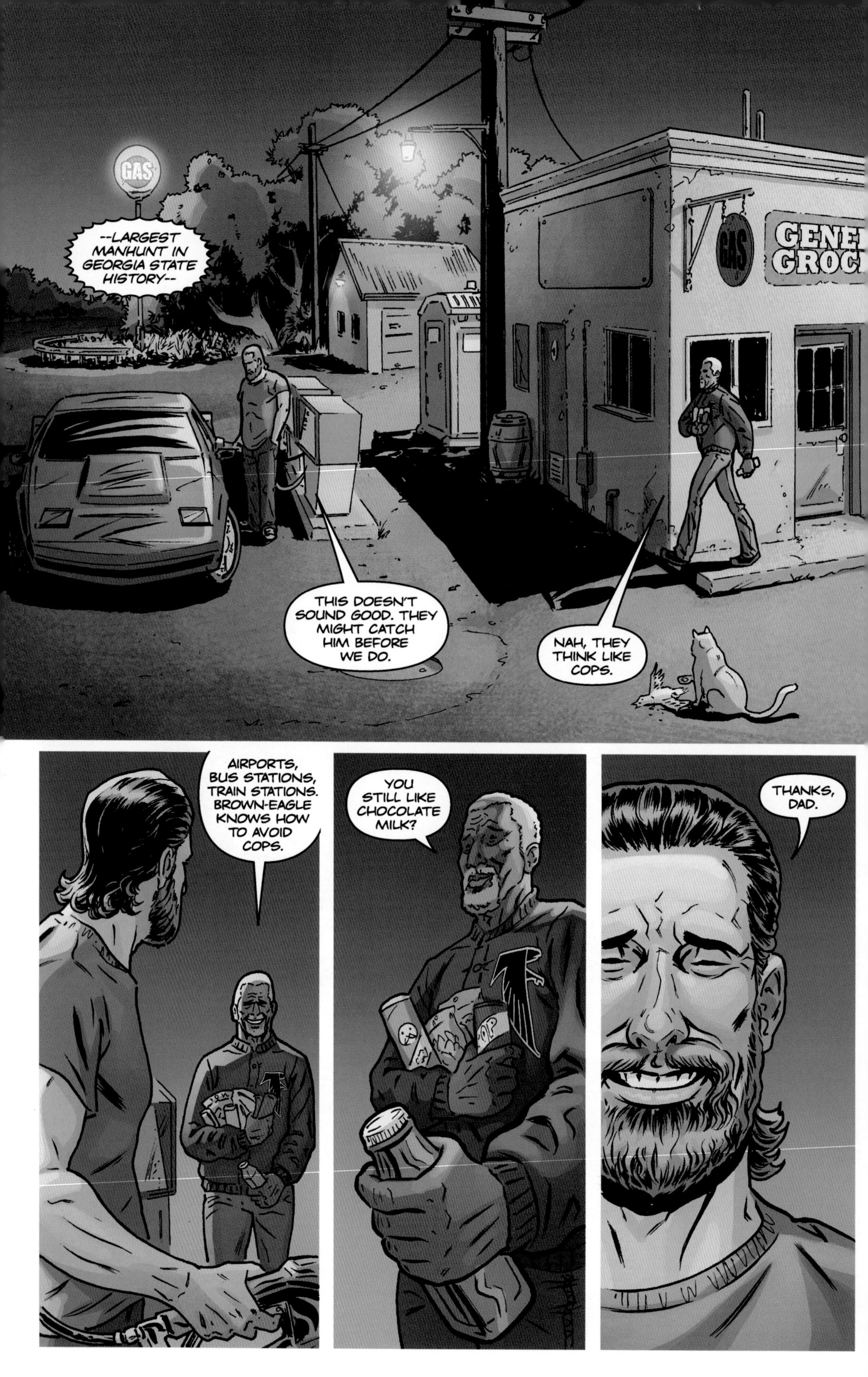
GAS
--LARGEST MANHUNT IN GEORGIA STATE HISTORY--
GAS
THIS DOESN'T SOUND GOOD. THEY MIGHT CATCH HIM BEFORE WE DO.
NAH, THEY THINK LIKE COPS.
AIRPORTS, BUS STATIONS, TRAIN STATIONS. BROWN-EAGLE KNOWS HOW TO AVOID COPS.
YOU STILL LIKE CHOCOLATE MILK?
THANKS, DAD.

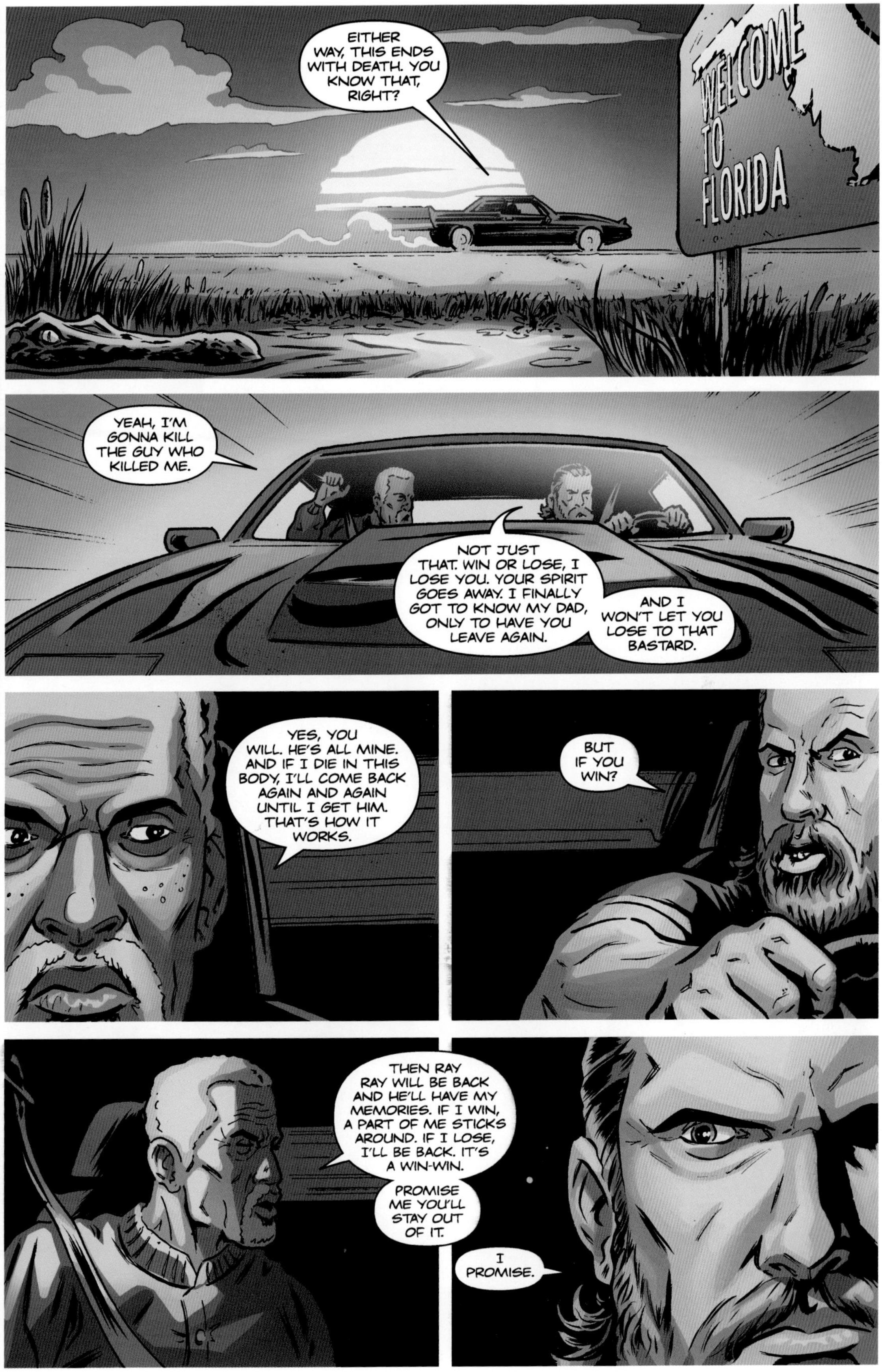
EITHER WAY, THIS ENDS WITH DEATH. YOU KNOW THAT, RIGHT?
WELCOME TO FLORIDA
YEAH, I'M GONNA KILL THE GUY WHO KILLED ME.
NOT JUST THAT. WIN OR LOSE, I LOSE YOU. YOUR SPIRIT GOES AWAY. I FINALLY GOT TO KNOW MY DAD, ONLY TO HAVE YOU LEAVE AGAIN.
AND I WON'T LET YOU LOSE TO THAT BASTARD.
YES, YOU WILL. HE'S ALL MINE. AND IF I DIE IN THIS BODY, I'LL COME BACK AGAIN AND AGAIN UNTIL I GET HIM. THAT'S HOW IT WORKS.
BUT IF YOU WIN?
THEN RAY RAY WILL BE BACK AND HE'LL HAVE MY MEMORIES. IF I WIN, A PART OF ME STICKS AROUND. IF I LOSE, I'LL BE BACK. IT'S A WIN-WIN.
PROMISE ME YOU'LL STAY OUT OF IT.
I PROMISE.

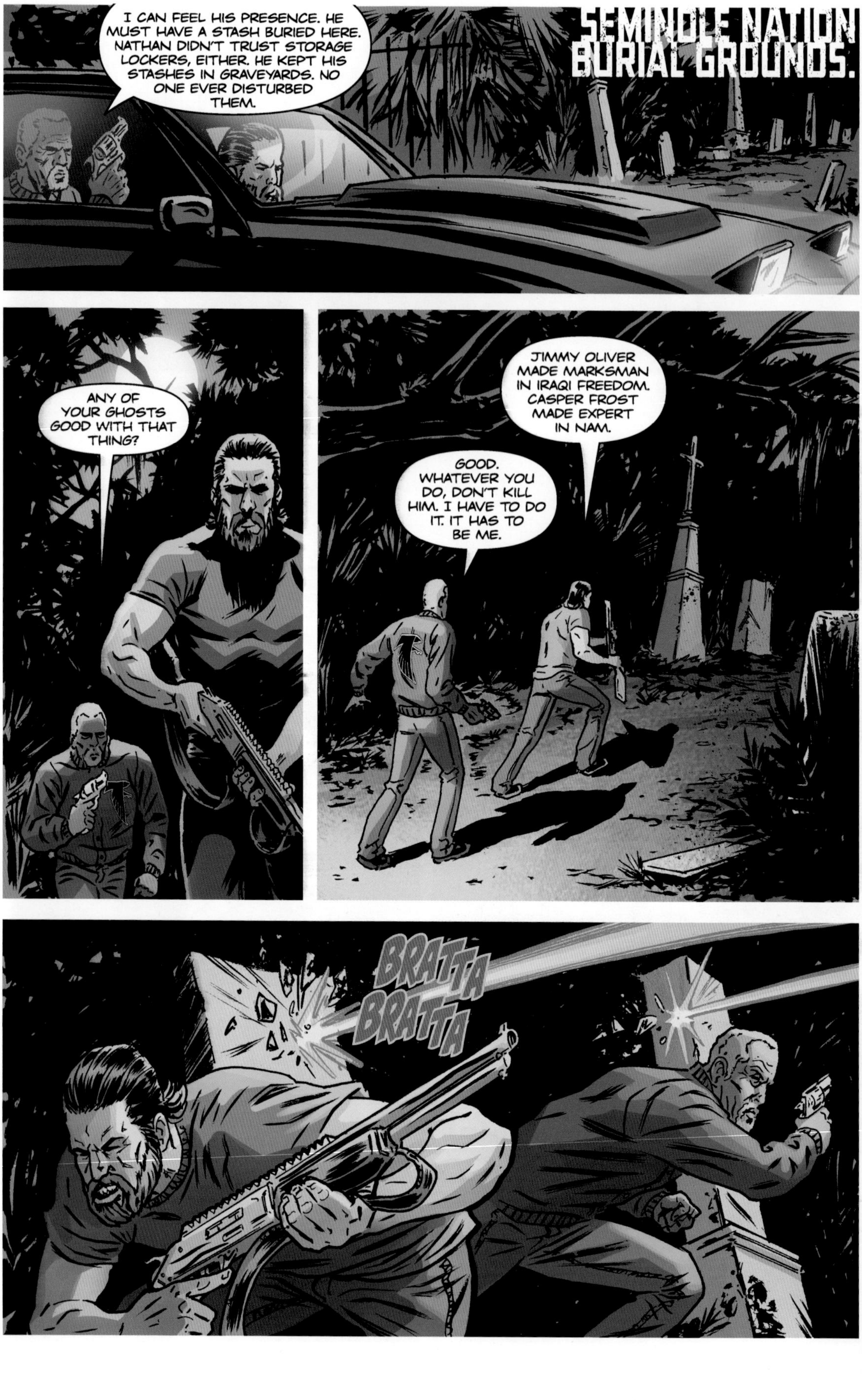
SEMINOLE NATION BURIAL GROUNDS.
I CAN FEEL HIS PRESENCE. HE MUST HAVE A STASH BURIED HERE. NATHAN DIDN'T TRUST STORAGE LOCKERS, EITHER. HE KEPT HIS STASHES IN GRAVEYARDS. NO ONE EVER DISTURBED THEM.
ANY OF YOUR GHOSTS GOOD WITH THAT THING?
JIMMY OLIVER MADE MARKSMAN IN IRAQI FREEDOM. CASPER FROST MADE EXPERT IN NAM.
GOOD. WHATEVER YOU DO, DON'T KILL HIM. I HAVE TO DO IT. IT HAS TO BE ME.
BRATTA BRATTA

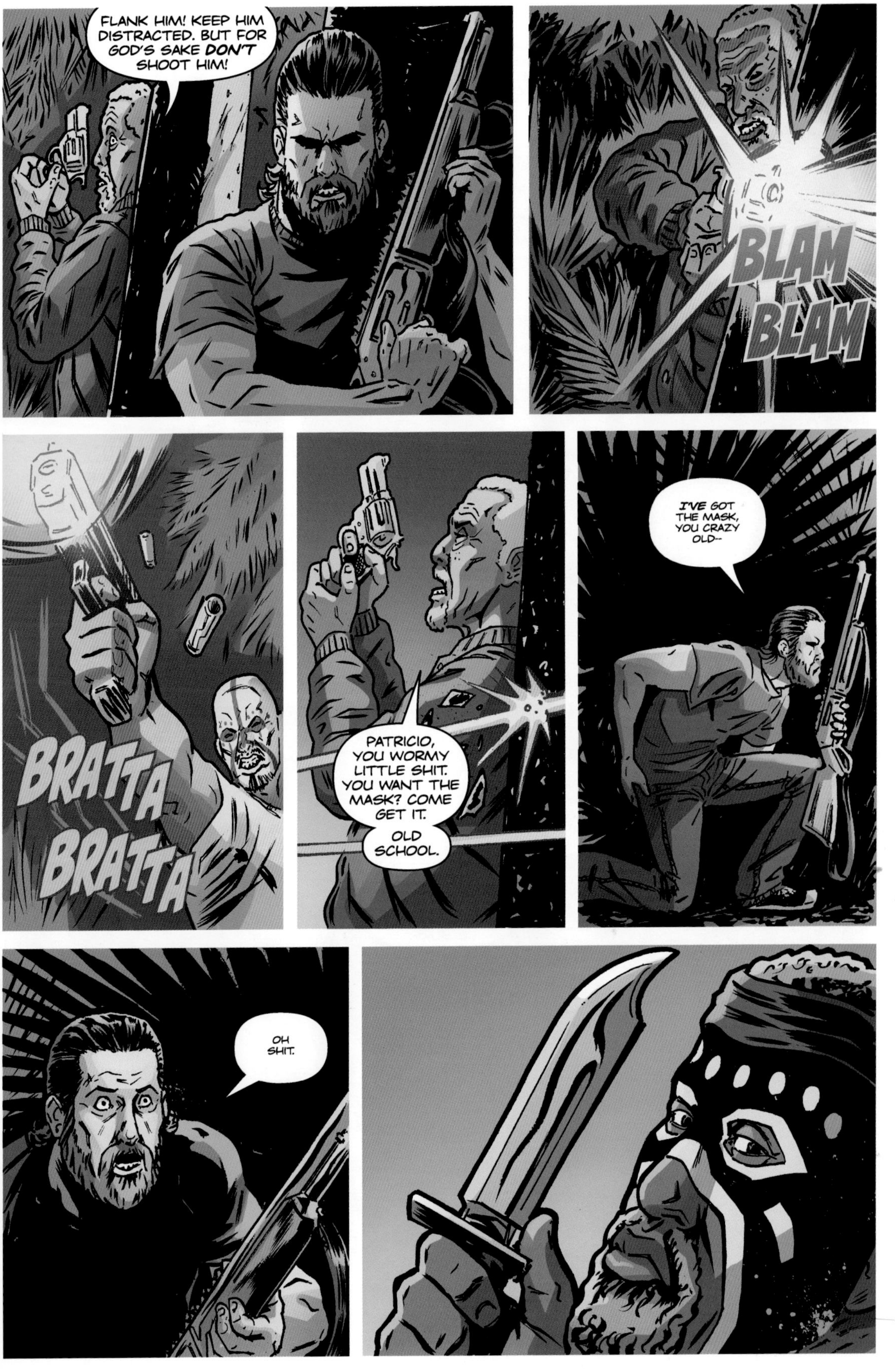
FLANK HIM! KEEP HIM DISTRACTED. BUT FOR GOD'S SAKE **DON'T** SHOOT HIM!
BLAM
BLAM
BRATTA
BRATTA
PATRICIO, YOU WORMY LITTLE SHIT. YOU WANT THE MASK? COME GET IT.
OLD SCHOOL.
I'VE GOT THE MASK, YOU CRAZY OLD--
OH SHIT.

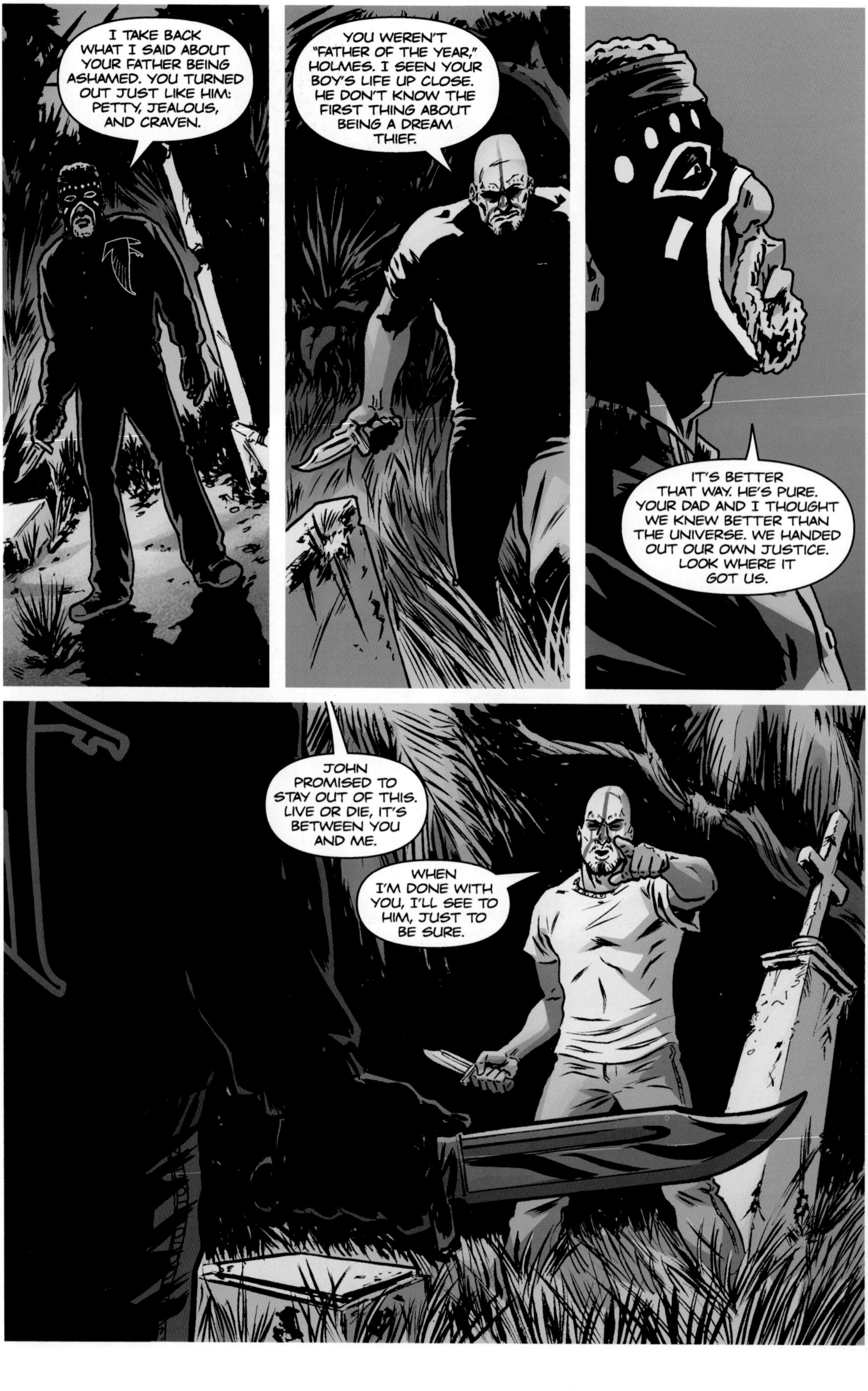
I TAKE BACK WHAT I SAID ABOUT YOUR FATHER BEING ASHAMED. YOU TURNED OUT JUST LIKE HIM: PETTY, JEALOUS, AND CRAVEN.
YOU WEREN'T "FATHER OF THE YEAR," HOLMES. I SEEN YOUR BOY'S LIFE UP CLOSE. HE DON'T KNOW THE FIRST THING ABOUT BEING A DREAM THIEF.
IT'S BETTER THAT WAY. HE'S PURE. YOUR DAD AND I THOUGHT WE KNEW BETTER THAN THE UNIVERSE. WE HANDED OUT OUR OWN JUSTICE. LOOK WHERE IT GOT US.
JOHN PROMISED TO STAY OUT OF THIS. LIVE OR DIE, IT'S BETWEEN YOU AND ME.
WHEN I'M DONE WITH YOU, I'LL SEE TO HIM, JUST TO BE SURE.

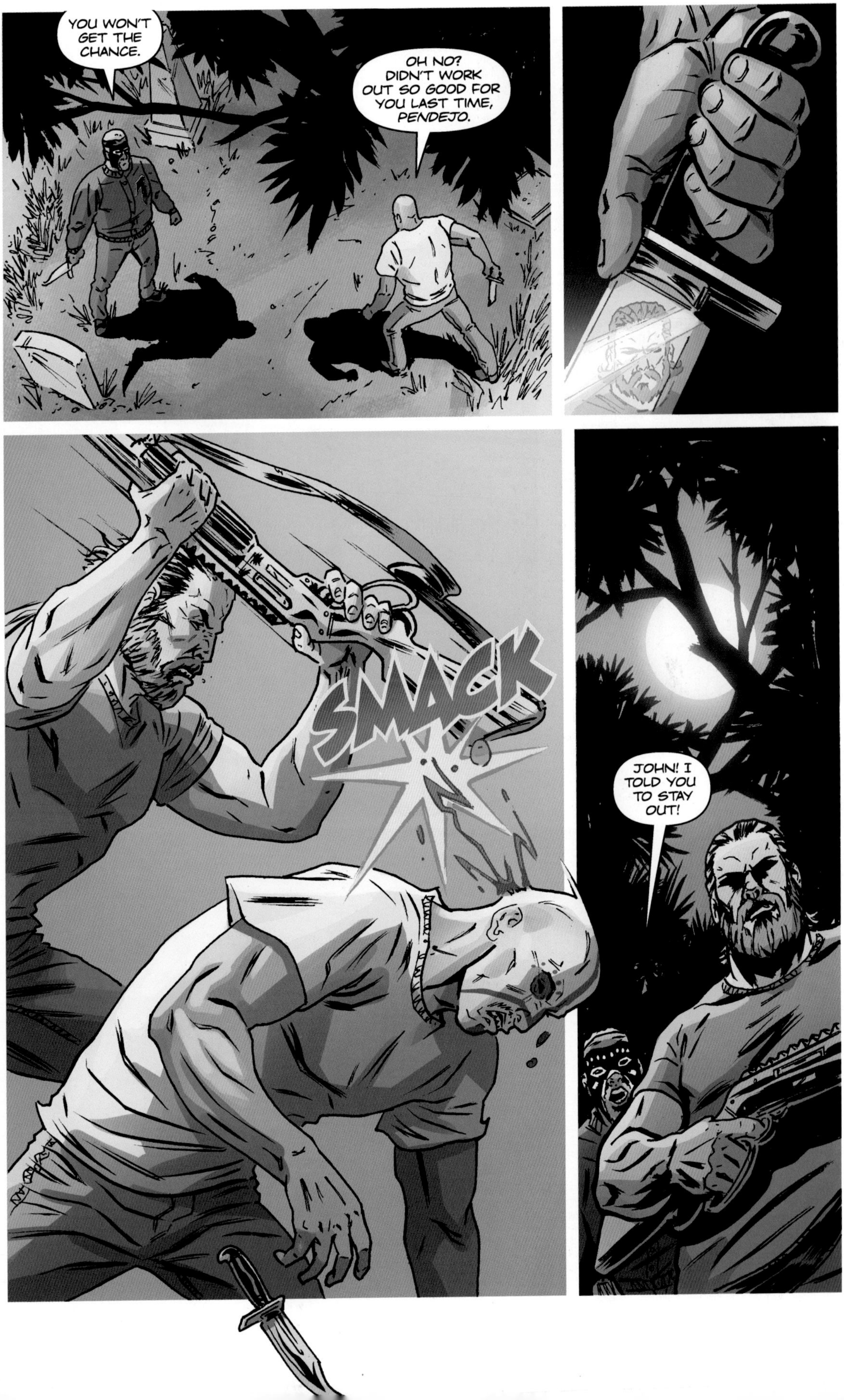
YOU WON'T GET THE CHANCE.
OH NO? DIDN'T WORK OUT SO GOOD FOR YOU LAST TIME, PENDEJO.
SMACK
JOHN! I TOLD YOU TO STAY OUT!

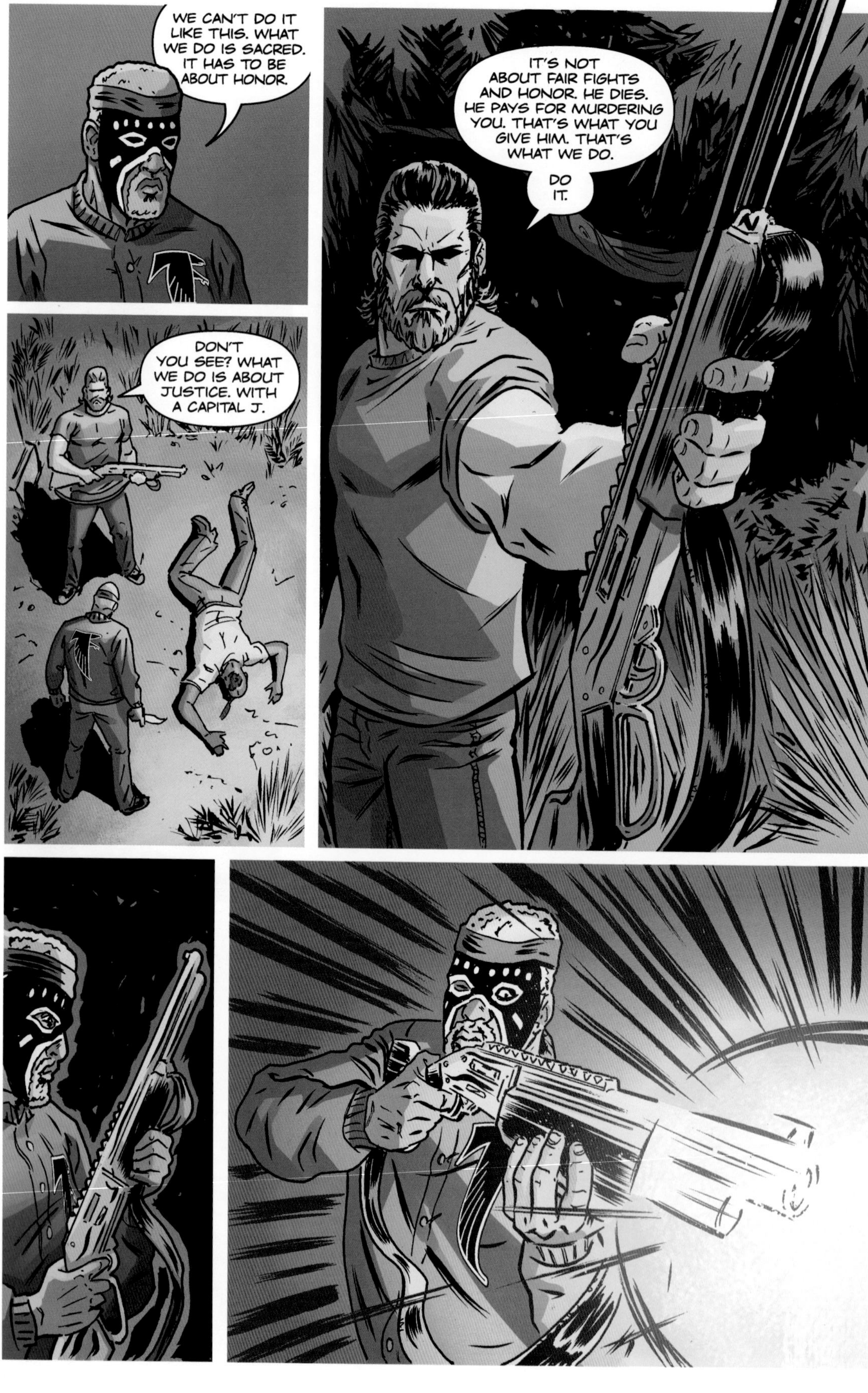
WE CAN'T DO IT LIKE THIS. WHAT WE DO IS SACRED. IT HAS TO BE ABOUT HONOR.
DON'T YOU SEE? WHAT WE DO IS ABOUT JUSTICE. WITH A CAPITAL J.
IT'S NOT ABOUT FAIR FIGHTS AND HONOR. HE DIES. HE PAYS FOR MURDERING YOU. THAT'S WHAT YOU GIVE HIM. THAT'S WHAT WE DO.
DO IT.

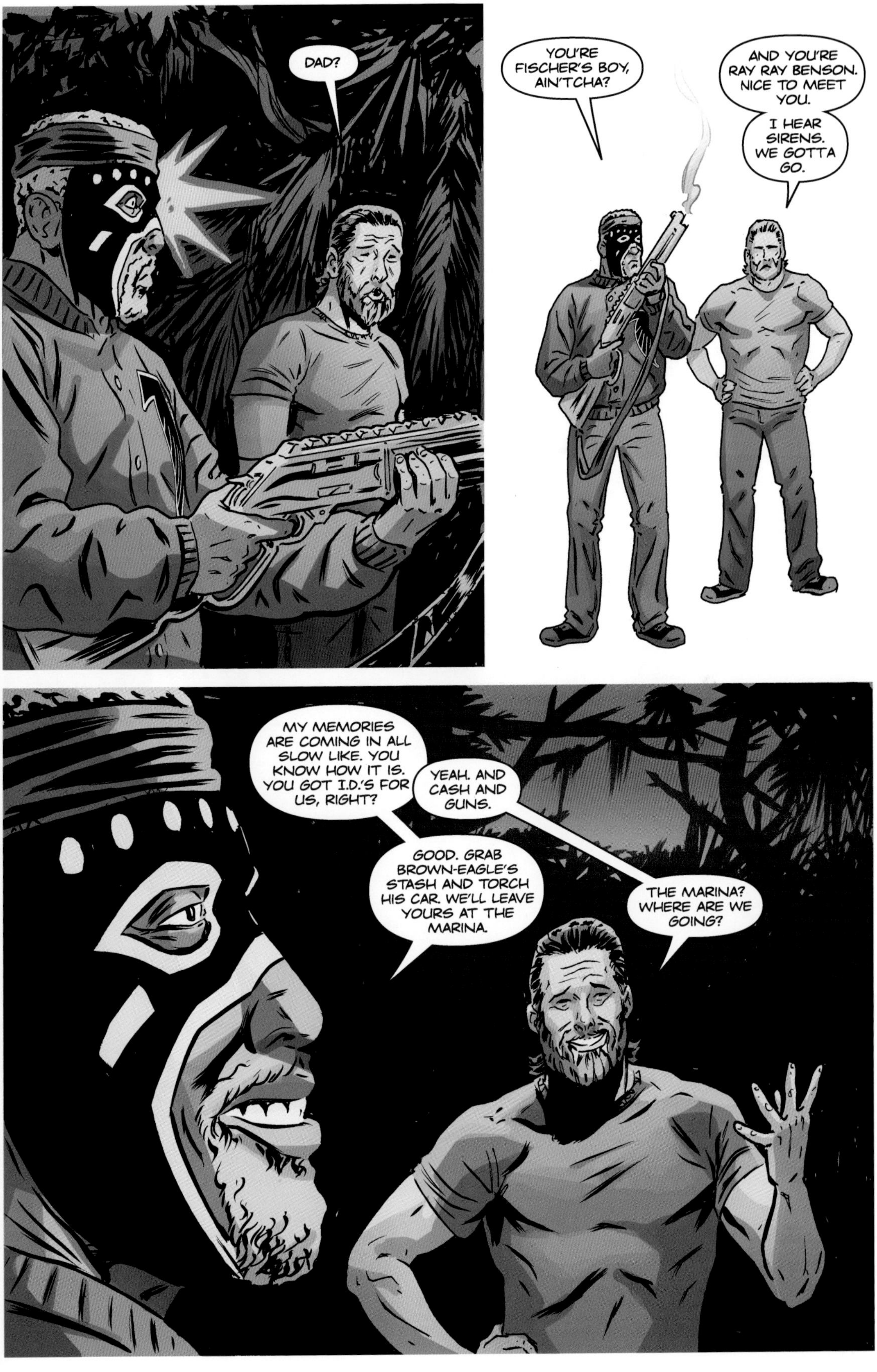
DAD?
YOU'RE FISCHER'S BOY, AIN'TCHA?
AND YOU'RE RAY RAY BENSON. NICE TO MEET YOU.
I HEAR SIRENS. WE GOTTA GO.
MY MEMORIES ARE COMING IN ALL SLOW LIKE. YOU KNOW HOW IT IS. YOU GOT I.D.'S FOR US, RIGHT?
YEAH. AND CASH AND GUNS.
GOOD. GRAB BROWN-EAGLE'S STASH AND TORCH HIS CAR. WE'LL LEAVE YOURS AT THE MARINA.
THE MARINA? WHERE ARE WE GOING?

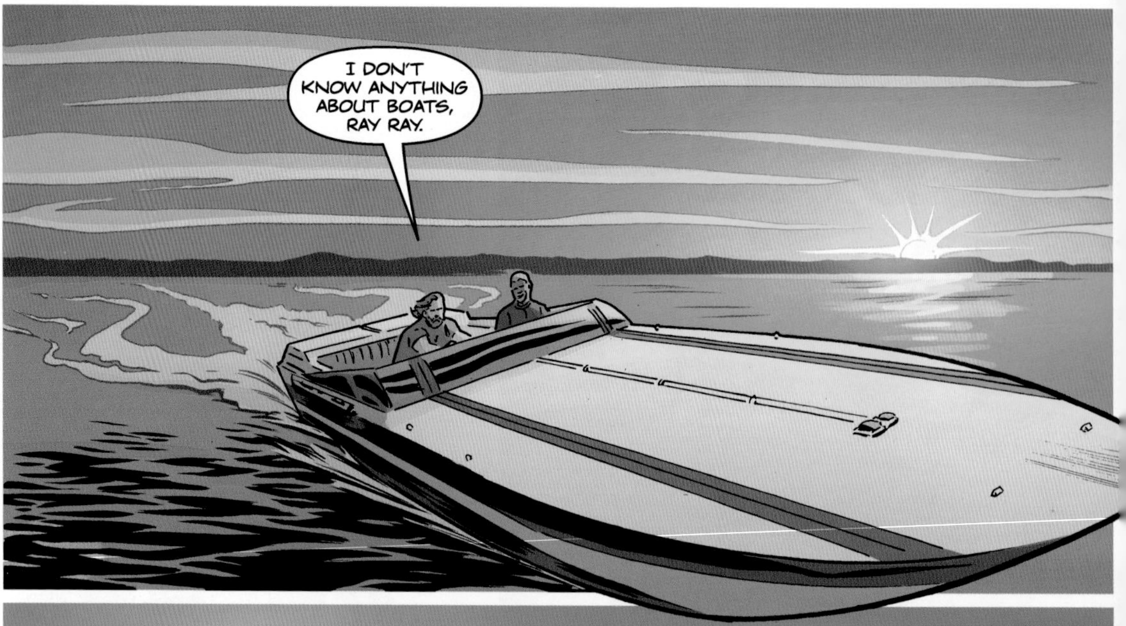
I DON'T KNOW ANYTHING ABOUT BOATS, RAY RAY.

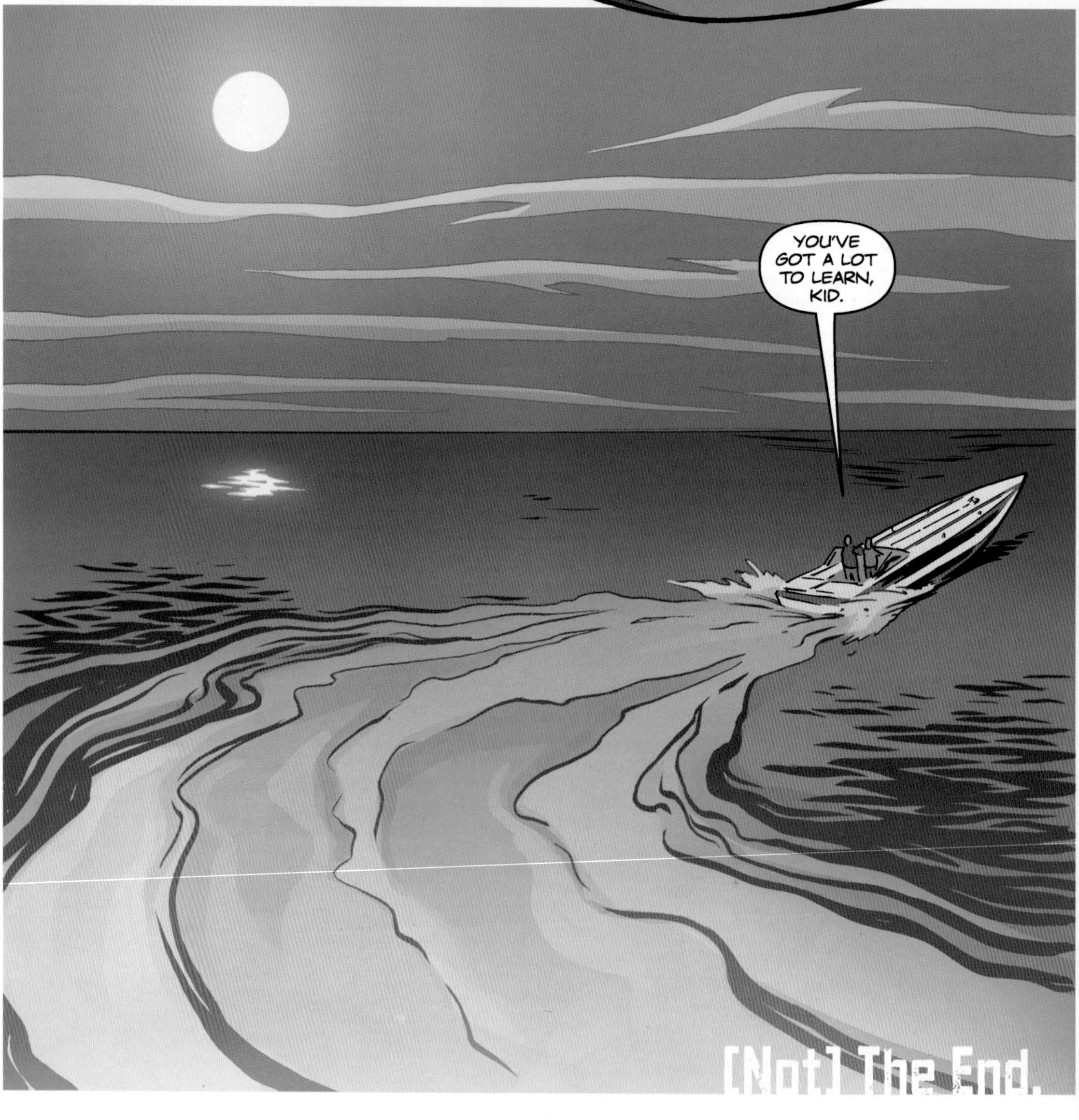
YOU'VE GOT A LOT TO LEARN, KID.
[Not] The End.

PINUPS

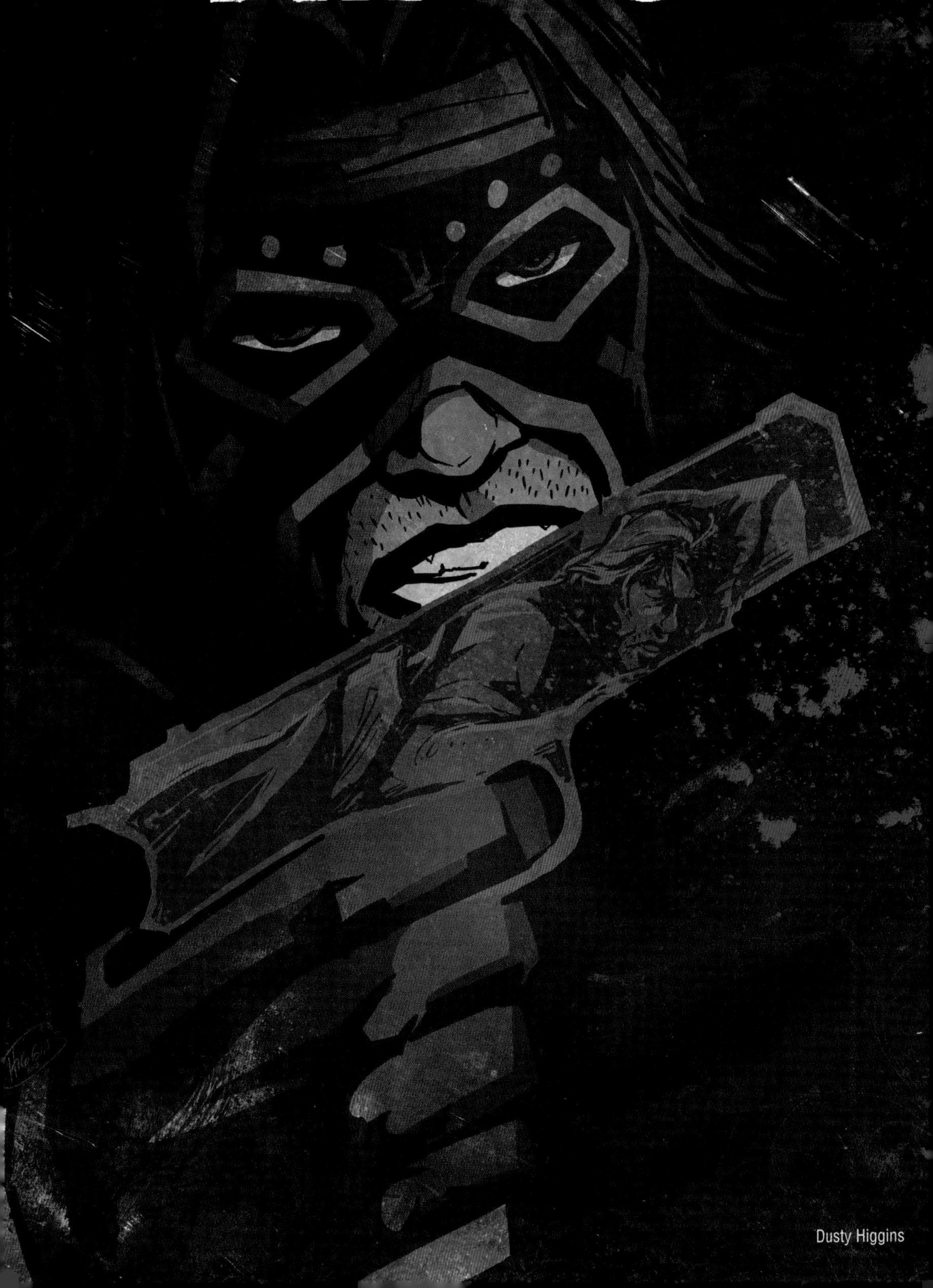

Dusty Higgins

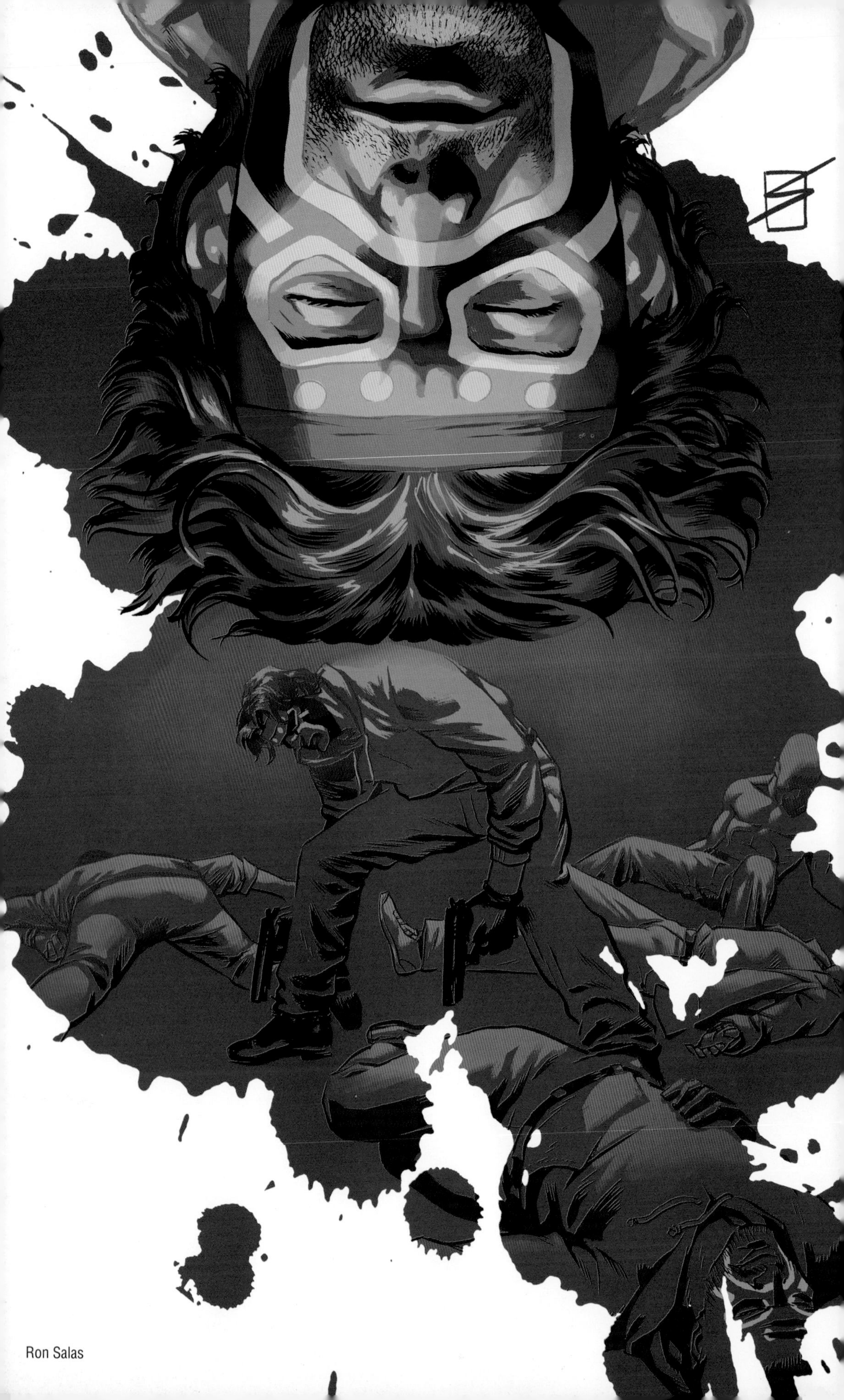

Ron Salas

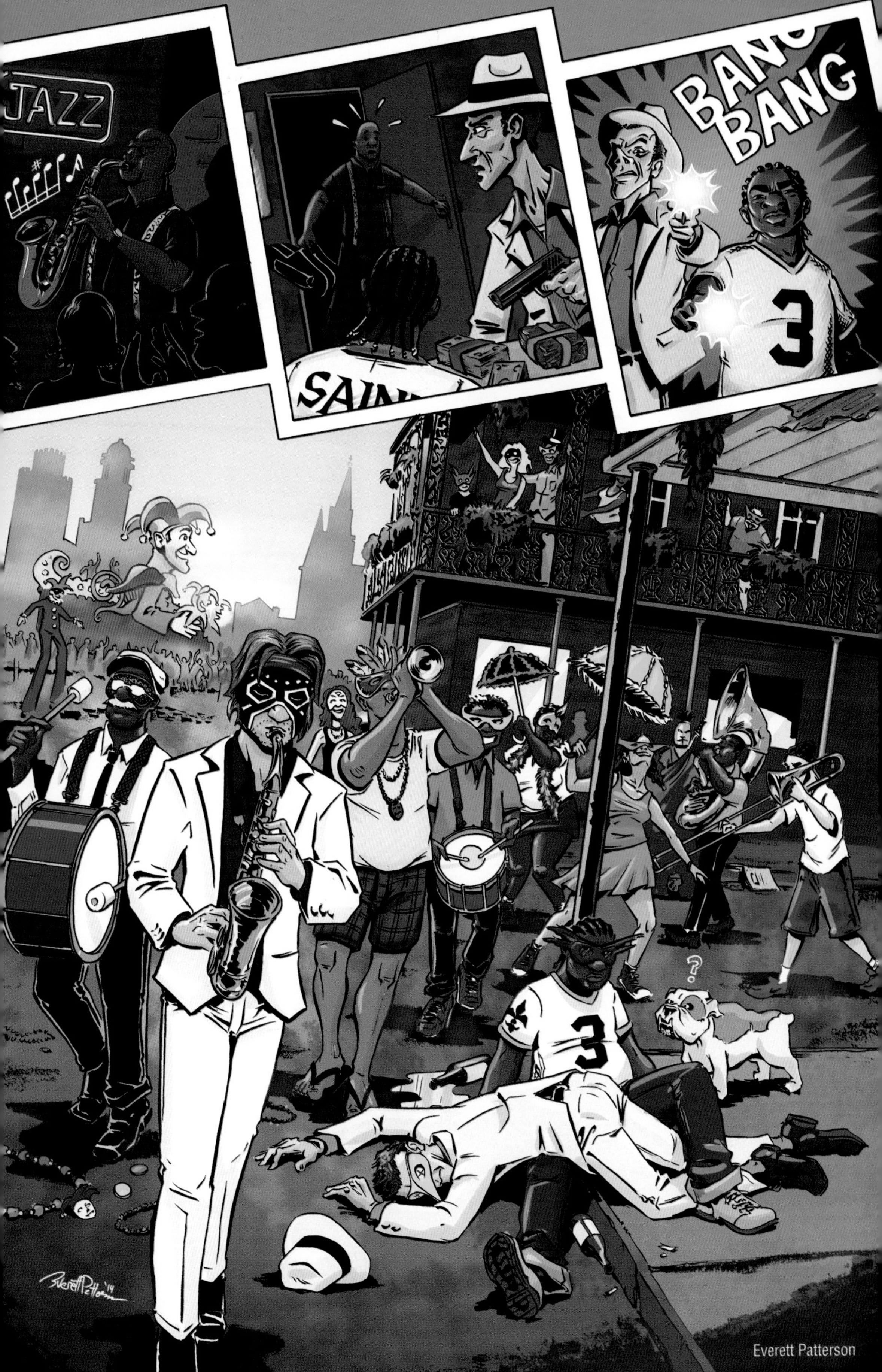
JAZZ
SAIN
BANG
BANG

Everett Patterson

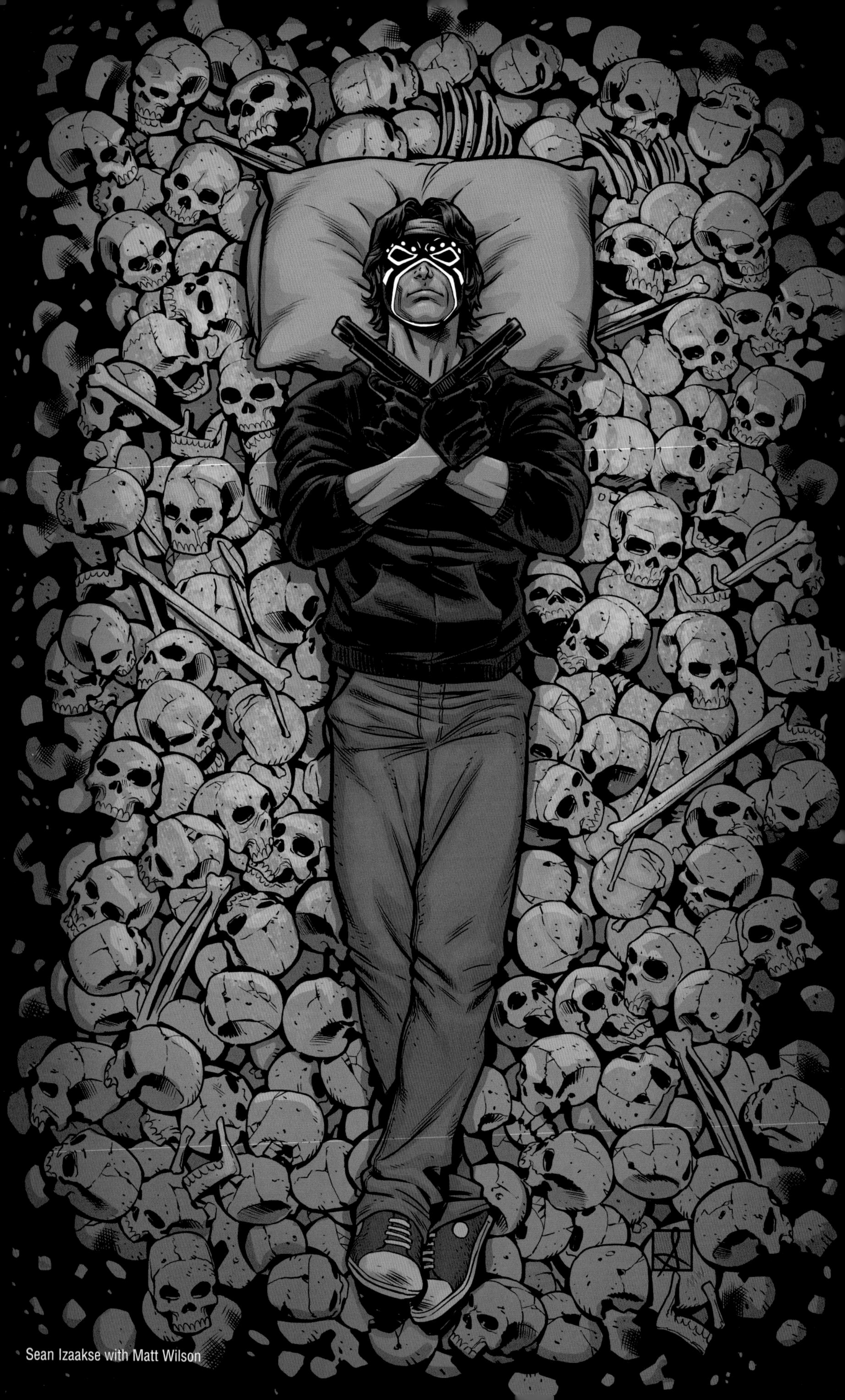

Sean Izaakse with Matt Wilson

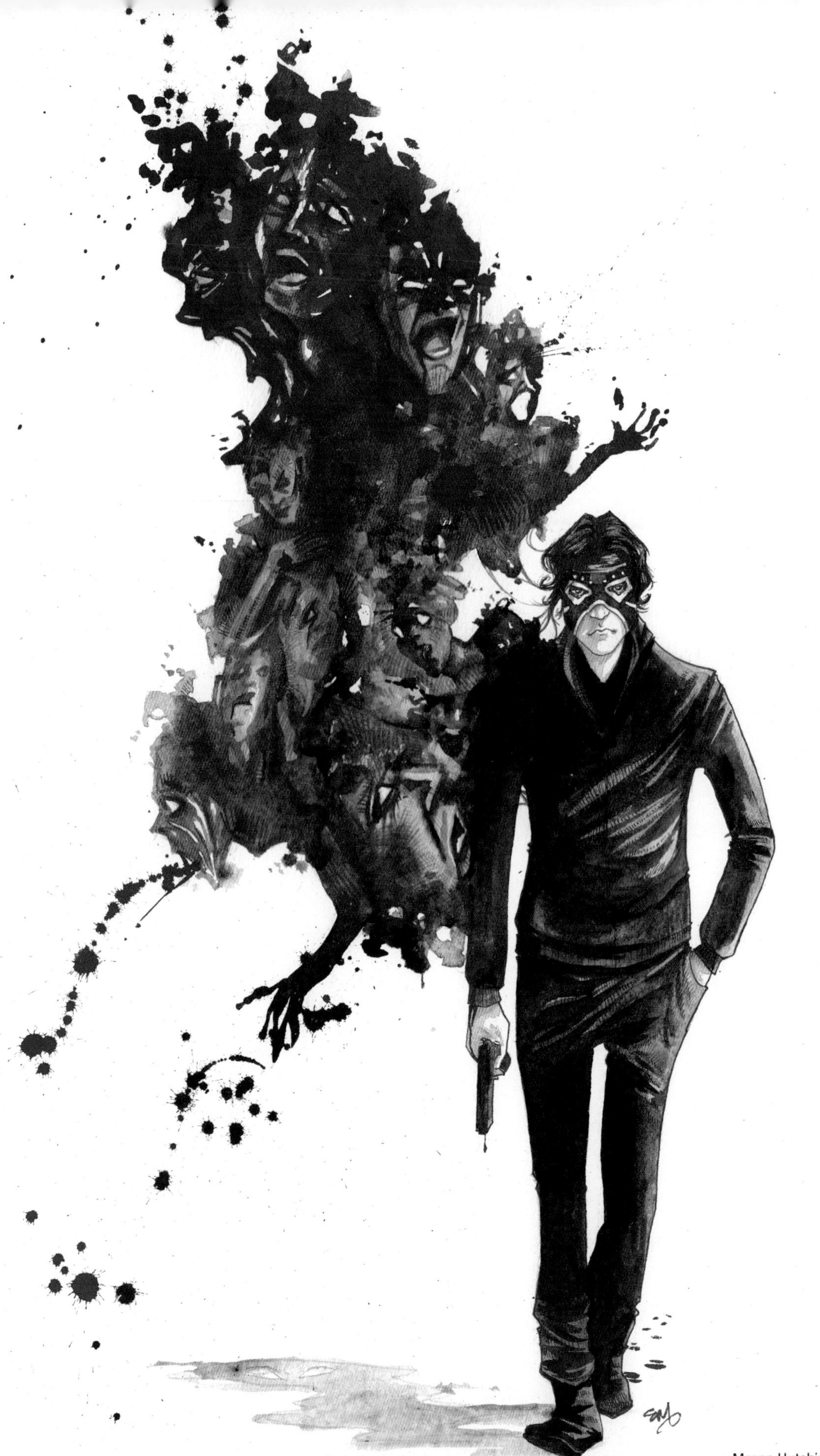

Megan Hutchison

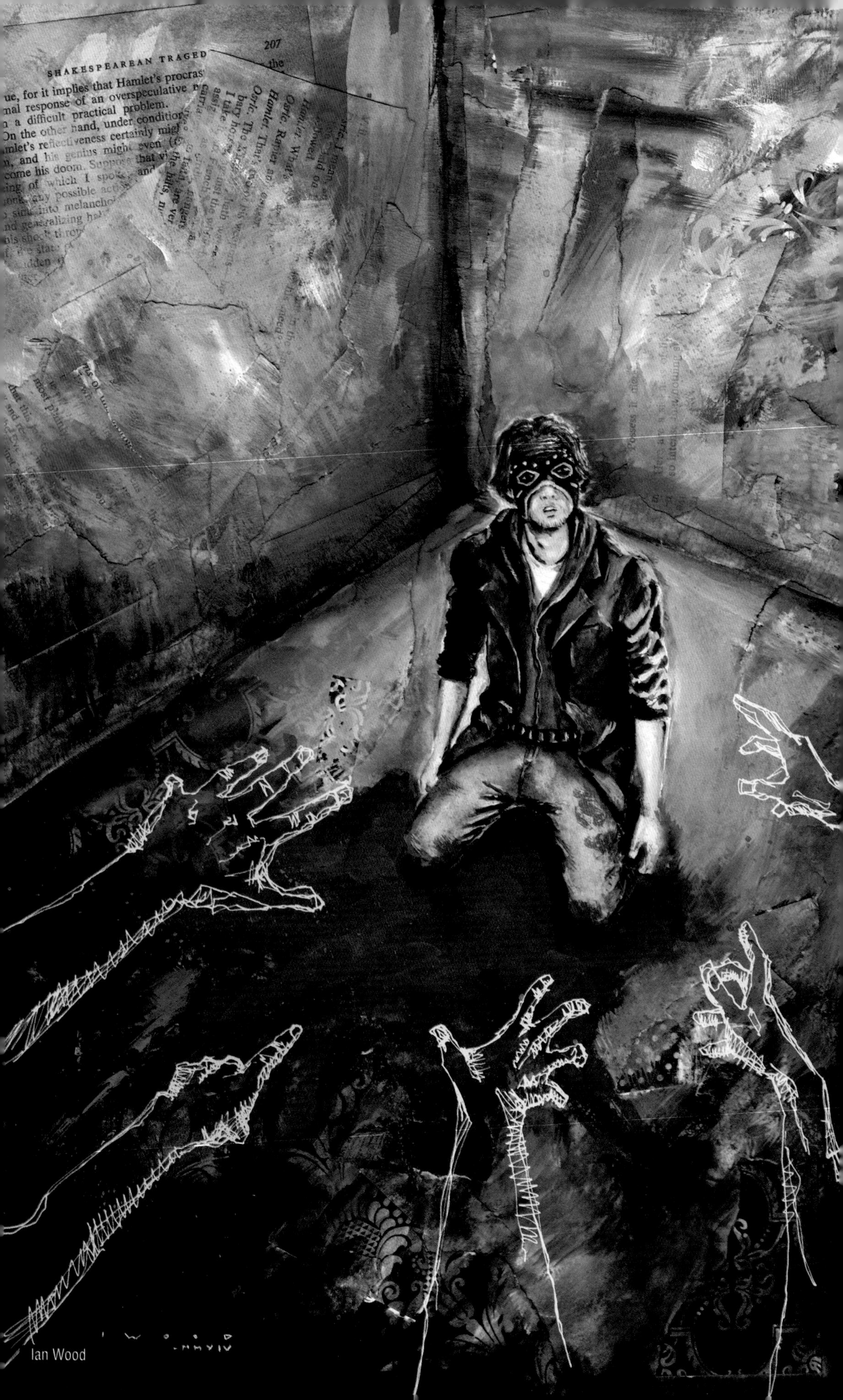
207
SHAKESPEAREAN TRAGED
ue, for it implies that Hamlet's procras
nal response of an overspeculative
n a difficult practical problem.
On the other hand, under condition
mlet's reflectiveness certainly migh
n, and his genius might
come his doom.

Ian Wood

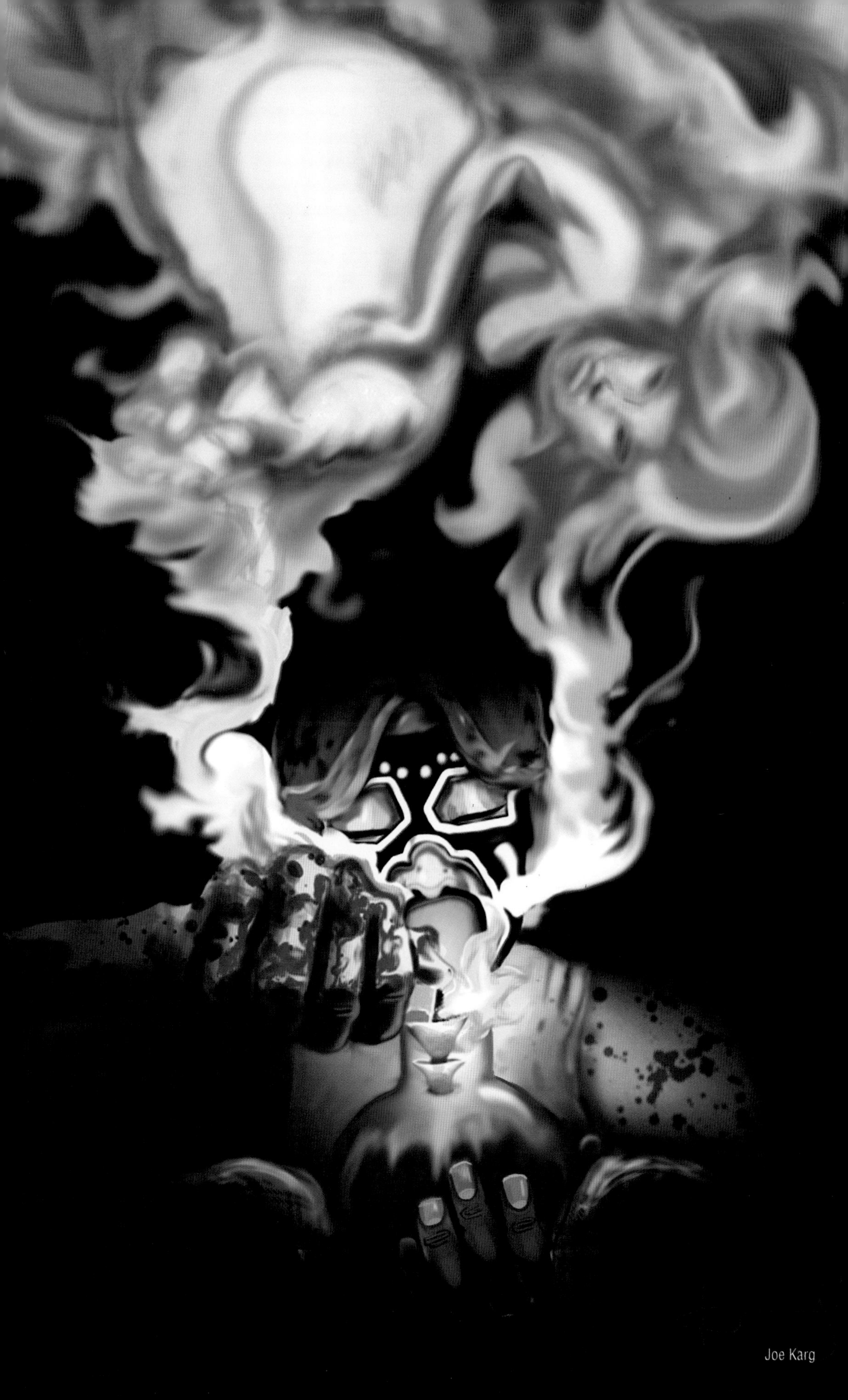

Joe Karg

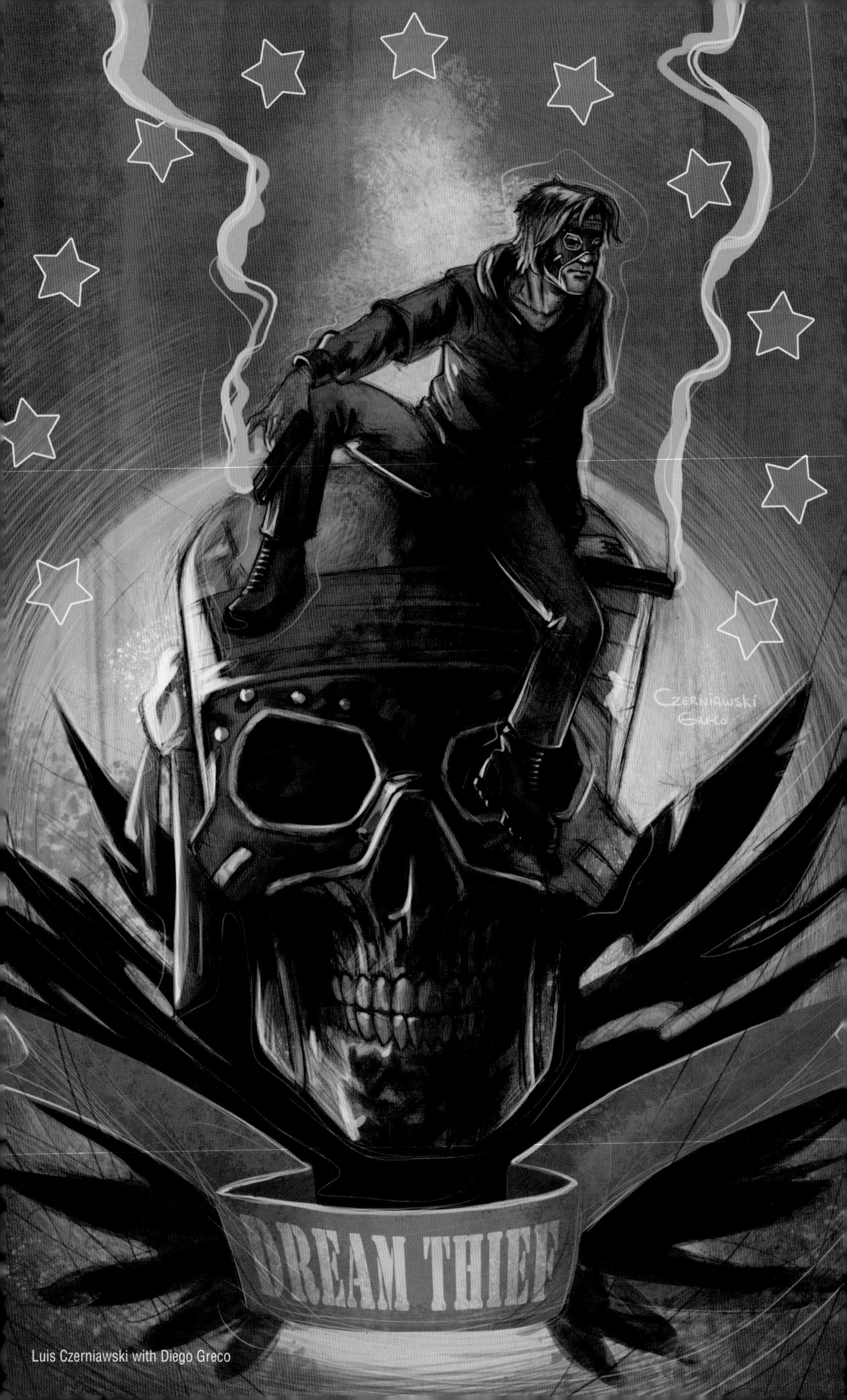
DREAM THIEF
CZERNIAWSKI
GRECO
Luis Czerniawski with Diego Greco

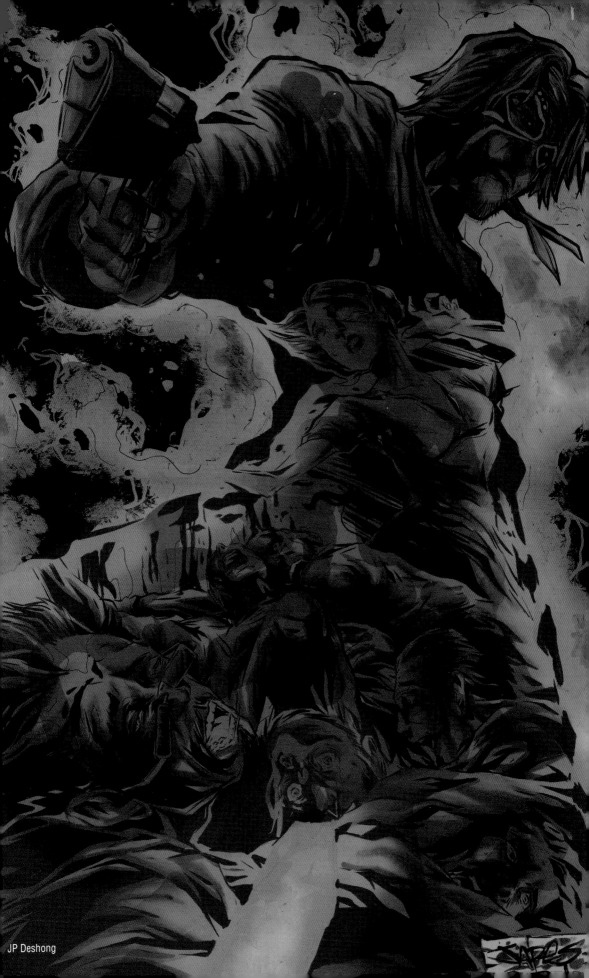

JP Deshong

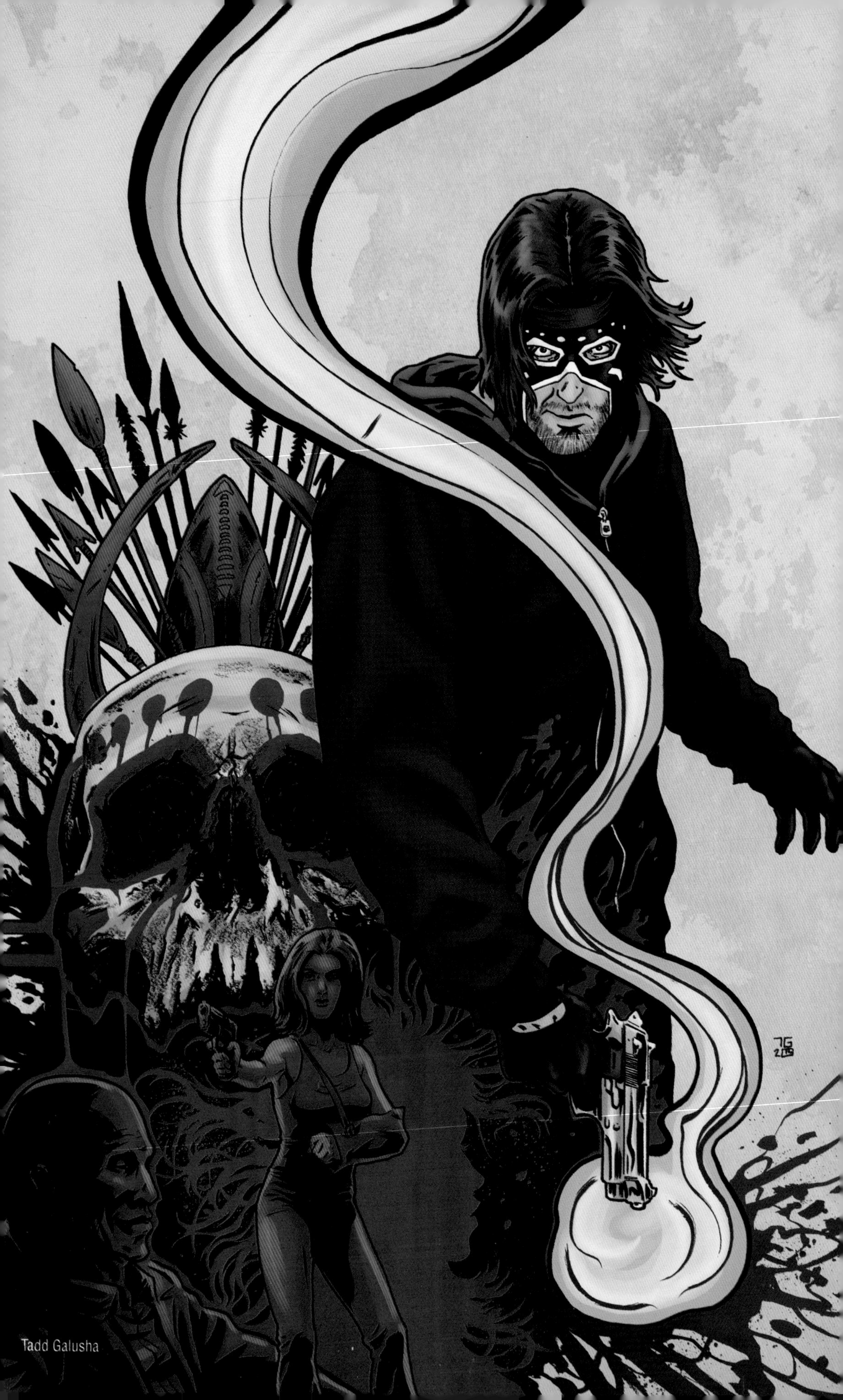
TG
2/19

Tadd Galusha

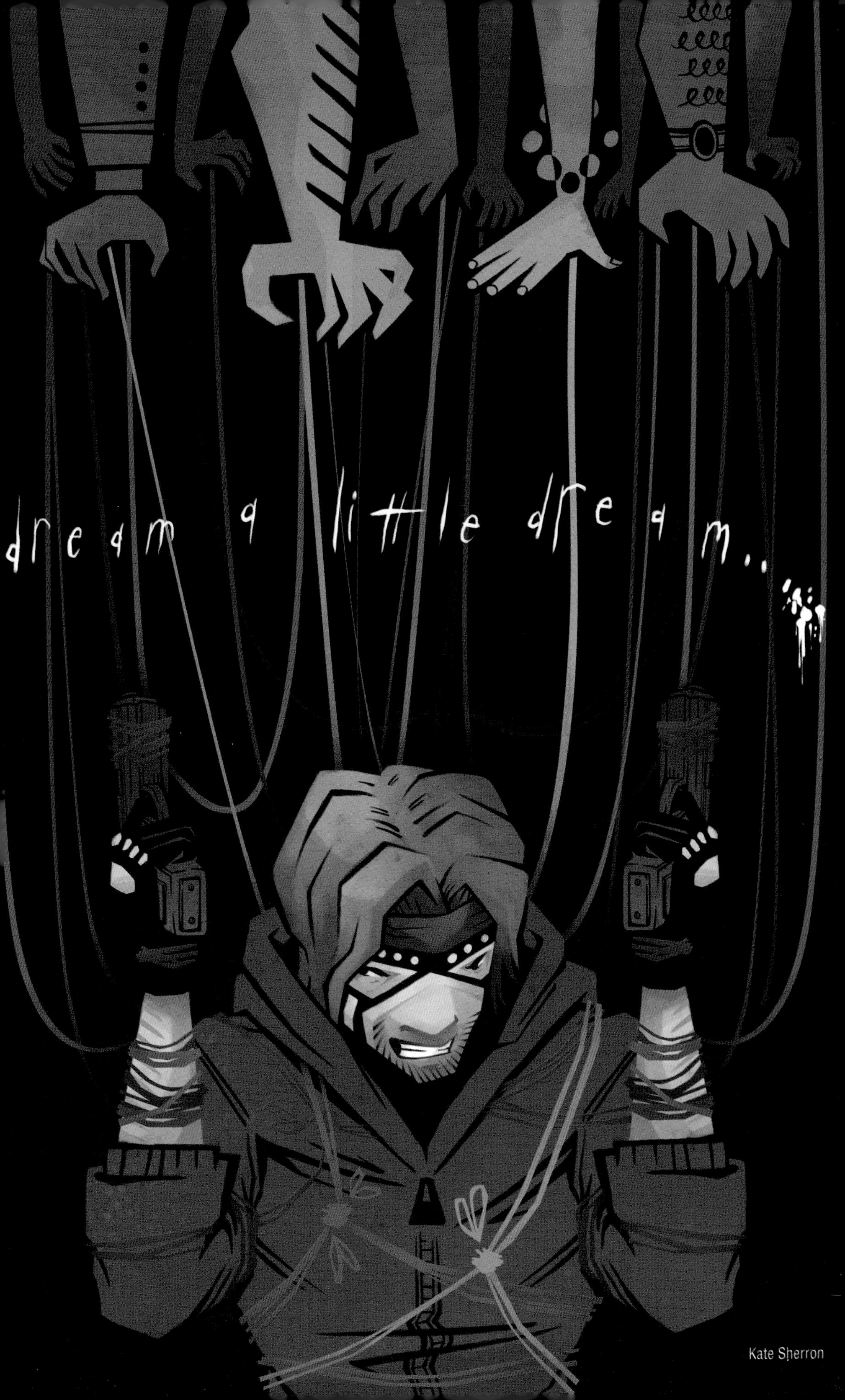
dream a little dream...

Kate Sherron

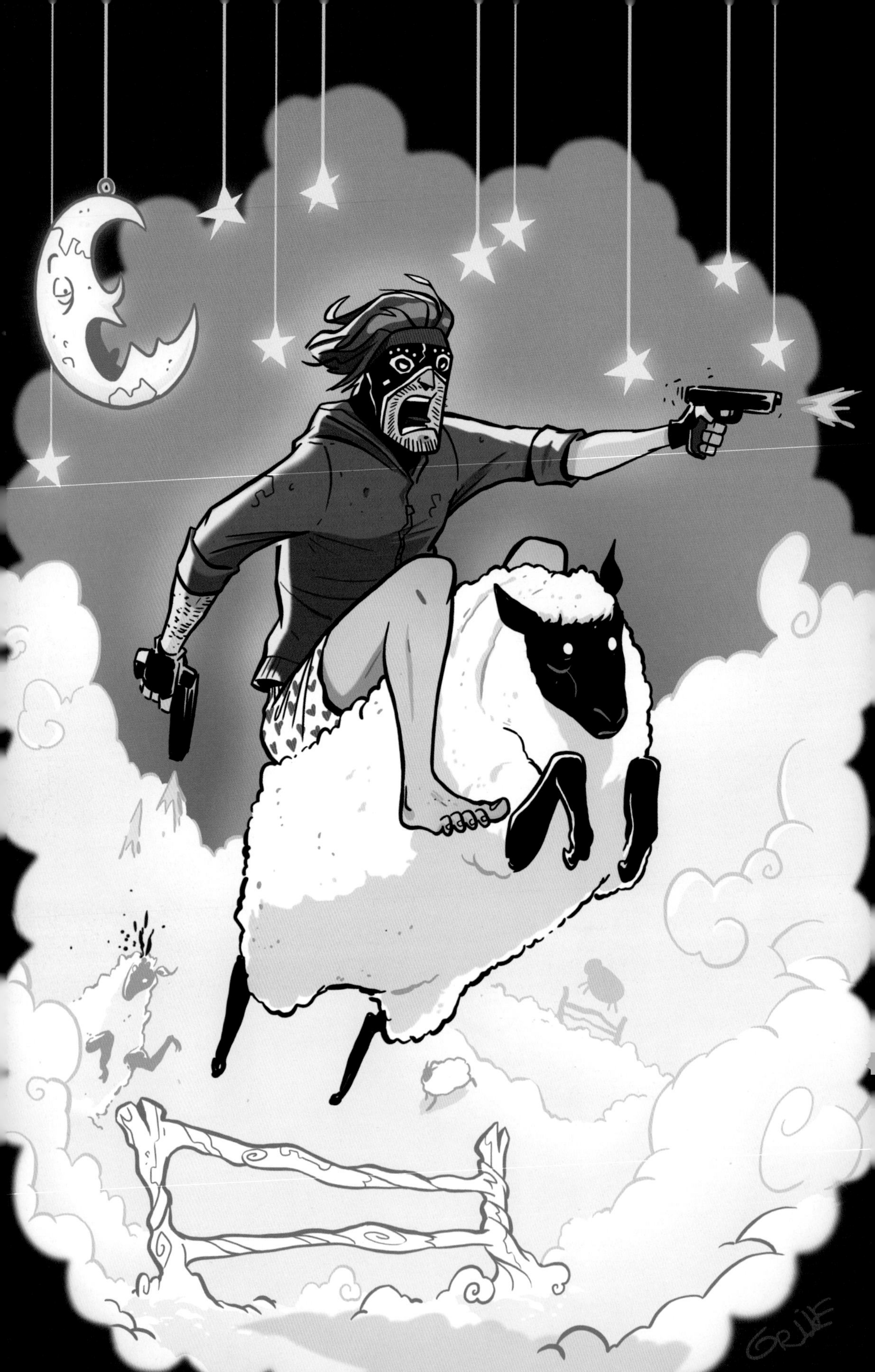

Chris Grine

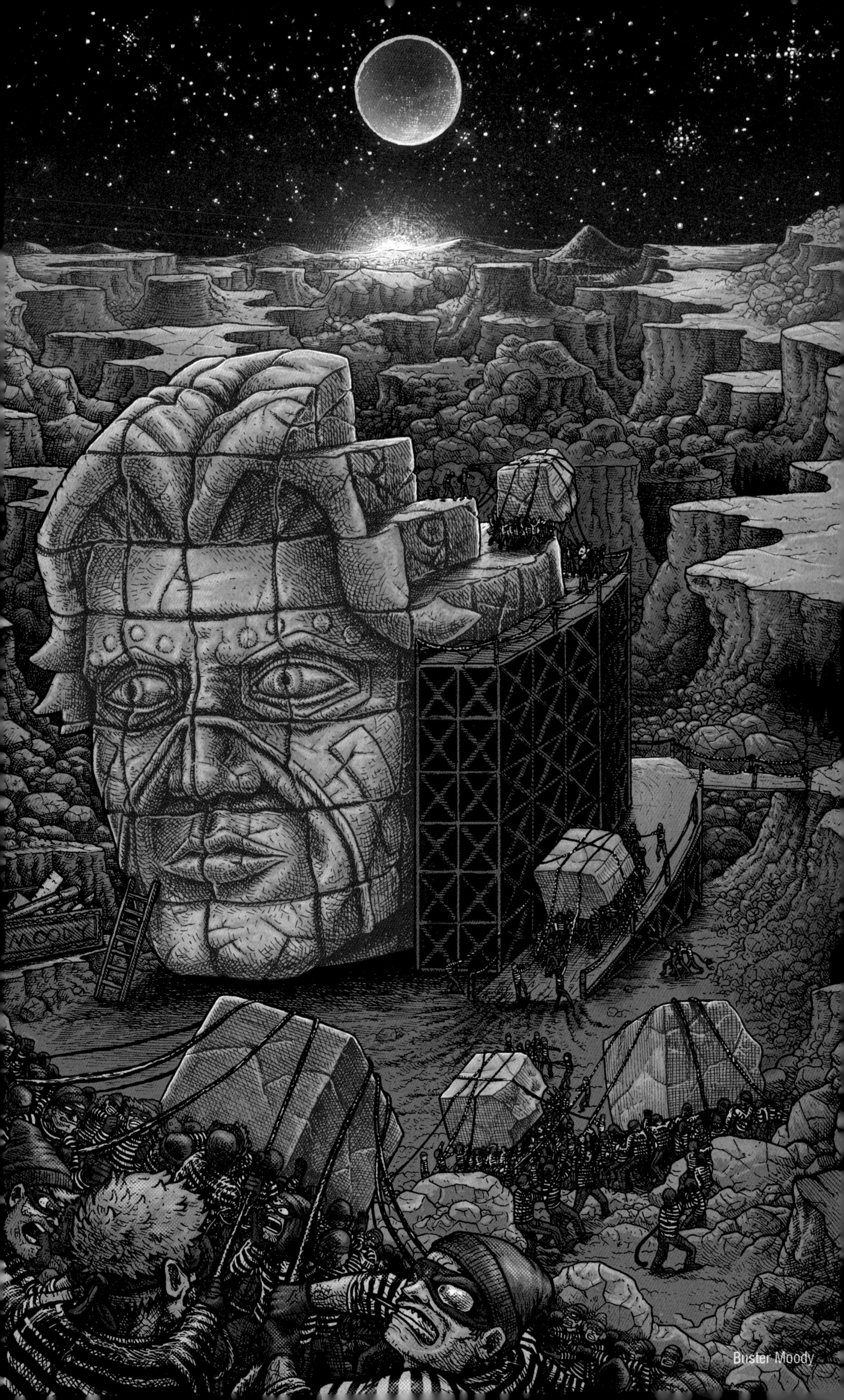
Buster Moody

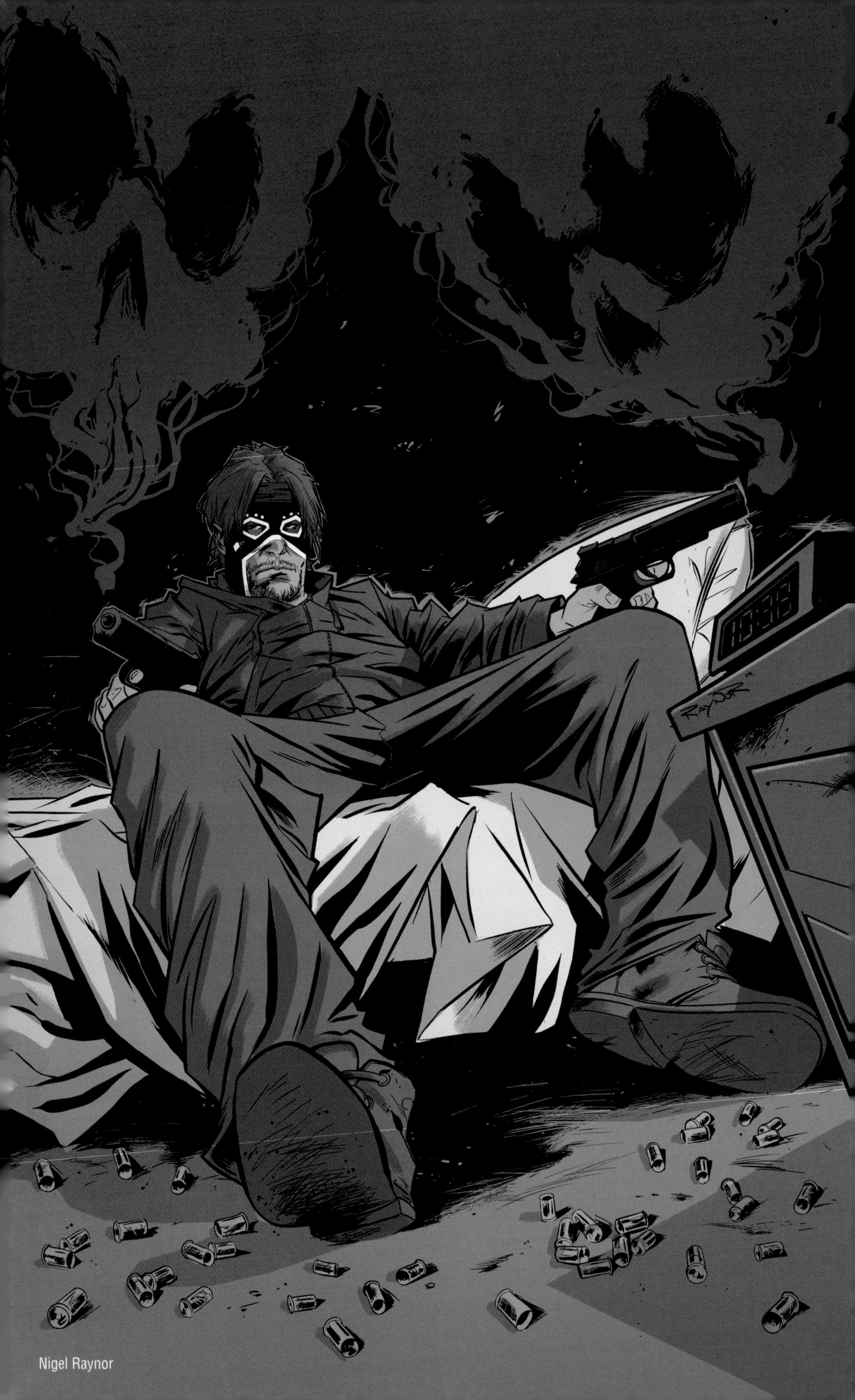

Nigel Raynor

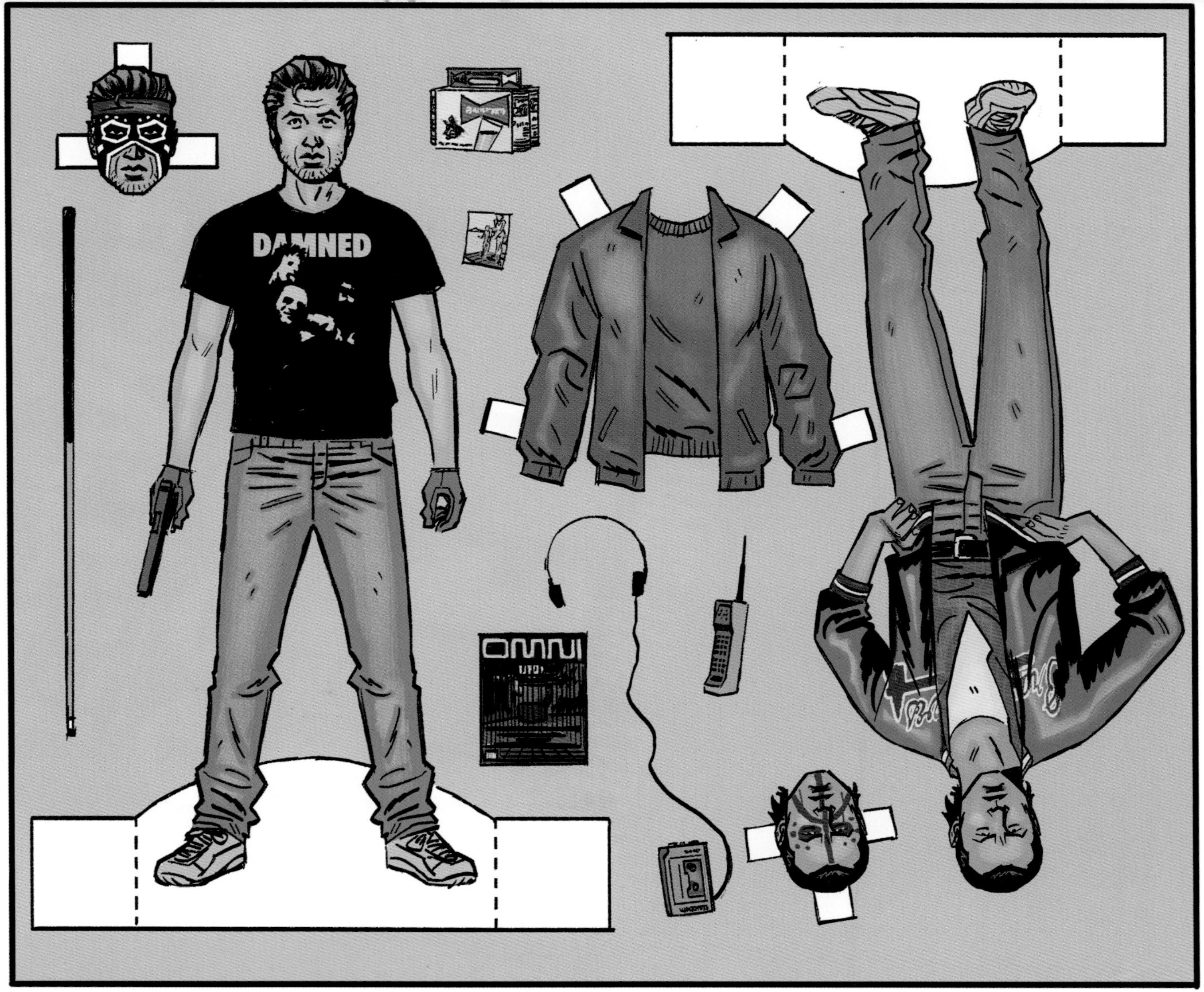
DAMNED
OMNI

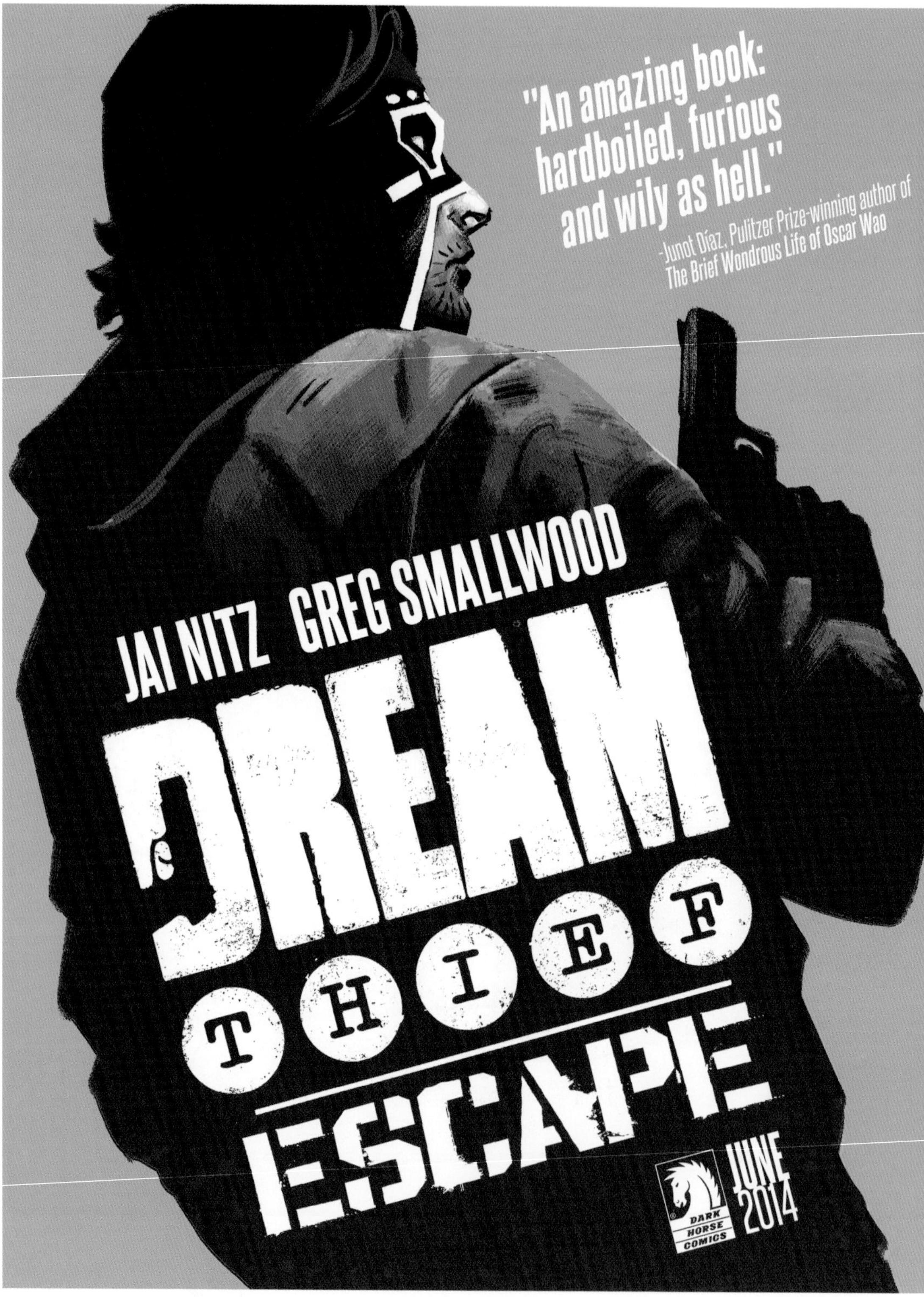
"An amazing book: hardboiled, furious and wily as hell."
-Junot Díaz, Pulitzer Prize-winning author of The Brief Wondrous Life of Oscar Wao
JAI NITZ
GREG SMALLWOOD
DREAM THIEF
ESCAPE
DARK HORSE COMICS
JUNE 2014

DIRECTIONS:

1. Tear out page.
2. Cut along dotted line (ask your parents before using scissors).
3. Punch holes on sides of mask and tie string.

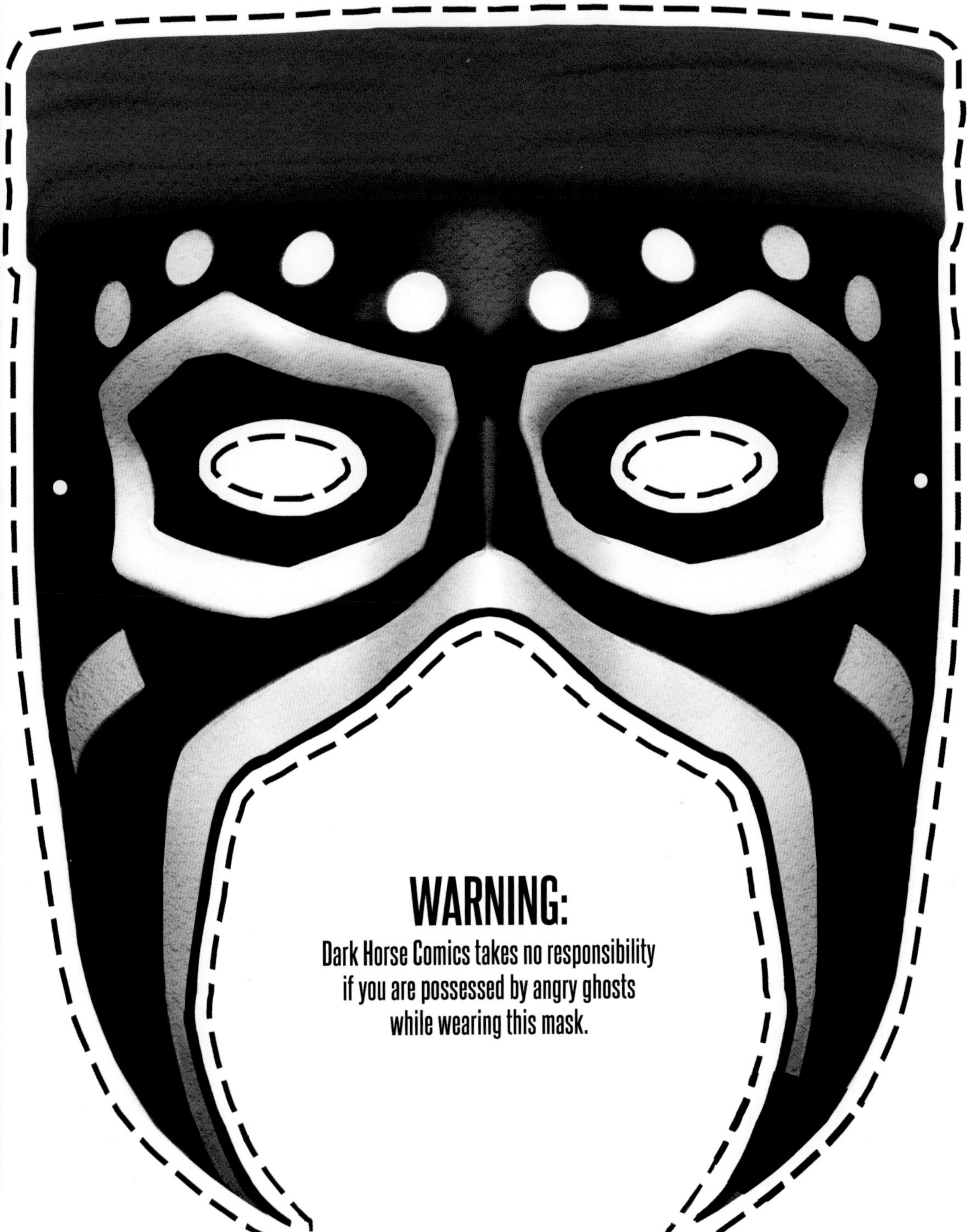
WARNING:
Dark Horse Comics takes no responsibility if you are possessed by angry ghosts while wearing this mask.

JAI NITZ is an American comic book writer who has written for Dark Horse, Marvel, DC, Image, Disney, Dynamite, and other publishers. He won the prestigious Xeric Foundation grant in 2003 for his self-published anthology *Paper Museum*. He won the Bram Stoker Award in 2004 for Excellence in Illustrated Narrative for *Heaven's Devils* from Image Comics. He also works as a professor at his alma mater, the University of Kansas, teaching courses on comic books and film. He lives in Lawrence, Kansas, with his girlfriend and two sons.

GREG SMALLWOOD grew up drawing comics in Leavenworth, Kansas. A self-taught artist, he was nominated for the 2014 Russ Manning Promising Newcomer Award for his work on *Dream Thief* Volume 1. When not drawing, Greg relaxes by surfing the Internet and eating Cheetos.

TADD GALUSHA is an American sequential illustrator. He's worked with an assortment of studios and companies doing storyboards, backgrounds, illustration, and comics. When not working, he can be found wandering in the Cascades.

TAMRA BONVILLAIN is a colorist, originally from Augusta, Georgia, who has worked on titles from Dark Horse, Image, Dynamite, and Boom. She attended the Kubert School in Dover, New Jersey, graduating in 2009. She has recently moved back to the South for some reason.

PROJECT BLACK SKY

X

Duane Swierczynski and Eric Nguyen
A masked vigilante dispenses justice without mercy to the criminals of the decaying city of Arcadia. Nonstop, visceral action, with Dark Horse's most brutal and exciting character—X!

VOLUME 1: BIG BAD
978-1-61655-241-1 | $14.99

VOLUME 2: THE DOGS OF WAR
978-1-61655-327-2 | $14.99

VOLUME 3: SIEGE
978-1-61655-458-3 | $14.99

GHOST

Kelly Sue DeConnick, Chris Sebela, Alex Ross, Ryan Sook, and others
Paranormal investigators accidentally summon a ghostly woman. The search for her identity uncovers a deadly alliance between political corruption and demonic science! In the middle stands a woman trapped between two worlds!

VOLUME 1: IN THE SMOKE AND DIN
978-1-61655-121-6 | $14.99

VOLUME 2: THE WHITE CITY BUTCHER
978-1-61655-420-0 | $14.99

CAPTAIN MIDNIGHT

Joshua Williamson, Fernando Dagnino, Eduardo Francisco, and others
In the forties, he was an American hero, a daredevil fighter pilot, a technological genius . . . a superhero. Since he rifled out of the Bermuda Triangle and into the present day, Captain Midnight has been labeled a threat to homeland security. Can Captain Midnight survive in the modern world, with the US government on his heels and an old enemy out for revenge?

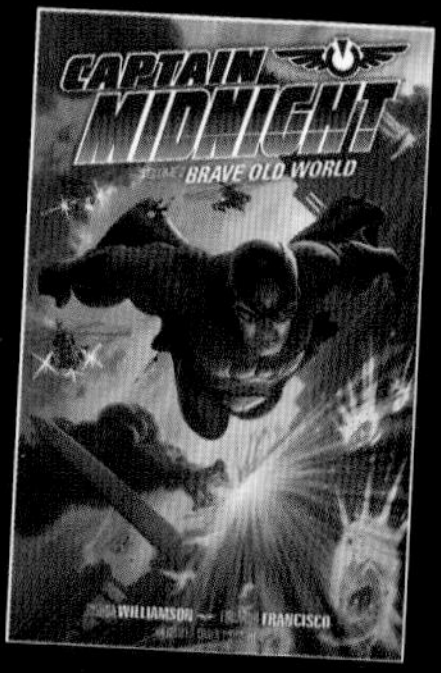

VOLUME 1: ON THE RUN
978-1-61655-229-9 | $14.99

VOLUME 2: BRAVE OLD WORLD
978-1-61655-230-5 | $14.99

VOLUME 3: FOR A BETTER TOMORROW
978-1-61655-231-2 | $14.99

SUPER:POWERED BY CREATORS!

"These superheroes ain't no boy scouts in spandex. They're a high-octane blend of the damaged, quixotic heroes of pulp and detective fiction and the do-gooders in capes from the Golden and Silver Ages." —Duane Swierczynski

SLEDGEHAMMER 44
Mike Mignola, John Arcudi, and Jason Latour
ISBN 978-1-61655-395-1 | $19.99

DREAM THIEF
Jai Nitz and Greg Smallwood
ISBN 978-1-61655-283-1 | $17.99

BUZZKILL
Mark Reznicek, Donny Cates,
and Geoff Shaw
ISBN 978-1-61655-305-0 | $14.99

THE BLACK BEETLE
Francesco Francavilla
VOLUME 1: NO WAY OUT
ISBN 978-1-61655-202-2 | $19.99

THE ANSWER!
Mike Norton and Dennis Hopeless
ISBN 978-1-61655-197-1 | $12.99

BLOODHOUND
Dan Jolley, Leonard Kirk, and Robin Riggs
VOLUME 1: BRASS KNUCKLE PSYCHOLOGY
ISBN 978-1-61655-125-4 | $19.99
VOLUME 2: CROWBAR MEDICINE
ISBN 978-1-61655-352-4 | $19.99

MICHAEL AVON OEMING'S
THE VICTORIES
Michael Avon Oeming
VOLUME 1: TOUCHED
ISBN 978-1-61655-100-1 | $9.99
VOLUME 2: TRANSHUMAN
ISBN 978-1-61655-214-5 | $17.99
VOLUME 3: POSTHUMAN
ISBN 978-1-61655-445-3 | $17.99

ORIGINAL VISIONS—
THRILLING TALES!